RETIRE

ONE WITH SELF, ONE WITH LIFE

Ten Lessons Learned Along the Journey

WILLIAM S. PALMER, PhD

For readers wishing to contact the author, he can be reached at
the following email address: bpalmer38@gmail.com.

Retire One with Self, One with Life

Ten Lessons Learned Along the Journey

William S. Palmer, PhD

ISBN (Print Edition): 978-1-09836-735-0

ISBN (eBook Edition): 978-1-09836-736-7

TABLE OF CONTENTS

ACKNOWLEDGMENTS

For Robbie, retirement companion extraordinaire.

For my first listeners and readers,
David Barbieri and David Pugalee.

And for Marcia Little, who contributed her photo,
"Sunrise: Ogunquit Beach, Maine," for the book cover.

BOOK INTRODUCTION

Retire One with Self, One with Life:
Ten Lessons Learned Along the Journey

When I reached age fifty, I began thinking seriously about retirement for the first time, typically by asking myself repeatedly the same questions, and sometimes in the same order. Will I have enough money accumulated to guarantee enough income for the rest of my life? Where will I choose to live? How will I spend my time? Who am I uniquely as an individual? Will my sense of self influence how I find purpose and meaning in a life without work?

One day while pondering my answers, I realized I had been asking and answering two critical questions last: Who am I uniquely as an individual? Will my sense of self influence how I find purpose and meaning in a life without work? At that precise moment, I understood that my answers to these last two questions would help me immeasurably in determining my answers to the preceding three.

By recognizing the importance of my own individuality and uniqueness, I was placing my retirement inquiries within a different and larger context, one with a strong psychological focus on my true or authentic self.

THE POWER AND FEEL OF AUTHENTICITY

I could always tell when I was being authentic by the way I felt. My strongest indicators of authenticity were my feelings of joy and happiness. During these moments, I experienced deeper and more intense feelings of connectedness and oneness, with myself, other people, even my surroundings. These feelings were immensely self-satisfying, to the degree I often felt as if my heart were singing and my soul soaring. In such moments, I became one with self, one with life.

Throughout most of my personal and professional life, I have found much purpose and pleasure in life when I experienced these moments of enjoyment, fulfillment, and well-being. These feelings occurred naturally, I observed, when I meshed my true self or authentic self with my everyday experiences and responsibilities.

I had learned early in life, then, that heightened feelings of joy and happiness happened when I aligned my authentic self with my everyday actions. If I continued to mesh my authentic self with my everyday options and choices in my retirement, I thus concluded I likewise would find much purpose and pleasure in a life without work.

THE FIRST BOOK PREMISE

Within this book, I am making two major premises. The first one involves the authentic self. *When we choose to live true to self in retirement, we are more likely to experience enhanced feelings of joy, happiness, and self-fulfillment, memorable and noteworthy moments of connectedness and oneness, aspects of self and daily living most of us desire and seek.*

One major problem, however, is that the recognition of the authentic self at any stage of life is not always an easy task to accomplish. Many of us have forgotten the authentic self within. Unfortunately, many of us are not even conscious of this personal loss. Perhaps we neglect the authentic self because it is invisible and formless.

THE AUTHENTIC SELF

In recent years, the term "true to self" has become used synonymously with the term "the authentic self." Throughout history, the term "the authentic self" has been defined and used in more precise ways, and by experts from many fields, as discussed in detail within lesson one in this book.

In a most general sense, the authentic self has been described by existentialist philosophers to contemporary scholars as who we are at our most basic core, our individual and genuine self, the composite of all our unique qualities.

Each of us possesses our own authentic self. Each of us has many individual traits, among them our special abilities and interests, skills and talents, world knowledge and experiences, who we are deep within. The sum of our individual qualities is our true self, our authentic self.

Often, we ignore critical features of the authentic self because many outside pressures are constantly at work, attempting to block us from becoming who we genuinely are and want to be.

OUTSIDE PRESSURES BLOCKING AUTHENTICITY

Along the way in our individual lives, we have allowed, often unknowingly, a wide array of outside pressures to block us from living more authentic lives. When we succumb to these pressures, we live differently from, and inconsistently with, our authentic self, and sometimes for so long we suppress and neglect, even forget about, our authentic self still deep inside. By surrendering to these pressures, we often unknowingly become *other than* who we truly are, *other than* who we truly want to be.

Therefore, being an authentic self also involves an individual's realization, understanding, and capacity to come to terms with those external forces and pressures attempting to block us from becoming who we truly want to be.

Before and during my retirement, I continued to explore the full range of my individual and unique authentic self, from my own personality and emotions to my interests and abilities. I engaged frequently in much self-examination, increasing my time spent in reflection, in efforts to become more aware and self-knowledgeable. As I considered how I could effectively use my authentic self in retirement, I spent many hours journal writing.

USING JOURNAL WRITING TO
EXPAND SELF-KNOWLEDGE

I often wrote questions in my journal and later answered them in writing, questions such as these: Who am I uniquely as an individual? What do I want to do in my retirement consistent with my unique self? What kinds of barriers may try to block me from reaching my retirement goals?

From these questions, I generated and attempted to answer many additional questions like these: What will deeply and profoundly matter to me in retirement? What core beliefs will I value the most? Will I be willing in my retirement to act on my beliefs and values? How can I remain true to self not only daily but continuously over time?

During my journal writing, I learned I had many more options and choices in retirement than I previously realized. Equally important, I often better understood how I could make, and needed to make, choices and decisions in retirement consistent with and inclusive of my own beliefs, with my own authentic self.

In and throughout my retirement, I have remained true to self. By staying true to self, I have experienced many moments of joy and happiness, of self- satisfaction and fulfillment. Often, in these moments, I have experienced an increased sense of significance, of increased self-worth.

Further, as I aged in my retirement, I have explored new opportunities to learn and grow. In particular, I learned how to remain true to self while at the same time experiencing different stages of developmental aging as they emerged in my retirement. We all pass through different stages of development as we age in the second half of life. Many of us, however, remain unaware of these stages.

THE SECOND BOOK PREMISE

A second premise I am making is concerned with the many personal and powerful benefits we receive when we become aware of developmental stages of aging in retirement. *During the second half of our lives, knowledge of our individual developmental stages of aging suggests ways for us to better change and adapt, to stay active and involved, to learn and grow in our later years. Moreover, these stages typically bring with them new and different opportunities for us to find deeper purpose and meaning in and along the retirement journey.*

FOUR STAGES OF DEVELOPMENTAL AGING IN LATER LIFE

There is no one fixed system representative of the developmental growth of everyone. Yet, research conducted by Gene D. Cohen shows most of us vary only slightly in our passages through four developmental phases in the second half of life. Cohen chooses to identify stages of developmental aging as "phases."

According to Cohen, the first phase of aging happens before most of us retire, at midlife. Cohen identifies this phase as Midlife Reevaluation, a phase which occurs from the late forties through the fifties. This first phase of developmental aging in the second half of life typically occurs before most people are retired, as it happened in my life, as I first attempted to ask and answer those retirement questions of most importance to me when I reached age fifty.

Cohen identifies the second phase of aging as Liberation, a phase accompanied with a strong desire for more freedom, and occurs from the late fifties into the seventies. This second stage of developmental growth in the second half of my adult lifespan began just before I retired.

Cohen identifies his third phase as Summing Up, a time when many older adults possess a strong desire to give back, and occurs when we are in our late sixties into our early eighties.

Retirees during this phase search for ways to make greater contributions to others and society at large.

The fourth and last phase, one Cohen calls Encore, occurs in our early eighties to the end of life. Cohen describes this phase of aging as a time of continuation, with a strong desire to remain living with vitality and purpose, even when confronted with severe aging, adversity, and loss.[1]

MY STAGES OF DEVELOPMENTAL GROWTH IN RETIREMENT

When I first retired, I thought naively that I would stay the same kind of retiree throughout all my remaining years. However, approximately ten years after I retired, I changed, and somewhat dramatically.

Not surprisingly, all four of my developmental stages were very much like those phases previously identified and described by Cohen. Further, my stages lasted for similar lengths of time, for approximately ten years. Each of my stages held much potential for personal growth. Moreover, my awareness of these stages gave me many opportunities to take an active role in my retirement as each stage emerged.

When I was in my fifties and first contemplating retirement, I entered Cohen's first stage of developmental aging in the second half of life, Midlife Reevaluation. In this stage, I attempted to ask and answer profound questions concerned with many retirement issues, especially how I might continue to find purpose and meaning in a life without work.

Ten years later, at age sixty-three, I retired and entered my second stage of adult development in my second half of life, one I called Freedom and Adventure, a stage similar to Cohen's Liberation phase of aging. During this stage, I possessed a strong desire for more time to devote to myself as my own agenda, my own daily itinerary, a life filled with much freedom and adventure in retirement.

FREEDOM AND ADVENTURE

Essentially, in this second developmental stage, I wanted to be free to do anything and at any time I chose. I wanted freedom and time to pursue new and different adventures and opportunities in retirement, with the potential for reaching new moments filled with opportunities to experience joy and happiness, new moments of connectedness and oneness.

Soon, in my early life in retirement, I was experiencing many moments of celebration and surprise, moments with unusually high levels of personal freedom, fulfillment, and enjoyment. I seized opportunities when they presented themselves. I filled my retirement days with moments of spontaneous living.

At the same time, I desired greater experimentation and innovation in my new stage of life. I acted on my new convictions, found new and desired adventures, and developed new relationships.

I left my career behind, became a snowbird, moved to two different geographic areas of the country, discovered new communities in which to live, and established new friendships.

I began and maintained a debt-free approach to financial independence. I developed new skills and interests. I assumed new and different leadership roles. I discovered ways to maintain a continuous positive perspective on life as I engaged in new and varied daily activities. I lived an active lifestyle as I pursued everyday activities of much purpose and pleasure.

REFLECTION AND REVIEW

In my early seventies, I entered my third stage of developmental aging, a stage I identify as Reflection and Review, a stage similar to Cohen's phase Summing Up.

In this third stage, I begin to change, behaviorally and developmentally, in unexpected and yet refreshing ways, to turn more deeply inward, with new and unanticipated dimensions of myself emerging.

During this third stage, I began to question more frequently what was and was not now important to me and, in particular, what I now could do to serve a greater good in my remaining years. I was searching for more powerful and purposeful ways to finding deeper purpose and meaning in my retirement.

By making increased use of reflection as I reviewed my life, I began to understand how and why I was changing my behaviors and shifting my values as I aged. In addition, I began finding new ways of making greater use of higher levels of awareness as I evolved into a more transcendent, transformed, and mindful self.

Now, after twenty years of a lived retirement, I am at present entering my fourth, and most likely my last, developmental stage of aging, one I call Contentment and Integration, a stage consistent with Cohen's Encore phase.

In the conclusion to this book, I explain how this fourth developmental stage is different from my previous three. Further, I describe how I plan to integrate all four of my developmental stages as I continue to age.

TEN LESSONS LEARNED IN RETIREMENT

Of all the lessons I learned in my retirement, ten remain the most memorable, the most personally satisfying and significant. They are the ten lessons I learned as a result of experiencing powerful moments of connectedness and oneness, moments when I felt as if my heart was singing at its loudest and my soul soaring to new and extraordinary levels, memorable and noteworthy moments of living one with self, one with life.

They are the ten lessons that have contributed the most to my personal growth and development along my twenty-year retirement journey. As a result of learning these ten lessons, I have found and cultivated deeper purpose and meaning as I have aged in my retirement. I have made my retirement years some of the best, if not the best.

The first five lessons I learned in retirement occurred during my second developmental stage, Freedom and Adventure. In these lessons, I answer questions about retirement similar to the ones I originally asked when I was at age fifty: What kind of a person did I want to be in retirement, and why was living true to self, one with self, so important to me? What lifestyle did I want to pursue in retirement and where did I geographically want to live? How could I manage my retirement accumulations to live financially independent for the rest of my life? How would I find purpose and meaning in my life? What interests and activities would give me the most purpose and pleasure in retirement?

The next five lessons I learned occurred in my third stage of aging, Reflection and Review. The lessons I learned during this stage focus primarily on my changing and evolving self in retirement as I experienced deeper transcendent change and developmental growth.

The lessons I learned in this stage involve reconnecting with my spiritual past; confronting and mastering major life transitions in retirement; witnessing positive aging while aging; becoming more mindful of my own aging experiences; and making peace with the present moment.

In these last five lessons, I discovered what it means to serve a greater good as I both witnessed and experienced remarkable moments of joy, goodness, connectedness and oneness. Many of these moments were truly exceptional, extraordinary moments when I reached higher levels of consciousness not previously experienced.

BOOK FOCUS

This book is my retirement memoir chronicling how I grew psychologically and developmentally in retirement by engaging in much inner exploration, reflection, and self-examination. Along my twenty-year retirement journey, I have become increasingly conscious of new and multiple dimensions of my authentic self, inner resources with much potential for continuous growth.

This book also is my retirement story describing how I welcomed and nurtured these different aspects of my authentic self as they emerged. Further, this book is my retirement story illustrating how this new self-knowledge guided me to unanticipated challenges and possibilities, unanticipated opportunities to cultivate new and deeper purpose and meaning in my remaining years.

BOOK STRUCTURE

Structurally, this book is divided into two parts, with Part One representing my second stage of developmental growth in aging and Part Two, my third. The lessons I learned in each developmental stage are numbered and identified. Each lesson is followed by a retirement story which captures the essence of each major lesson learned.

I have written each chapter primarily in narrative form, in first person active voice, because this book is my retirement memoir. In those places in the book where more factual clarification and verification of the content seemed to be needed, I have made use of appropriate references.

BOOK RATIONALE

While there are many retirement books autobiographical in nature, I know of no other book that traces for readers a life in retirement lived over time, over twenty years. I know of no book that illustrates for readers how the meshing of one's true self with how we choose to live in retirement frequently results in extraordinary moments, deep and meaningful moments of oneness filled with love, joy, happiness, and fulfillment.

I know of no other retirement book that places psychological and developmental aspects of aging in retirement within research-established stages of growth. I know of no other book that embeds within its retirement framework those basic questions most readers want answered: Financially, do I have enough money accumulated to retire? Psychologically, am I ready to retire? Where do I want to live in retirement? What will I do with more free time?

I know of no other book that shares with readers ten powerful lessons learned in retirement filled with remarkable moments of oneness, moments including examples of positive change and transformational growth. Moreover, I know of no other retirement book that clarifies for readers the significance of reflection and self-awareness in retirement as we search for deeper purpose and meaning as we age. *Retire One with Self, One with Life* is such a multi-layered retirement book.

BOOK PURPOSES

I understand there is no one retirement journey, no one retirement story. There is no one retirement mold that fits all. Nevertheless, there is much information all of us can glean by reading about a retirement lived over time, a retirement story rich with options and examples readers may not have considered.

Specifically, one major purpose of this book is to share with readers the concept of the authentic self, what it means to be true to self in retirement. Another related purpose is to share with readers how the leading of an authentic life in retirement can become a powerful and often deliberate force in finding purpose, meaning, and happiness. A further purpose of this book is to underscore for readers how retirement is not a static process. We do not retire and stay the same. We have many opportunities to change and grow as we experience different stages of developmental aging in retirement. Finally, whether readers be retired or not, *Retire One with Self, One with Life* provides an array of useful and beneficial recommendations for improving self-growth and positive development in most stages of life, regardless where readers presently may find themselves along the adult lifespan.

It is the application of my retirement lessons in the lives of other individuals that will be different and unique. Readers will at times make use of my retirement lessons in similar ways, at other times in different ways, and often in new and refreshing ways. Because we each are our own authentic self, there are endless possibilities.

I hope, at a minimum, readers find as much pleasure while reading my retirement memoir as I did while writing it, a retirement journey still evolving, still unfolding.

PART ONE:

FREEDOM AND ADVENTURE

LISTEN TO THE MESSAGES HIDDEN DEEP WITHIN THE HEART

The Reemergence of the Authentic Self

In late December of 1999, my partner Robbie and I were traveling by train with our friend David, heading from Raleigh, North Carolina to Washington DC, to celebrate the New Year and the beginning of the New Millennium. Little did I know that I would soon begin another journey, a more difficult journey, a journey inward to determine whether I should retire sooner rather than later in life.

From my briefcase, I removed the yet unread afternoon mail. As I perused the different envelopes, I noticed two letters from my retirement companies, most likely reporting my recent accumulations. I opened the envelopes, read the content, and studied the graphs. The 1990s had been powerful investment years. My retirement funds had increased steadily throughout this decade, and with unimaginable financial gains.

After completing some basic calculations, I knew it was true what my financial advisor lately had been suggesting to me: Finally, I had accumulated enough retirement funds to last a lifetime, even longer. Finally, after years of teaching and investing, I had the option now to retire and reap the benefits of financial independence.

For many years, particularly throughout the past decade, I had planned to retire as soon as I financially could. I had enjoyed a long and basically successful academic career, but now I desired time in my remaining years to explore a new and different life.

THE DIFFICULTY IN DECIDING TO RETIRE

Although I financially could retire comfortably, emotionally I could not bring myself to make this decision. Something deep inside, feelings of doubt, discomfort, and unease, were preventing me from readily accepting my desired retirement as a logical and viable option. For unknown reasons, I felt as if I first had to give myself permission to retire, and at this present moment, I could not.

For many subsequent months, I still did not clearly understand the reasons for my reluctance to retire. However, I knew I did not want to retire prematurely and later regret it. On the contrary, I wanted to be as logical and objectively reserved as possible in making one of the most important decisions of my life. Thus, I began to use journal writing to further explore the reasons for my retirement hesitations.

THE USE OF JOURNAL WRITNG FOR SELF-DISCOVERY

For many years, I had used a variety of methods to become more reflective and self-aware, more self-knowledgeable. During these introspective moments, many of my subconscious thoughts sometimes emerged on their own. They occurred naturally, "out of the blue." During other times, they occurred after prolonged and deeper reflective thinking.

I often used journal writing to capture my unconscious thoughts as they popped into my thinking and awareness, objectifying them by writing them on paper, to see and later study. I also wrote personal questions in my journal to use as prompts for events happening in my life. I often wrote answers to these questions and read them later, sometimes over and over.

By asking myself select questions, writing down my uncensored answers, and studying my written responses over time, I was able to discover and understand new aspects of myself previously unexplored, a process sometimes called "writing for discovery."

Throughout the spring of 2000, I sorted and sifted through my responses to a variety of personal retirement inquiries. I began by asking myself and answering in my journal writing responses to these two basic retirement inquiries: (1) What would I be relinquishing if I were to retire, and on the other hand; (2) What would I be gaining in my life by retiring sooner rather than later in life?

WHAT WOULD I BE RELINGUISHING BY RETIRING?

As I wrote my responses, many benefits of my long career flowed forth, easily and naturally.

A NOTEWORTHY ACADEMIC CAREER

Without question, I would be leaving behind a life in academia of which I was most proud. After completing undergraduate school in 1960, I taught in one capacity or another. I taught English at the high school level for eight years. During this time, I traveled extensively abroad. I participated in two educational trips to Europe and two world trips during the summer months. For three of these years, I lived and taught in Melbourne, Australia. Upon my return to the States, I completed both my Master of Arts and Doctorate Degrees at The University of California, Berkeley. While attending Berkeley, I was employed as a Teaching Assistant.

After graduation in 1970, I commenced my university-level teaching career. I quickly advanced in the university ranks, from Assistant Professor to Associate Professor in two years, and from Associate Professor to Full Professor in the following four.

First, I was appointed an Assistant Professor at The University of Delaware for two years, before being appointed and promoted to Associate Professor at Penn State University. Then, the following year, I was offered a position as Department Chair at the University of North Carolina at Chapel Hill, where I was appointed Full Professor with tenure four years later, in

1977. Thus, I became a professor at one of the top-tier academic institutions in our country.

For the following twenty-eight years, I remained a Professor of Curriculum and Instruction in the School of Education, where I specialized in the teaching of courses in Literacy and English Education. I also taught two graduate seminars, both focused on teaching doctoral students about different aspects of educational research, content designed to assist them in the completion of their doctoral proposals and dissertations.

For a total of forty-one years, I had invested much time and effort in studying, training, and advancing myself in academia. It seemed frivolous, even silly at times, for me now to disregard these personal educational invest- ments and accomplishments, to toss them aside, and to retire relatively early just because financially I finally could. Moreover, I would be bringing my present professional and academic life as I knew it to a complete end, and with this finality and choice would come the surrendering of a series of other career-related benefits.

A PLEASANT WORKSPACE

I would be leaving behind a pleasant workspace and environment. Since the first days of my career at Carolina, I was assigned a spacious office with multiple windows on the top floor of Peabody Hall. From my office win- dows, I had a direct view to my right of the historic Carolina Inn with its imposing colonial architecture. To my left, I could see the busy intersection of Cameron and Columbia Streets, all just a few blocks from Franklin Street and downtown Chapel Hill. I felt honored to be a faculty member at such a prestigious university and a resident of Chapel Hill, a lovely campus town, often devotedly referred to by alumni as "The Southern Part of Heaven."

A MULTIFACETED CAREER

I would be ending my teaching career and daily contact with students. I loved the multifaceted nature of my work, from teaching and advising exceptionally bright students to directing their theses and dissertations, from reading and writing scholarly articles to attending conferences and presenting papers. It would not be easy to say goodbye to my professional roles and the status and pride that came with the completion of each.

A STRONG SOCIAL NETWORK

I would be leaving behind most of my social network. In my office suite, I looked forward to personal and professional conversations with many of my colleagues. We often covered topics ranging from world news to sports events and The Tar Heels, from campus activities to university and in-house politics. I also valued my friendships with faculty members in other disciplines and program areas within the School of Education, university-wide, and from other local and national universities.

LIFELONG LEARNING OPPORTUNITIES

Through my academic career, I experienced many opportunities to become and remain a lifelong learner. One activity I enjoyed immensely was attending many and varied university-sponsored lectures. At Carolina, it seemed as if there were a lecture of interest every day and evening somewhere on campus. While attending these lectures, I often met and mingled with numerous and renowned speakers, from noted international scholars and media personnel to accomplished artists and politicians.

A DAILY WORK STRUCTURE AND
PROFESSIONAL IDENTITY

I would be ending my daily work structure. I lived only a few blocks from campus in a townhouse in the historic district. Most days, I walked to campus, taught a class, attended meetings, visited a school to observe a teaching intern, went to lunch with a colleague, held office hours, and exercised late afternoons at a local gym.

In the evening, I either attended a social event, a university function, taught an evening class, or worked at home. Indeed, my academic work and position at Carolina reinforced my sense of place and belonging which, in turn, often resulted in strong feelings of self-worth. Thus, by retiring, I would be relinquishing more than a structure to my life that work provided. I would also be ending my professional identity.

A GUARANTEED INCOME

With my retirement, I would be terminating my tenure and steady stream of guaranteed income. As a result, I would have to learn how to pay myself an annual salary, and I would need to manage my retirement accumulations so that this money lasted for the rest of my life.

A PRIMARY PURPOSE IN LIFE

Most importantly, I would be relinquishing a sense of significance, a primary purpose in life. On numerous occasions in my career, I experienced powerful feelings of meaning and fulfillment after something magical, exciting, and powerful happened: A class went extremely well; a doctoral student finally designed a potential and promising dissertation study; a student or groups of students comprehended new information; faculty discussions challenged and enriched the academic perspectives of those present.

A CHARMED AND AUTHENTIC LIFE

For most of my teaching and academic years, I not only experienced a noteworthy career, but a life I described to my close friends and colleagues as charmed and authentic. To those who would listen, I often reminded them I had never viewed my life in academia as work because I enjoyed it so much, just about every minute of it. I frequently paraphrased for them a line from Robert Frost's poem, "Two Tramps at Mud Time": *My vocation and avocation are one, like two eyes that meet and see one vision.*

As an authentic self in my career, I was capable of meshing naturally my genuine self with my academic career. As a result, I experienced many moments filled with happiness and fulfillment, moments of joy and pleasure, moments of harmony and balance, moments lived one with self, one with life.

These good times in teaching and academia became what I further called my golden years in my career. I had time, and was expected to take time, to study, learn, teach, conduct research, and publish—requirements of my profession I enjoyed. The completion of these tasks resulted in many moments of professional success. My sense of work fulfillment and job satisfaction did nothing but grow and expand as the years passed. If I were to retire, I would be relinquishing a position in academia which provided me with a strong sense of significance, a primary purpose in life.

WHAT WOULD I BE GAINING BY RETIRING?

Then, there were my answers to the second question: What would I be gaining by retiring sooner rather than later in life? My first response was obvious.

MORE TIME WITH ROBBIE

From the start of our relationship in 1984, my life partner, Robbie, displayed an array of outstanding characteristics: high intelligence, exceptional problem-solving ability, and wide background experiences and interests. In addition, from the first time we met, he made evident his many levels of goodness and commitment to our relationship.

Throughout our long life together, I cannot recall one boring moment we ever experienced, most likely because we were regularly engaged in separate or mutual activities, learning new information, creating new projects, listening to and learning from others, helping others, giving our time and support to noteworthy causes. We both were always busy, in our careers and in our personal lives, together and separately.

Robbie owned an antique business in Durham, North Carolina. His career required him to know much about art, architecture, antiques, collectibles, and quality reproductions. His world of work included much travel, particularly on weekends, to buy and sell inventory. During most weekdays, he sold inventory at his shop.

Through Robbie's antique business, we met many interesting and accomplished customers and patrons. We also became friendly with numerous antique dealers, a sub-culture of highly specialized and accomplished individuals. From many of these individuals, we purchased select inventory for our own private collection and use. We frequently referred to these possessions as our "objects of desire."

Throughout our relationship, Robbie and I participated in activities and events beyond our own individual worlds of work. We met new friends, joined and participated in community activities, read good books, cooked, dined out, exercised daily, attended lectures, entertained in and outside our home, renovated our home, traveled together, bought music, went to the movies, and attended concerts, plays, and lectures.

Moreover, we both enjoyed the beach and life at the beach. In addition to our Chapel Hill townhouse, we bought a beachfront condo in Atlantic Beach, North Carolina, to use on weekends and long vacations. Later, we bought another condo in Ogunquit, Maine, to use during summer months. Although I did not know it at the time, we were both experiencing and discovering what a life without work might be like for the both of us, sometime in the distant future.

During my early years in academia, I committed much time in my life to my career advancement. Now with Robbie as my life partner, I began shifting away from a life primarily devoted to my career to a more balanced, peaceful, and comfortable private life. I was finding and cultivating new meaning in everyday living and gaining a deeper appreciation for all the small and simple things in life. In short, I was experiencing with Robbie many moments of joy or bliss in everyday living.

Further, I felt most fortunate to have found and cultivated similar ways of experiencing joy and bliss in my personal life as I had found in my professional career: a life of continuous inquiry, lifelong learning experiences, rich cultural experiences, and a strong and varied social network.

MORE TIME ENGAGED IN A LIFE OF BLISS

Robbie and I frequently reminded each other of our good fortune: We shared what we called lives of joy, lives of bliss. I attributed our fulfillment and contentment to our mutual abilities to stay present with one another, to accept each moment together with authenticity that emerged naturally and often. In addition, I also had been born and raised with an unusual gift of joy.

Joy was a personal trait I possessed and experienced regularly since childhood. Daily, I planned and participated in a variety of activities, and I looked forward to my involvement in these activities with anticipation and excitement. These activities ranged from socializing, participating in plays, sports, and youth clubs to learning new information and sharing it with other people.

Throughout my life, joy had become for me a gift of resiliency, intellectual searching, and creativity. As I matured into adulthood, my gift of joy guided me to think and act in different ways, and often to take risks I would not have otherwise taken.

In time, I came to understand my gift of joy, of finding immense pleasure in everyday living, was a personal and vital source of strength and power. No matter what challenging circumstances were occurring in my life, my responses to these events were influenced in no small way by my large reservoir of joy.

With the use of my natural gift of joy, I was able to experience with Robbie an unusual and enriching life of bliss. If I were to retire, I would have more time to devote to Robbie and our shared lives of bliss.

FREEDOM FROM UNPLEASANT WORK OBLIGATIONS AND CONSTRAINTS

By the mid-1990s, I became increasingly aware of a feeling I previously had believed would never happen: I was losing some of my earlier zest for my academic life and career. I did not possess any longer the same level of resiliency needed to bounce back, to find new purpose and pleasure in my teaching and academic work.

NEW DEMANDS, NEW RESPONSIBILITIES

As I continued in my career, I faced many new demands and responsibilities in the gradual but changing nature of my work. With the passage of even more time, many more career-related changes continued to occur, slowly diminishing my previous feelings of joy, adventure, scholarship, and creativity.

With these changes, I experienced many shifts in administrative leadership styles and ideologies, new unpleasant in-house politics, and what appeared as increased jockeying for power and control by different colleagues and faculty.

The sense of constancy and collaboration in my previous work lessened, replaced by the reinvention of past and tried leadership conditions, often inadequately conceptualized. As my career progressed over the years, my golden and charmed authentic life in academia began to slowly fade and disappear, becoming fond memories of the past, eroded in part by new and questionable changes in working conditions and professional climate.

In the last two years of my career, the nature of my work changed again, only this time more profoundly, primarily because of the sudden influence of an ever increasing and powerful national movement—the accountability movement.

THE ACCOUNTABILITY MOVEMENT

The accountability movement in our country started in the early 1970s. Now two decades later, the influences of this movement were finally infiltrating institutions of higher education everywhere, and with much force. One major goal of this movement was to make universities more accountable, more business-like in the measurement of productivity, from grant writing and teaching performance to scholarly endeavors and field-based experiences.

First slowly but later steadily, my workplace climate became far different from what it was during my golden years.

During my golden years in academia, faculty members often sauntered though the halls, chatted with colleagues in other departments, joined one another for coffee and further conversation, shared educational articles on the spot, or meandered across campus from one building site to another, to attend a lecture or presentation, while at the same time meeting all their necessary university responsibilities.

Now, however, my once peaceful, collegial, and collaborative working environment, with much time for contemplation and the life of the mind, with time for all kinds of scholarly productivity, became greatly diminished, if not gone forever, replaced by endless paperwork, committee work, and new supervisory and accountability-driven teaching assignments.

Even the physical pace and movement of faculty within my building changed. I often observed many of my colleagues now rushing through the hallways quickly and often frantically, in efforts to attend on time a daily series of endless and overlapping committee meetings, new assignments, and new accountability-related supervisory field experiences.

Rather than participate in my work with zest, excitement, and joy as I had done so often in the past, I now found myself pulling away whenever possible from my work and workplace, and with this pulling away, I felt a much deep and inner loss for my past golden life in academia, my past charmed life of work.

THE LOSS OF MY AUTHENTIC SELF

During the summer of 2000, Robbie and I had spent a memorable summer in Maine, enjoying every moment living and traveling along the coast, with occasional trips to Boston, New York City, Montreal, and Nova Scotia. When August arrived and it became time to return to Chapel Hill and the beginning of Fall Semester, I did, but with a heavy heart, with feelings of much reluctance and regret.

During the orientation for new students and faculty, I remember sitting in the back row of a large auditorium on a lovely sunny day, next to an open window that looked outside onto well-maintained campus lawns and surrounding shrubbery.

The speeches and introductions appeared endless. I was momentarily thinking how I would rather be free, outside in the sun, when I heard my inner voice say, "This is not the work I want to do anymore. This is not the way I want to spend the rest of my life."

Later in the day, I sat alone in my office, overwhelmed with feelings of guilt, despair, stagnation, even hopelessness. I felt trapped, stuck in meaningless work, trapped in an endless cycle of committee work, paperwork, and teaching responsibilities, most of them unpleasant, work I no longer enjoyed or valued.

I hungered for greater work-related fulfillment. I felt empty and disillusioned. My sense of self-worth had diminished. I felt defeated, unable to resolve and eliminate these new and rather alarming feelings of loss, loss of my past charmed life in my career and academic work.

For the rest of Fall Semester, I plodded along in my career, accommodating these uncomfortable feelings as best as I could. I was struggling to fix things, to make the nature of my work bearable and meaningful, and I no longer could. After a long and successful career, for the first time, I now felt like a failure in my formerly loved and cherished career.

Something was seriously out of balance, not just with the conditions of my work, but in the way I was thinking and feeling about myself and my career. Something was happening inside me, hidden and unresolved. Something was happening to my values and beliefs, and they all seemed related to the loss of my most basic essence, my authentic self.

THE LOSS OF INTEREST

My interest and continued investment in my teaching and career had diminished, first gradually but later with snowballing force. Every chance I had to remove myself from my work and workplace, I did. I began spending more time and longer weekends at my condo on the ocean in North Carolina. During long holiday breaks, I retreated to my home near the ocean in Maine.

THE LOSS OF JOY

My strongest indicator something was out of order with me and my work was my loss of joy. Joy in my life and work had always been a constant, a rare gift, one of my strongest attributes. My gift of joy, of finding immense pleasure in work and everyday living, was a vital source of personal strength and power. No matter what negative and challenging circumstances were occurring in my life, my response and resiliency to these events were influenced in no small way by my abundance of joy.

Now at the end of my academic career, I was facing for the first time a challenge in life I had not experience before: the loss of joy. My loss of joy and interest in my work were also deeply embedded in another and larger loss, my loss of soul.

THE LOSS OF SOUL

At the time as I was experiencing these unpleasant feelings of loss, I happened to read Thomas Moore's masterful book, *Care of the Soul: A Guide for Cultivating Depth and Sacredness in Everyday Life*. In this book, Moore reminds readers that we make use of our soul in everyday living. By using our unique characteristics, we express our authentic or genuine self. Our individual self reflects what is in our soul and explains our personal depth and substance, our true values, beliefs, and behaviors.

Moore also reminds readers that our self-concepts are inextricably linked to the content in our souls, and our work reflects our self-concepts. He further states the conditions of our work have much to do with the disturbances of our soul because our work is an important reflection of our sense of self. Most importantly, Moore warns readers that whatever aspects of our true self we neglect for too long become a personal source of suffering.

Moore further suggests an option for dealing with our feelings of loss: Examine these feelings of loss until we grasp a greater comprehension of our inner conflicts and potential ways of resolving them. A major conclusion Moore reaches is that care of the soul often comes from living congruently with the messages coming from deep within the heart and not at odds with them.[2]

Something suddenly clicked in my thinking. Could I be living at odds with unconscious messages hidden deep within my heart? Could aspects of my thinking be incongruent, at odds with one another? Could I be living at odds with my true self, my authentic self?

THE AUTHENTIC SELF

I recalled one of my favorite courses in 1968 when I was a doctoral student at The University of California, Berkeley. It was a foundations course in philosophy, a course in which the professor traced philosophical thought over 3000 years.

During this course, I first learned about the emphasis many philosophers placed on the need to know one's authentic self. Early Greek philosophers, for example, debated topics ranging from the meaning of the motto "know thyself" to what Socrates meant in his famous quote, "The unexamined life is not worth living."

PRESSURES BLOCKING THE AUTHENTIC SELF

It was the later existentialist philosophers, however, who captured my interest the most. Many of them concluded the choice to be authentic was up to us individually, to act and become who we individually truly are and want to be, an authentic self.

Certain existentialist philosophers believed the authentic self was more than the degree to which an individual assumed responsibility for being true to self. The individual first had to determine if actions taken in life and society were congruent with the individual's genuine beliefs and desires.

I remember reading and discussing with excitement how Jean Paul-Sartre believed that the authentic self was reliant on the ability of an individual to find authentic faith in self, and thus become true to self despite those pressures outside of self, pressures which often attempt to block the way, pressures that attempt to make and keep us *other than* who we truly are and want to be. I also recall reading Soren Kierkegaard similarly noting the following about the authentic self: The capacity to live authentically required individuals to come to terms with individually specific, external forces and influences which are different from, or *other than*, and inconsistent with one's true or authentic self.

For years, other philosophers, psychologists, and scholars from other fields have informed us of a wide range of these outside pressures that attempt to block us individually from our authentic self. While outside pressures are many and varied, most come from a common core of sources influential in most of our lives, and often in unconscious, subtle, and deliberate ways. These sources typically want us to be more like them, or a different kind of person, or to ignore our individual beliefs and values and replace them with other and often opposing views.

Most of these outside pressures come from sources closest to us: our family members, friends, our cultures and society, our schools and education, and our politics and religious beliefs, by themselves or in combination.

DEFINING THE AUTHENTIC SELF

From existentialist philosophers to contemporary scholars, the authentic self generally has become defined as who we are at our most basic essence, the sum of our individually unique qualities, and the alignment of our authentic self with our actions so that we are not living different from, *other than,* and inconsistently with our true self.

Here is how the psychologist, Phillip C. McGraw, defines the authentic self:

The authentic self is you that can be found at your absolute core. It is the part of you that is not defined by your job, or your function, or your role. It is the composite of all your unique gifts, skills, interests, insights, and wisdom. It is all your strengths and values that are uniquely yours and need expression versus what you have been programmed to believe that you are "supposed" to be and do. It is the you that flourished unself-consciously, in those times in your life when you felt happy and most fulfilled.[3]

Each of us, then, possesses our own special authentic self. Each of us has many individual and unique traits, among them our specific abilities and interests, skills and talents, world knowledge and experiences, who we are inside at our most basic core. The sum of our unique qualities becomes our true self, our basic self, our authentic self.

In the preceding quote, McGraw reminds us we are much more than how we have been defined by outside pressures. We are more than how we are programmed by our work and defined by our work. We are more than what others think we are supposed to be and do. When we live true to self, we do not allow these pressures to block our way. Instead, we express our authentic strengths and values, and as a result, feel happy and fulfilled.

BEING AND LIVING *OTHER THAN*

The term living or being *other than* implies someone is not living or acting authentically. Instead, the person has succumbed to different outside pressures blocking, or attempting to block, the person from being an authentic self and living an authentic life.

Being and living *other than* was what Sartre says happens to us when we allow these outside pressures to keep us from maintaining authentic faith in self. Living *other than* true to self, according to Kierkegaard, happens when we remain oblivious to those external forces and influences which are inconsistent with, different from, or *other than* our authentic self. More recently, living *other than* is what McGraw reminds us we do when we allow outside pressures to program us to become who we think we are supposed to be, rather than who we want to be and become.

TWO OUTSIDE PRESSURES TO REMAIN *OTHER THAN*

Had I, now at the end of my career, become *other than* in my thinking and behavior? Had I become at odds with my authentic self in my work? Had I stopped doing things in my work that were meaningful to me, things at which I was proficient? In becoming *other than*, had I suppressed, even forgotten about, my authentic self within?

Now, at the end of my career, I was increasingly becoming aware of subtle, often unexpressed, but still significant *other than* outside pressures attempting to influence my decision to continue working. Had I become programmed over the years to believe I was supposed to be somehow different from what my authentic self now wished? Had I succumbed to different kinds of outside pressures blocking me from my own conscious awareness? Were these pressures attempting to influence my decision to stay working rather than retire? Had I become who I thought I should be rather than who I wanted to be?

While there may have been many outside pressures blocking me from my authentic self, I immediately thought of two outside pressures to remain the same, to remain *other than* who I now wanted to be and become.

REMAINING WHO I WAS SUPPOSED TO BE

Many of my current colleagues were in similar financial circumstances as I. They had worked for many years and accumulated enough funds to retire comfortably. Only most of these colleagues planned not to retire early or anytime in the immediate future. Rather, they intended to work well beyond age seventy, to acquire even more retirement savings. Further, many of my colleagues seemed to have acquired the ability to balance their careers with their personal lives, to continue working without dissatisfaction and regret.

Inwardly, I felt a pressure to be and behave like these professors, to devote my life to a noteworthy career, even without this pressure ever being directly expressed. My colleagues' desire for a continuous and long career was the way I was supposed to be.

REMAINING WHO I WAS PROGRAMMED TO BE

Although I now often felt like a failure in my work, I also knew feeling like a failure and being a failure were two separate issues. While I was presently working with less interest and joy in my career, I was still accomplishing more than just maintaining the status quo. Even in my recent moments of deep despair, I managed to meet my work responsibilities. I was heavily programmed to be successful in my work, and my recent and exemplary Post-Tenure Review was one testament to this programming,

During the beginning of the 2000 academic year, I participated in a mandatory Post-Tenure Review for all Senior Faculty. The process and the paperwork were extensive. Within a self-prepared document, I compiled a review of what I accomplished in my career for the past five years and stipulated what I planned to accomplish for the next five years.

Categories for documentation over the past five years included publications and other scholarly activity, teaching assignments, teaching evaluations, service, and advising. My report was read and reviewed by a post-tenure review committee comprised of colleagues within other program departments. A final report was later sent to my Dean and myself.

In their evaluation, the committee rated me an outstanding professor in all categories, concluding that I was a faculty member with an exemplary record. The following semester, I received one of the highest increases in merit pay I had ever received throughout my many years of tenure.

My feelings of validation and worth, however, were short-lived. Soon, my feelings of loss and misery returned, leading me to conclude I was particularly good at doing work I no longer enjoyed nor valued—work, for still unknown reasons, I could not bring myself to leave behind.

COMPREHENDING MY INNER CONFLICT

I did understand some basic aspects of my inner struggle. I knew, for example, I was feeling a deep sense of loss, of my past self and work, and presently much unhappiness with the present conditions of my work.

In contrast, for most of my past career, I had enjoyed every bit of my work. I had remained successful by including numerous aspects of my authentic self with my past academic tasks and daily living experiences, finding in the process much joy and fulfillment. Without question, these moments of meshing my authentic self with my work were the times in my career and life when I felt most happy, whole, complete, living what I called a charmed and authentic life.

Then, gradually, things began to change. Not only had my conditions of work changed but I also had changed. By the end of my career, I had become a person who now wanted to retire in full and live a life of bliss, as I had been enjoying with Robbie for some time, especially during long holidays and summer vacations, an insight of which I was not yet fully conscious.

BREAKTHROUGH

Many years ago, a friend had reminded me of this personal observation: Breakthroughs in our thinking happen in a flash, and in that flash, we are changed forever.

In a flash. That is exactly what happened to me one spring evening in 2001. A breakthrough in my thinking happened in a flash. In that moment,

I was changed forever. I finally understood what was holding me back, preventing me from deciding to retire.

For much of that day, I had been pondering why I could not bring myself to retire with a sense of logic and assurance. I had continued my internal debate by asking myself a series of "what if" hypothetical questions and writing my answers in my journal.

Eventually, I wrote this question: If conditions in my present work were the same today as during my golden years, would I still want to retire?

My response came immediately, "Yes."

In a flash, I finally understood the nature of my inner conflict, my previous inability to retire with comfort and ease. Even if the nature of my work were to change, to become like it was during the golden era of my academic life, my academic career was no longer what I now wanted.

COMPREHENDING MY INCONGRUENT THINKING

My conflict was the result of an inner struggle between two opposing ways of thinking and behaving. On one hand, I was fighting to maintain who I thought I should be, the person who I was trained and programmed to be, my professional identity with its title and responsibilities.

On the other hand, by continuing with my career, I had been suppressing what was hidden deep within my heart, the person I now wanted to be, my authentic self. In and throughout my academic career, I had always been much more than my exemplary post-tenure review, my professional identity and career accomplishments. Most importantly, I was my authentic self, that part of me not defined by my professional title and identity, that inner part of me that is also in need of constant expression.

There it was, the incongruency in my life, the reason for my inner conflict. Instead of honoring my authentic self, I was choosing to do just the opposite. I could not comfortably make the decision to retire because I was allowing who I thought I was supposed to be to block me from acting, from doing what I now wanted to do, retire and begin a new and different life in my remaining years, potentially one filled with new freedom, adventure, and purpose. As a result, I had become in my work *other than* my true self, *other than* who I now genuinely wanted to be. I had been in conflict with and suppressing my basic and most powerful essence, my authentic self.

MY FIRST LESSON LEARNED: LISTEN TO THE MESSAGES HIDDEN DEEP WITHIN THE HEART

I had just learned my first major lesson in my impending retirement, the importance of listening to the messages hidden deep within the heart, messages coming from the authentic self.

While I had been struggling to conform, to be more like my colleagues who decided to stay working until much later in their careers, I differed from most of these colleagues in significant ways. I wanted to retire, now, not later. Moreover, I was ready to retire. I had worked continuously for forty-one years. My heart was no longer in my work. I had achieved the professional goals I set out to accomplish. There were no advantages for me to continue with my career.

I had accumulated enough retirement funds to retire comfortably and be financially secure. I could pay myself a salary comparable to my present salary, even more if I ever needed. Moreover, I would have more time in life to do anything I wanted, at any time, and without the interruption of required work. I had the support of Robbie, who would become my retirement companion. Most importantly, I would have more time to find and cultivate what I now genuinely wanted, a new life in retirement.

I also realized the present conditions of my academic work were not the major reasons for my inner conflict. While they were influential catalysts for use while considering other options in my life, they were not the primary reasons for my decision to retire. I want to retire, and I was ready to retire.

In a flash. My desire to begin a new life in retirement finally became so clear I had no choice but to listen to and follow the messages coming from deep within: *Take the leap. Live the life you now want and value. Live fully in retirement the blissful life you and Robbie have been embracing for years. Stop fighting these possibilities moving you in a new direction. Trust your judgment and the process of being and becoming your authentic self. On the other side of your momentary doubt and discomfort is a new life waiting in retirement.*

THE REEMERGENCE OF THE AUTHENTIC SELF: RETURNING FEELINGS OF ONENESS

As soon as I wrote and sent my Dean notification of my intent to retire, I immediately experienced a flood of positive and powerful feelings, among them returning joy, excitement, freedom, anticipation, of being whole again, of being one with self, one with life. I was alive again, vibrant, and enthusiastic, eager to begin a new and major transition in my life. I had reconnected with my authentic self.

I wasted no time in making use of these powerful feelings of oneness as I entertained new opportunities for a new life in retirement. I wanted to maintain my sense of joy. I wanted to find and develop a new sense of purpose, a new sense of significance, to matter in new and exciting ways. I wanted my heart to sing and my soul to soar again as it had done during the golden age of my career. In a flash, my life changed forever. I finally could give myself permission to retire, to begin a new life in retirement, one congruent with my authentic self.

My decision to retire, nevertheless, still required much courage. There was finality in the decision. Once I retired, there would be no turning back. I would be leaving my long academic career behind, and most likely forever. There would be no longer a guaranteed salary as in the past; no tenure; no university office space, and fewer daily professional contacts. There would be no longer the daily contact and work with graduate students, nor teaching assignments or work structure.

Most of all, I would be choosing to end my professional career and life. I would be terminating my professional career with its status and prestige, a career for which I had worked for many years to obtain. I would be choosing to forfeit my professional identity. I would be no longer Dr. William S. Palmer, Professor, The University of North Carolina at Chapel Hill. Rather, I would be just Bill, a man in search of a new and purposeful life in retirement.

Beyond courage, it would also take much wisdom to relinquish a secure and established past to face an uncertain and unknown future. I had lost joy and passion in my work, but I had maintained both in my shared life of bliss with Robbie. If I were to start a new life filled with new sources of pleasure and purpose, now was the time to begin such a journey. Now was the time to honor my authentic self. Now was the time for me to retire.

LINGERING DOUBTS

A few months later, I officially retired on June 30, 2001. A lingering question was whether I would find in retirement sources of purpose as significant as those I once experienced in my career. Although I believed strongly I would, I must have had some subconscious doubts.

Out of nowhere one evening before I had written and submitted my retirement notice, I heard my inner voice silently recite and sing the beginning words from a poem by Emily Dickenson: *I'm Nobody! Who are you? Are you—Nobody--too?*

This incident happened more than once and when I least expected it, and only stopped once I finally retired. I now suspect that all kinds of doubts and fears were raising their ugly heads in my subconscious, especially the fear that I was making a terrible mistake, that looming ahead for me was a lonely, empty, and insignificant life. The opposite, however, was about to happen—the beginning of a new and powerful life in retirement, a new and exciting stage of life in which I would learn many more life-changing lessons.

In the last few weeks before I officially retired, I was about to learn a second important lesson in retirement: what it actually would mean to retire true to self, and the significant changes I would need to make in my present life if I were to achieve this goal.

RETIRE TRUE TO SELF

After the Pink Full Moon: Coming Out and Staying Out

In April of 2001, two months before I retired, I attended a small cocktail party at the home of a colleague. As he prepared drinks, his wife reminded the guests that tonight was a special time of year, for it was the evening of the pink full moon.

Several guests wanted to know more. What exactly was a pink full moon? The hostess did not seem to know, except to add that the pink full moon was brighter and shinier than most full moons.

Another colleague came to her rescue, adding that the pink full moon did not appear often, only on occasion. Then, another guest contributed a more detailed description, one giving credit to Native Americans who named the pink full moon because of a ground weed, a phlox plant that blooms in the spring.

Eventually, a seemingly more knowledgeable colleague spoke. She reminded us that it is what the pink full moon symbolizes that is most important. The pink full moon was about the changes in nature at this time of year, and how these transformations are like the changes that occur over time in our individual lives.

My colleague continued to elaborate, informing us that winter was behind us, and we were now experiencing the winds of spring, natural forces spreading seeds and pollen for new plants of all colors, including pink—all symbolizing rebirth and new beginnings, potential for much boldness and authenticity in everyday living.

I listened intently. Indeed, the pink moon under discussion shared many similarities with my life. Soon I would be fully retired. The spring of my life had arrived. I had endured and survived the dark and cold of winter. If only symbolically, the pink full moon was a powerful reminder of the many new, exciting, and bold possibilities ahead, awaiting me in retirement.

A BRIGHT AND SHINY CAREER

As the pink full moon was bright and shiny, so had been most of my professional career. I had numerous and memorable opportunities to study, learn, teach, and travel. In time, I became an expert in my field, gave speeches nationally and internationally, consulted widely, and met many fascinating and accomplished people from differing areas of life. Like the pink full moon, however, I also possessed another side—a somewhat hidden and silent side.

SILENT AND HIDDEN

Since a young age, about the age of seven, I knew I was gay, what then was labeled a homosexual. My earliest feelings about being gay were based on the fear of what would happen if anyone ever found out, including my family. Even as a young child, not yet exposed to a lot of the norms in society, I knew I was not supposed to be having these same-sex feelings, that something was wrong with the way I was thinking, so wrong that I should keep these thoughts to myself.

During that same year, 1945, I remember going one afternoon to the movies with my parents. Before the movie started, a newsreel was shown first, just before the previews of upcoming movies. World War II was in the process of ending, and many of the newsreels focused on different events in the War and at the end of the War.

The newsreel this particular day contained a segment showing men with triangle badges on their shirts in prison camps, men who were being called "homosexuals." I remember whispering to my father sitting next to me what the word "homosexual" meant, and he whispered back, "Men who like other men instead of women."

That Saturday in 1945 became a defining moment in my young life. I learned a person with same-sex preferences had a name: homosexual. I also learned there were other people in the world like me.

At age seven, however, the impact of seeing men in jail because they were homosexual left this indelible message: If you are a homosexual and if anyone finds out, you will be sent away to some place for punishment. Based partially on this fear, I began my long silence about being gay.

GROWING UP GAY

For most of my school years, from grammar school throughout high school, I was different from my peers, both in appearance and behavior. I was extremely thin, somewhat over-active, effeminate with a high-pitched voice. Although I excelled in sports like track and baseball, I could not seem to readily change my physical and behavioral characteristics. Because I was often teased and bullied by my peers, in time I came to feel that I was not only different, but also defective, in need of fixing.

SILENT, BUT WITH SELF-ACCEPTANCE

As I aged, I thought much about my sexual identity. I kept thinking I might be passing through a phase in my life, that I might change and become heterosexual as I matured. However, by age fifteen, I knew my feelings were not just a phase, that I could not change my same-sex feelings, and, most importantly, I did not want to change them. I had accepted the fact that I was gay and would remain gay for the rest of my life.

With this self-acceptance came a powerful release of long pent-up anxiety, and in its place, a sense of peace. I was out to myself, and with my inner feelings of self-acceptance, I felt more at ease, with myself and others.

I remained silent about being gay because I wanted to avoid further hurt, rejection, and retaliation from my peers. Further, I did not want to experience any direct oppressive and punitive anti-homosexual treatment by society, heavily prominent in the 1950's when I was in high school, and into the 1960's, when I began my teaching career.

POWERFUL SOCIETAL PRESSURES
TO BEHAVE *OTHER THAN*

During my high school days, I faced many societal pressures to become *other than* my true self, *other than* my gay self. During the 1950s, many young men postponed going to college, choosing instead to serve in the military. However, at this time in history, the military had characterized homosexuality as a lifestyle incompatible with military service, thus putting a ban on gays from serving.

Also, in the 1950s, President Eisenhower signed an executive order banning homosexuals from working anywhere in the federal government, citing homosexuals as a security risk.

Thus, enrolling in the military would not have been an option for me. I did not know what I would be doing for a future career, but I did not think it would be connected to the federal government. At this time in my life, these two governmental rulings did not have much of a direct and personal impact on my life.

However, in 1952, when I was in ninth grade, I read in a newspaper that the American Psychiatric Association had listed homosexuality as a mental disorder, what the article called a sociopathic disturbance. I recall responding emotionally, if silently. I knew intuitively I was not mentally ill. I was gay, not suffering from a "sociopathic disturbance."

Regardless of my feelings, inwardly I felt much fear, even as a young adult. If someone with authority found out I was a homosexual, I believed I could be categorized as mentally ill, and potentially even institutionalized.

DECIDING TO LIVE *OTHER THAN*

During my high school years, I reached a critical conclusion. If I were to survive and succeed in the world of work, I would need to do more than remain silent about my sexual preference. I also would have to change my thin and awkward appearance and my feminine tendencies.

Throughout most of my high school years, I started to eat more and exercise more, hoping to gain weight and physically fill out. In addition, I took speech classes, primarily to learn to speak in a lower register, and I did. I even won some speaking competitions. I also joined the drama club, hoping through acting classes I would find opportunities to act more masculine in my behavior.

In my drama class, I enjoyed the various roles I was assigned, and I felt safe and even accepted by many of the other students. I was working diligently to do a better job of blending in, of adjusting to the expectations of others, particularly the mainstream heterosexual world. I was working hard to hide my homosexuality, to be and become *other than* my true gay identity.

THE POWER OF A TEACHER'S INFLUENCE

I was guided toward a successful future career with the help of one of my middle school teachers. Her name was Mrs. Athens, and she was my eighth-grade English teacher. During my school years, Mrs. Athens became one of my most memorable teachers.

She was an example of a teacher who took the time to make me feel special and valued. She often pointed out my academic strengths and contributions. She nurtured my intellect and creativity and in return, strengthened my wobbly self-esteem.

CONSIDERING TEACHING AS A CAREER

During work with a guidance counselor in high school, I discussed with her the possibility of one day becoming a high school teacher. Privately, however,

I worried if the students I might teach one day would detect I was gay and thus rebel and taunt me, instead of finding me a capable teacher worthy of respect.

In my sophomore year, I decided to try a test-run at teaching, to experience teaching firsthand and to evaluate student responses and reactions to me and my teaching.

I returned one afternoon to my former junior high school, to meet with my eighth-grade teacher, Mrs. Athens, with an important request. I informed her I was thinking about becoming a teacher one day and asked if she would let me try to teach a class of her students, to determine if I could teach content with some degree of success. Most of all, I wanted to experience firsthand the reactions of her students toward me.

Over a period of three weeks, I taught one of Mrs. Athens's English classes in the late afternoon, after completing my high school courses. During each of these teaching experiences, no student giggled, made negative remarks, nor misbehaved. Mrs. Athens gave me helpful feedback and additional strategies to try, and she invited me back a second and third week to teach her classes.

During the third week, she left the classroom, but I could see her standing outside the door, looking into the classroom from the side window. I could see her, but the students could not. Still, no inappropriate student reactions, no laughing, no misbehavior.

I was teaching eight grade students, on my own, and they were staying with me. I was only two years older than most of them. My self-confidence and assurance soared. One day, I thought, I might become not only a classroom teacher, but a teacher who might make a positive difference in the lives of future students.

COLLEGE DAYS: BECOMING A CHANGED SELF

During my undergraduate days in college, I had moved away from my hometown, met lots of new students, made new friends, and became quite popular and active in numerous student organizations. At the same time, while I made efforts to disguise my gay identity, I still knew I displayed at times gay and effeminate tendencies more than masculine behaviors.

However, no one openly rejected me during my college days. I cannot recall any direct incident of personal attacks, slurs, or name-calling based on my sexual orientation or physical characteristics. Finally, I was fitting in, feeling accepted and embraced by my peers, and developing at the same time new levels of self-confidence.

HIDDEN IN THE WORKPLACE

When I finally became a certified high school teacher in 1960, I similarly did not experience any incidences of rejection based on my physical behaviors. I had learned well how to fit in, how to remain silent about my homosexuality, how to hide my gay identity to the best of my ability. At this time in our country's history, my decision to remain hidden and silent made much sense, for it was the 1960s.

In the 1960s, the dominant view of homosexuality was one of disease and psychological impairment. In states like Florida, special investigative committees were created to collect information on teachers suspected of being homosexual or lesbian, and to remove them from their teaching positions, a standard practice that lasted in Florida until the 1970s. Consequently, I remained silent about my homosexuality during my eight years as a school teacher.

A SHIFT IN TERMINOLOGY

By the time I began teaching high school in the 1960s, the word "homosexual," viewed by many in our society to be a term too harsh and clinically distancing, was slowly replaced with what many in society felt was a kinder and more appropriate synonym, the word "gay."

BEING GAY IN A UNIVERSITY SETTING

Throughout my years as a university professor, I eventually shared with a few close colleagues my gay identity, and I sensed many other colleagues knew as well. However, I experienced no direct discrimination. If I had, I would not have advanced smoothly and quickly through the ranks to full professor and tenure. The university and tenure process, then and now, can be extremely brutal, time-consuming. Promotion and tenure procedures typically are filled with endless steps to demonstrate one's engaged scholarship, service, and teaching performance to an array of academic peers and university-wide officials.

The colleagues doing the evaluation are often professors and administrators with different and difficult academic personalities, research preferences, and academic biases. In addition, most have predetermined mindsets as to how a tenured and promoted colleague should appear, both as a person and on paper, within curricula vitae.

INCHING TOWARD MORE AUTHENTICITY

After my promotion to full professor with tenure, I felt more comfortable sharing the fact that I was gay with a few trustworthy and loyal friends and colleagues. While many of my other colleagues may have suspected I was gay, I was not ready to openly come out to them, primarily because I still remained fearful of rejection and retaliation.

THE GAY RIGHTS MOVEMENT

As I was starting my career at the university level, the Gay Rights Movement was making numerous and noteworthy societal advancements. Inwardly, I rejoiced when I heard and read about gay protests in New York City at the Stonewall Inn in 1969, and the subsequent first gay pride parade in 1970 on Christopher Street. After my first university appointment, Lambda Legal became the first legal organization established to fight for the equal rights of gay men and women.

Then, in 1973, the American Psychiatric Association removed homosexuality from its list of mental disorders. In 1975, the first federal gay rights bill was introduced to address discrimination based on sexual orientation. From the late 1970s on, gay men and women were elected to public office, and at local, state, and national levels.

In 1980, at the Democratic National Convention, Democrats added a strong and fundamental component to its core platform: All groups must be protected from discrimination based on race, color, religion, national origin, language, age, sex, or sexual orientation.

In the 1980s, the gay movement nearly ceased because of the AIDS epidemic. Government funding was lacking. Fewer people supported the gay movement than before. The gains previously made by the gay movement seemed to be quickly disappearing.

In time, many people, both gay and straight, became increasingly concerned and involved. A variety of citizens refused to stay silent while their family members and friends died daily from AIDS. Powerful organizations, like ACT UP, refused to be silenced when other organizations were belittling and defaming the gay community.

Soon, the gay movement came roaring back. In 1993 and onward, numerous marches occurred in support of gay and lesbian rights, like the march on Washington, where over 800,000 participated for gay rights and liberation. Also, starting in the mid-1990s, much national and political debate began, concerned with the rights of gay men and women to serve in the military.

In 2000, a year before I retired, Vermont became the first state to legalize civil unions between same sex couples.[4]

STILL CHOOSING TO REMAIN SILENT

Selfishly, I remained a passive participant in these powerful strides for gay rights. I still feared workplace and community bias and prejudice. I still believed I would be unfairly and poorly treated and harshly judged and rejected by my colleagues, even at the university level, even in a somewhat more liberal community.

TAKING BOLD AND AUTHENTIC ACTION

At a symbolic level, the pink full moon takes bold and authentic actions in the proliferation of new life, producing in the process much powerful plant growth. Like the pink full moon, I finally found an inner strength and desire to take bold and authentic action with much potential for further growth. After many years of remaining silent and hidden about my gay identity, I decided it was time to come out.

At the time of my retirement in 2001, society had a somewhat greater acceptance of gay individuals in gay relationships than earlier in my life. I just needed to find an appropriate time and level of comfort before I came out. That time and place came suddenly and unexpectedly, at a university retirement reception, where I was one of five honorees.

The reception was a rather large gathering of university leaders, university-wide faculty members, graduate students, local school administrators, as well as local teachers, an event held in a large banquet hall on campus.

Each of the five retiring faculty members, all male, was seated separately at large tables, with each given the opportunity of inviting family members and special friends to sit at his table and nearby tables.

Our Dean commenced the celebration by requesting each of the retiring professors to introduce himself as well as the people at his table. We were seated alphabetically by our last name, from left to right across the large ballroom. I could quickly deduce that I would be the fourth honoree to introduce myself and my guests.

The first honoree started by introducing himself and his wife and the others at his table. I realized that the pattern of introduction would be the same for all retiring honorees, except me, and I was right. All introductions prior to mine went something like this: the introduction of the professor, his wife, his children and other family members and friends present.

At my table, I had my partner Robbie. Sitting next to me was my god-child, Ashley. There were no family members at my table, but I did invite a group of my best friends, my favorite colleague on campus and her husband, three colleagues from other universities, and three former doctoral students, all themselves now university professors.

A LONG-AWAITED MOMENT OF ONENESS: COMING OUT

When it came time for my introduction, I knew what I felt compelled to do, to introduce Robbie as my lifelong partner. It was finally time for me to come out, and to everyone present.

If my colleagues and people in attendance could not accept me at this stage of my life, I had little to lose. Because I would be retiring in a few weeks, I could handle any short-term and negative consequences. This evening seemed the perfect time to share openly what I had worked so hard over the years to keep silent: who I really was, my authentic self, a gay colleague. When my turn arrived, I introduced myself and turned to face the people in attendance. I told them I had someone special to introduce, Robbie, my life partner for the past eighteen years.

I looked at Robbie sitting at my table. He looked so handsome and impressive in his Seville Row suit, but I also quickly noticed that he turned his head downward, as if embarrassed. I immediately understood why. I had not told him ahead of time I would be introducing him, nor as my partner. I did not know prior to this evening that I would be coming out. I was now outing him as well as myself, and at first, we were both uncomfortable, uncertain how those in attendance would react.

I asked Robbie to stand. He slowly rose and when he did, the room erupted with a deafening roar of approving applause, the most applause of the evening for any given introduction, comment, or speech.

Robbie's face beamed with a big smile, and I felt overwhelmingly joyous that I was finally out as gay and being validated by my colleagues and the guests present at the farewell party to my long career. Silently, I recalled the quote attributed to Robert Browning: "A minute's success pays the failure of years."

A feeling of unimaginable approval and acceptance surfaced deep inside. I felt at once lighter and freer, as if a heavy physical burden finally had been lifted. I felt the delight of self-honesty, of finally acknowledging and honoring my authentic self with everyone present. In a flash, I felt free of the self-imposed restraints that kept me silent about my gay identity for most of my life.

Now that I was out and feeling momentarily assured and accepted, I no longer wanted to retreat, to hide my gay identity, to remain silent. I wanted more than ever to stay out, to remain one with self, one with life.

STAYING OUT

A few days before I officially retired, an incident happened with a colleague that tested my recent commitment and resolve to stay out, to remain true to self. I was sitting in my office, still feeling pleased with my recent decision to come out, still basking in the feelings of recognition, validation, and acceptance.

A colleague who had not attended my retirement reception but heard about it came into my office, greeted me, and proceeded to tell me all about another retirement party he had attended the previous evening, one across campus in another department. He continued to elaborate, informing me of the many prominent people who spoke at this colleague's reception, all the exemplary things they said about the person retiring. Before he finished, he let me know that this was the kind of retirement party he would like one day.

I thought for a moment about my colleague's motives in sharing this information with me. I knew the type of retirement reception he had described was just the kind he would want. My colleague's intent may have been only to share this story with me. Nothing more. We were not close as friends, but we often did share information quickly, on the run, as we were coming and going to and from our offices.

Nevertheless, I felt my colleague was indirectly trying to say something else to me, and for some other reason. He seemed to be minimizing my retirement reception in comparison to the one he recently had attended, and I believed I knew his reason.

Since my retirement reception, many other colleagues had commented to me how happy, relaxed, and at ease I now appeared. I was finally feeling free and in control of my own life, living more as my true self, and it was obvious to others who knew me. I believe this colleague also noticed the difference in me but, unlike other colleagues, he appeared to have a more difficult time accepting my feelings of new freedom and independence.

He appeared to be indirectly attempting to discount my retirement reception and, at the same time, marginalizing my new sense of self-acceptance and assurance. Regardless of this colleague's precise intent, here was an excellent opportunity for me to clarify my new sense of self, honestly and boldly. I responded to him, quickly and appropriately, and without being offensive.

First, I thanked my colleague for sharing the details of another colleague's retirement reception. I acknowledged that it must have been a most impressive event. Next, I moved on to the crux of my intent. I informed him why I valued more, and for different reasons, my own retirement party in comparison to his friend's reception the night before.

My retirement reception, I explained, served as an opportunity for me not only to come out, but to stay out, and in the process to stay true to self. I concluded by informing my colleague that no amount of powerful people or speeches could ever top my newfound feelings of authenticity.

He smiled, mentioned he was late for a lunch engagement, and left without any further comment. My direct and honest response momentarily surprised me. In the past, rather than be self-affirming, I typically would had chosen to remain silent, quiet, and compliant, as if in agreement.

In contrast, I now found much personal satisfaction in expressing what I really thought and how I genuinely felt. Finally, after all those years spent hidden and in silence, I was now out and determined to stay out, learning how to live my life honestly and openly.

OUT IN POSITIVE WAYS

As a gay man out and in retirement, I wanted to remain a good role model for others, to defy the gay myths and stereotypes. I wanted to contribute to the reduction of homophobic feelings held toward gay men and gay relationships. At the same time, by remaining out in positive ways, I wanted to protect my self-esteem.

What I could do minimally, I concluded, was to present myself to other individuals in as many positive ways as possible, to feel good about my social identity as I solidified it. As a gay man, I had no desire to be antagonistic nor offensive to opposing members of the straight world. Rather, I wanted to use the best behaviors and strategies possible to oppose gay discrimination and bias.

OUT AND LIVING IN LARGER GAY COMMUNITIES

In our plans to become snowbirds in retirement, Robbie and I eventually planned to relocate to communities with larger gay populations. We wanted to live in or near gay enclaves and form new gay connections and friendships. During our travels, we had met many gay couples who spent summers in Maine and their winters in gay-friendly places such as Fort Lauderdale, Florida; Tucson, Arizona; Palm Springs, California; and Puerto Vallarta, Mexico. In our retirement, we wanted to experience a similar kind of immersion in the gay lifestyle.

OUT WITH ROBBIE AS A GAY COUPLE

Most importantly, I wanted Robbie and me to be accepted as a gay couple. We had lived together in a powerful relationship as a gay couple for many years. It was who we were and wanted to be.

Whatever I choose to do with my life ahead in retirement had to be congruent with my authentic self, who I was at my basic core: a gay man in a long-term and gay relationship. I understood there may be any number of social pressures to be *other than* my gay and authentic self, and I wanted to be prepared to deal with and resolve these pressures consistent with my newly accepted and genuine identity.

MY SECOND MAJOR LESSON LEARNED: STAY TRUE TO SELF

Thus, I learned my second major lesson as I approached retirement. If I wanted to remain true to myself, I not only had to come out, to claim my gay identity, but I also had to stay out, to not be tempted to revert to my past behavior of remaining silent and hidden.

As I approached my life in retirement, I wanted to protect myself from living half-truths and other barriers to authentic living. I wanted to remain proud and positive in my relationship with others. I wanted to be honest with others, to protect my self-esteem, to stay true to self. As I learned this second major lesson, I also comprehended a new and important insight.

In my early retirement years, I had often asked myself this question: Why did my momentary and short-lived loss of my authentic self at the end of my career appear more devastating and intense, more self-directed and self-rejecting, in comparison to my long-lived societal rejection for being gay? I now believe I know the answer.

Throughout my early life as I tried to hide my gay identity, I assumed many people, whether they knew me or not, might reject me if they knew I was gay. However, and this is my important point, *I rarely if ever rejected myself for being gay*. I was gay, and I accepted the fact I was gay. In other words, I did not reject myself for being gay nor try to fight the fact that I was anything but gay. I just kept silent about my gay identity to avoid further hurt and retaliation. There is a critical difference, however, between hiding one's true self, and rejecting one's true self, and this difference is significant.

I was not rejecting myself for being gay by remaining silent for many of my past years. Instead, I was able to remain gay and accept myself as gay while choosing, at the same time, to remain silent about being gay, to remain in control of my gay identity and lifestyle.

In contrast, my momentary loss of my authentic self in my last few years of my academic career was a powerful example of unnecessary, painful, and devastating self-rejection.

For a few months before I retired, I believed my inability to meet the conditions of my work with joy and pleasure was my fault. As more time passed, the more I blamed myself. For the first time in my long and successful career, I felt like a failure in my work. I had become *other than* who I truly was and wanted to be.

The self-imposed and unnecessary self-rejection I brought to this situation felt real, and soon became, if only momentarily, somewhat debilitating. I was choosing to be an artificial self rather than my true self. My authentic self only re-emerged after I realized I was not a failure but being *other than,* struggling to continue with work I was supposed to do but work I no longer wanted.

With this insight, I understood I had another choice, to retire and become one with the life I wanted. After acting on this choice, my feelings of loss and failure immediately disappeared. I reconnected with and became again my authentic self. Further, I pursued my goal of becoming a snowbird in retirement.

TAKING MORE BOLD ACTION: BECOMING SNOWBIRDS

Robbie and I would soon begin our lives as snowbirds, and we were ecstatic about the new possibilities in our retirement adventure. We were a gay couple, on a journey to find a home in new and more densely gay communities. We finally were doing what Thomas Moore reminds us is possible when we allow ourselves to exist true to self: "We *sting* the world with our own vision and challenge it with our own ways of being."[5]

THE DIFFICULTY IN DOWNSIZING

For two years after retirement, Robbie and I remained in Chapel Hill for the winters, spending most of our time preparing to begin our retirement journey as snowbirds. We had much liquidation to do. In both Robbie's business and in our private lives, we had collected much, accumulated much.

In Robbie's business alone, he had three large storage units filled with inventory, as well as inventory in his three-level shop. We spent many weekends bringing inventory to various auction sites, selling it from our home, online, and to friends.

At the same time, we started to sell the antiques, collectibles, and paintings in our private collection. At one time, we owned 125 paintings by the North Carolina artist Stephen White. We kept only six. In our kitchen alone, we had accumulated over seventy-five "kitchen animals," most of them collectible statuary. We sold all but one.

There were many moments when we tested each other's patience. While Robbie was away from home during the day, I often cleaned out our closets and sorted things into "keep" or "throw out" piles, and later tossed the items in the "throw out" pile into the garbage bins for next day removal.

After Robbie had returned home, I later walked into the kitchen and there on the table were all the items I earlier had discarded. I got the message. We both had to decide together on what to keep, sell, give away, and throw away. We often did not agree, and compromising was not always easy.

Nevertheless, in time, we sold all of Robbie's inventory and most of the items in our own collection. In addition, we had sold a rental condo we owned and leased for twenty years, our beach condo, and our lovely Chapel Hill townhome in the historic district.

Over many years of buying and accumulating clothing, furniture, artwork, antiques, and collectibles, we now owned only two vehicles—a car and a van—and a few select items we decided to keep and transport to our Maine home. We had money in the bank, each other, and our two cats, Miss Belle and Mr. Boots, all of us eager to begin our retirement journey.

DEPARTURE DAY

In June of 2003, we spent our last night in Chapel Hill at the home of neighborhood friends. When we left the next morning for Maine, Robbie drove the van and I drove the car, with our two cats as my companions.

Waving goodbye to our neighbors, we drove tandem down McCauley Street, to Pittsboro Street, down Franklin Street, to Interstate 85, heading north. We were on our way, finally beginning our journey in retirement as snowbirds, leaving Chapel Hill as residents, most likely forever.

Here was my chance to live a new and exciting life. As we proceeded on our journey north, I thought about what ways of living and being I was bringing with me to my new snowbird lifestyle.

I still wanted to do a lot of what I once did in my teaching and career but in the context of retirement. If I were excited about something in my life each day, if I felt good about who I was and what I was doing in my life, then I would be living consistently with my authentic self, my major objective.

Robbie and I now faced a new and immediate challenge: finding our second home as snowbirds. We had already found our retirement home in Maine, a place we called Paradise North. Now we needed to locate and purchase our new retirement home in Florida, our Paradise South.

FIND HOME AND COMMUNITY

Paradise North, Paradise South

As snowbirds, Robbie and I wanted two retirement homes, one in the north and one in the south. Prior to the selection and purchase of each home, we did much preplanning, making extensive lists of specific criteria to guide us in our efforts. Of all our criteria, we gave priority to communities with large and gay-friendly populations.

STAYING AUTHENTIC, STAYING TRUE TO SELF

For most of our lives, we had lived primarily in a straight world, fitting in as best as we could as two gay men involved in a long-term relationship. We realized, of course, we would always be living in a predominantly heterosexual world, and we acknowledged a continued enjoyment and willingness to be included in and accepted by our mainstream culture.

In retirement, however, we now wanted more opportunities for participation, inclusion, and assimilation into communities with a notable blend and balance of both straight and gay individuals. Therefore, our first criterion for the selection of our retirement homes became gay-friendly communities.

PROVENANCE

In our search for our retirement homes, we had underestimated the role our individual and past living experiences would play in determining the exact location of each. For me, my strong sense of provenance, of being born and raised on the coast of New England, played a critical role in determining the exact location of our retirement home in the north.

I grew up in Portsmouth, New Hampshire, a coastal town in the Granite State. Although I had left home soon after college, I found myself periodically traveling home to Portsmouth for short visits and vacations. On one such occasion in the late 1970s, I was a Visiting Professor at the nearby University of New Hampshire in Durham.

One evening at a faculty function, a colleague's wife and I were talking about our roots, where we felt we most belonged. I informed her that Portsmouth was my hometown, a place where my heart was, a place where I felt I most belonged.

"There's a word that accounts for that feeling," she responded with a knowing smile. "It's called provenance."

Then she proceeded to share with me her definition of provenance. Just like a rare piece of art or antique, our individual life has its own history, its own record of ownership, its own provenance. Later in life, like at the time of retirement, many of us make use of our distinguished provenance. We return to live near where we were born, in part to reclaim our roots, our own authenticity.

I understood her message, and I agreed with her. No matter where I had previously lived over the past forty years, I felt most at home where I grew up, on the New Hampshire coast and ocean, with its rugged beauty and fresh salty sea air. If home were truly where my heart was, then home for me was somewhere along the coast in southern New Hampshire.

FINDING OUR RETIREMENT HOMES: SOME BASIC CRITERIA USED

Now out, we chose to live in gay-friendly communities, somewhere in the north and south. As snowbirds we were also in search of appealing weather, communities rated high for walkability, communities of charm and beauty, with lots of opportunities for participating in various social and cultural activities, and in affordable communities.

PARADISE NORTH: OGUNQUIT, MAINE

During summers in the mid-1980s, Robbie and I traveled through various states in New England to buy inventory for his antique business. Frequently, during these trips, we visited and stayed in one of our favorite coastal towns—Ogunquit, Maine.

Ogunquit was special in many ways, but it was a town with unusual significance to me because it was compatible with my own sense of provenance: a town on the southern coast of Maine, just thirteen miles north from where I grew up, a place near my roots, a place where I felt one with the land. This small and quaint town also met all our criteria for a retirement home in the north.

A GAY-FRIENDLY TOWN

For over 100 years, Ogunquit has been a renowned art colony visited by many tourists, many of them gay. Thus, for years, Ogunquit has had a reputation for welcoming gay visitors and including them as part of the town's culture and history.

Many gay individuals of all ages have chosen to move to Ogunquit, to become residents, either seasonally or full-time, because of its welcoming nature and acceptance of gay individuals. As a result, a rich blend of gay and straight citizens lives and works side by side in this small New England town. Furthermore, many gay men and women own many of the businesses in and around the downtown village and serve as members on the town's governing boards and agencies.

From our earliest visits to Ogunquit, Robbie and I were impressed with the genuine acceptance and respect gays and straights displayed toward one other, an early indication of an egalitarian community, one in which signs of equal rights were immediately apparent.

LOCATION

Ogunquit is a quaint village along the Southern Maine seacoast, a town with only a total of fifteen square miles. The town's physical and natural appearance has not experienced jarring change over the years, primarily because of local zoning restrictions.

Ogunquit has a present population of just over 900 full-time residents. Numerous tourists from all over the world visit this resort town throughout the four seasons, but particularly in the summertime. During the summer months, tourists increase the town population by thousands.

Ogunquit, pronounced Oh GUN quit, is derived from the Abenaki Indian language, and in translation means "beautiful place by the sea," and this small coastal town in York County lives up to its name.

In 1997, Robbie and I bought a condo in Ogunquit. Ever since, we have made this Maine village our summer home. To this day, I continue to experience much delight and pleasure during each returning visit.

We slow our driving pace as we enter the village from the south. Many of the buildings are eclectic in style and design. Most structures are typically New England in architecture, turn of the century Victorian and various clapboard structures, most freshly painted for the summer season by the time we arrive mid-May. As we proceed along US Route 1, we eventually arrive at a three-way intersection in the town's center.

To our right, Shore Road begins, leading to Perkin's Cove, a scenic fishing and artist colony site, and the Marginal Way, a walking path along the rugged cliffs and rocks above the ocean. Straight ahead is Beach Street, the entrance to Ogunquit Beach, the pathway to Ogunquit Beach, recently named one of the most beautiful small beaches in the country.

Our condo is on Main Street, to the left of downtown, a short distance away. We curve to our left and drive through Ogunquit Center. To our right, we pass the Village Market, a local gourmet grocery store. We pass several shops and businesses on both sides of Main Street. Soon we pass the Old

Village Inn. Across the street are several restaurants, ice cream shops, pizza eateries, as well as the Leavitt Theatre, a local movie theater. As we view the quaintness of the town, we sit back and relax, happy to be home for another summer season in the north.

APPEALING SUMMER WEATHER

Southern Maine has one of the most comfortable statewide summer climates in the country. Peak temperature occurs in July and averages about 70 degrees throughout the State. In the southern coastal area during a warm summer, temperatures can reach 90 degrees or higher, and for many days.

We live in Ogunquit each year from May 15th to mid-October. Thus, we get to experience some or all of three seasons, the end of spring, all of summer, and the beginning of fall. Summertime in Maine can be varied, but most of the time it is magnificent, with warm to hot days and ocean breezes to crisp but comfortably cool evenings, ideal for the wearing of sweaters.

A TOWN FOR WALKING

Throughout my life, I have enjoyed walking daily more than most other forms of exercise. Therefore, it was important to me to find in retirement a community that possessed many walkability features. Ogunquit met my walkability test. It is a community filled with footpaths and bridges leading to numerous and varied scenic places, from downtown to the beach and ocean, up and down hills on Shore Road, to the harbor and footpaths along the high and rugged rocky cliffs.

Our condo in Ogunquit is ideally located in town for walking. We are approximately one-third of a mile to downtown with its shops, hotels, and restaurants. We are less than a mile to the main beach. The walk to the Marginal Way and back to our home is just under three miles. If we desire longer walks, we can jaunt from our beach to the neighboring beach, Wells Beach, and back, for a total of just over five miles.

If we are even more adventurous and desire to walk six miles or longer, we can do a walking tour of the homes outside of town, up and along Berwick Road, along North Village Road, then down Tatnic Road, until we reach Main Street again in Ogunquit, and by turning right, head back to our condo.

We can complete different combinations of these different walking routes, or we can seek new walking paths outside of town in nearby towns and neighboring villages.

A TOWN OF CHARM AND BEAUTY: BECOMING ONE WITH THE LAND

The many places and locations of beauty in and around town are endless and depend on the viewing preferences of each individual resident or visitor. Not only is the scenery in Ogunquit visually appealing, but much of it seems to stay the same year after year. Essentially, there are four personal local sites of charm and beauty in Ogunquit that remain my favorites.

Beyond charm and beauty, these specific scenes buffer my sense of provenance, my feeling of being connected to and one with the land.

CONTINUITY: UPPER MAIN STREET

The pathway up the hill going out of town to the north of Ogunquit is now paved with bricks. It curves and winds its way in front of the Yellow Monkey and other guest houses and private homes on both sides of the street. At the top of the hill on the left, there is a large art glass business called Panache. On the right side is a large and lovely guest resort named Juniper Hill, surrounded by large well-manicured lawns, plants, shrubbery and trees. A large and impressive birch tree dominates the entrance to this resort, but it is the scene of the hill leading out of the town that possesses its own unique charm.

The composite of architecture, nature, and sometimes pedestrians moving up or down the hill is what I find memorable and visually pleasing: the homes with their different porches, balconies, and unique architecture and colors; the various forms of plant life; the residents and tourists moving up and down the hill, at different times of day during each of the seasons, all a co-existence of different shapes, sizes, angles, and colors.

Every summer, throngs of visitors travel up and down this hill, carrying beach chairs, umbrellas, and pushing carts and strollers full of beach gear and small children, making their pilgrimage down the hill to the beach in the morning and back up the hill in late afternoon.

Each season, I take time to sit alone on a bench at the bottom of the hill and watch the pedestrians coming down and going up the hill. I never tire from viewing this scenic spot year after year, for it is a site that symbolizes to me continuity, the continuity of beach-going in Ogunquit, a beautiful place by the sea.

One day while sitting on the bench at the bottom of the hill, taking in the spender of this view, a friend passed by and stopped momentarily to chat. I mentioned to him the pleasure I found each year in viewing the hill. I told him about the feeling of continuity I experienced while viewing this site. He listened intently and smiled, as if knowing something that I did not. He reached down, grabbed my hand, and literally led me into the nearby Old Village Inn.

Inside the Inn, my friend led me to the lounge and pointed to a framed Post Magazine cover hanging on the wall. A painting of my hill was on the cover, inclusive of the local homes and businesses, with tourists of all sizes and ages traveling homeward up the hill, carrying all kinds of beach paraphernalia.

My friend explained that the artist Norman Rockwell painted this exact scene in the early 1950s, this exact site I treasure so much. He further informed me this painting later became the cover on Post Magazine that same year. Continuity indeed. Now nearly seventy years later, just as Norman Rockwell captured this scene of the hill leading north out of town, the scene continues to delight and charm a new generation of residents and visitors to Ogunquit.

PERMANENCE: OGUNQUIT BEACH

Early in the summer season, I often walk a short distance north out of town to Ocean Street, turn right toward the ocean, cross the footbridge, and arrive toward the northern end of Ogunquit Beach. To my left in the distance is Wells Beach, and to my right, the three-mile-stretch of pristine, pale white, and soft sand shoreline for which Ogunquit Beach is famous. I am home on Ogunquit Beach, with the Atlantic Ocean on the horizon and waves crashing onto shore. Sailboats glide by, seagulls cry on nearby rocks, and lighthouses gleam in the far distance. The hues and shades of color change daily, and often in relation to the weather.

I walk the beach toward its main entrance on Beach Street. The Atlantic Ocean is on my left, and to my right is the coral reef with its high sandy dunes. The Josias River flows behind the dunes. A few wooden bridges lead from the dunes on the beach side to the river, a spot where many beachgoers sunbathe on windy days.

As I arrive at the main entrance to the beach, I see to my far left another of my favorite scenes in Ogunquit, a view of the former Cliff House Hotel, where I worked as a waiter during my college days. Directly in front of me, I delight in a panoramic view of the Marginal Way, a walking path along the ocean, with its array of private homes and resorts nestled on the top and sides of its cliffs.

I have visited Ogunquit Beach many times over my lifetime, and this panoramic view never seems to change. Nor do I find it ever less appealing. For me, there is a permanence to it, a permanence that reminds me of its relationship to my own sense of provenance. From deep inside while viewing this scene, I hear my inner voice recite a powerful and personal message: I am home, home here on Ogunquit Beach, home where I belong.

SERENITY: PERKINS COVE

I leave the beach and proceed back into town via Beach Street. I pass several hotels, restaurants, ice cream stands, and shops selling all kinds of items, from beach towels to boogie boards. On the left side is a large beach parking lot and straight ahead, a bridge that crosses over the Josias River. Straight ahead is Ogunquit center on the mainland. Once in town, I turn left and proceed down Shore Road, heading toward Perkin's Cove.

Perkin's Cove is considered by many as one of the most picturesque and serene parts of Southern Maine. It is a great place to meander and visit various shops. restaurants, and art galleries. The harbor began as a fishing village and eventually became a renowned artist colony. Artists from afar came to this site to take advantage of the beautiful light and exquisite scenery. To this day there is an unusual blend of local fisherman, artists, boats, tourists, art galleries, clothing and jewelry boutiques, and restaurants.

During my summer walks, I like to circle the cove early in the morning, stopping for a fresh cup of coffee in the back of the harbor closest to the water. Few tourists are around early in the morning, just me, the barista, and a few clanging buoys.

The ocean usually appears expansive and calm this early in the morning, and I find the various morning shades of blue and gray soothing. The shoreline borders the ocean with imposing ledges, cliffs, and tufts of verdurous green moss and other plant growth. In Perkin's Cove early in the morning, I find the setting a perfect place to sit and take in nature's beauty in every direction, to set the tone for what kind of day I want it to be and remain, serene and peaceful. Then, I head home, by way of the Marginal Way.

TRANSCENDENCE: THE MARGINAL WAY

A scenic trail, the Marginal Way runs from Perkin's Cove back to Ogunquit center. The path is a 1.25-mile paved walking trail along the town's ragged cliffs, with spectacular ocean and coastal views. The rocks and cliffs are geological wonders that have been studied by archeologists for many years.

The walk along Marginal Way is an opportunity for me to make use of many senses: the taste and smell of the sweet, salty sea air, the smell and sights of beach roses and other plants, the sound of large waves crashing onto shore and among the crevices and rocks below, the sight of lovely homes and mansions along and above the walking path.

Along the walk, I experience many moments of personal transcendence, moments inclusive of self-restoration, communion with nature, meditation, and spiritual prayer. The Marginal Way Preservation Society has placed benches along the walk for all visitors, especially those, similar to myself, who are inclined to pause, sit, relax, and think, to become quiet and at peace, to become one with nature.

My favorite stop is a bench at the highest elevation along the Marginal Way, just before the path turns downward in front of the Anchorage Hotel and alongside the Beachmere Inn. The view from the high elevation is exceptional, with cliffs and rock formations on three sides. To the far left, I can view Ogunquit Beach and to the far right below, I spot Perkin's Cove, all part of the shoreline of the vast Atlantic Ocean. Here, at this precise spot on the Marginal Way, I momentarily transcend myself. I become lost in the moment. I become at peace, one with self, one with nature, one with the universe.

OPPORTUNITIES FOR SOCIAL CONNECTIONS

Since we have lived in Ogunquit for the past twenty-three years, Robbie and I have made many friends of all ages in and around town, many of them gay, many of them straight. We have met most of these friends by participating in a variety of social events.

One of the reasons we believe we have such a fine group of personal friends in Ogunquit is that most of our close acquaintances all seem to want to make a difference. They seem to want all of us as friends and community members to experience a greater good in everyday living, and they demonstrate this remarkable trait in a variety of ways. While our friends overlap in the following categories, we classify them in general within the following dominant groups.

OUR CONDO ASSOCIATION

We have many friends where we live, in our condo association. In our condo complex, we have thirty condos, with half of the condos owned by other gay men and women. Most homeowners, gay or straight, share many of the same values as we do and work together to keep our condo community well-maintained, clean, and safe. We enjoy the company of our northern neighbors and consider many of them our extended family.

OUR BEACH FRIENDS

We also have our beach friends, those individuals we socialize with on our frequent visits to the beach. These friends invite us into numerous beach conversations on a regular basis, from what books to read, plays and movies to see, restaurants and cooking recipes to try, to what travel trips to take. They invite us regularly to walk with them on the beach, to play bocce ball, to run in upcoming road races, to join them for drinks after the beach, and later in the evening sometimes into their homes for dinner.

OUR HAPPY HOUR FRIENDS

We have our happy hour friends, acquaintances we meet in town during early evenings for cocktails and conversation. Many are visitors from surrounding communities in Southern Maine, while many are summer visitors who travel yearly to Ogunquit from faraway places, including other countries.

OUR FRIENDS WHO GIVE BACK

Perhaps the most important and personally powerful social activities in which we participate involve opportunities in Ogunquit to give back. Ogunquit may be small in geographic size, but it is a town with a gigantic heart, a town that genuinely enjoys giving back to a wide range of noteworthy causes.

Throughout the year in Ogunquit, there are many opportunities to participate in any different number of fundraisers. Robbie and I feel most fortunate to have friends who organize and attend with us many of these numerous events. The following are just a few examples of the fundraisers in which we have participated.

We have attended fundraisers for local and state political candidates. We enjoyed the whole experience of supporting Mike Michaud when he ran for Governor of Maine in 2015. A former President of the Maine Senate, Mike had come out the previous year and was running as an openly gay candidate for governor. Robbie and I fully supported his candidacy to the end.

We have attended fundraisers for GLAD, the Maine Gay and Lesbian Advocates and Defenders, an organization that fights discrimination in employment, housing, and public accommodations based on sexual orientation. GLAD also fights discrimination based on HIV status and gender identification and expression.

We have attended and contributed to the support of Equality Maine. This organization, founded in 1984, is the oldest and largest gay, lesbian, bisexual, and transgender organization in the State. In 2008, Maine Equality was a primary opponent of an attempt to revoke an antidiscrimination law in Maine. In 2009, Equality Maine announced a five-year plan that focuses on issues that affect LGBT youth, elders, transgender individuals, and people living in rural Maine.

We have attended fundraisers for the Frannie Peabody Center, an organization committed to the compassionate care of those affected by HIV/AIDS. Concerned with screening and prevention, mental health and substance counseling, this organization serves over 400 individuals statewide.

Robbie and I were especially impressed when we learned that the Frannie Peabody Center also provided housing support for people living with HIV/AIDS and the reason why. Housing stability is a key component of sustained health and the reduction of HIV transmission risk.

If we are fortunate enough to get tickets, we enjoy attending the Broadway Gives Back fundraisers. Held in Maine Street Bar in a small room with a stage, this event features different performers who appear in different productions during the summer season at Ogunquit Playhouse. The money donated goes to different and notable causes.

We donate and attend fundraisers for the Ogunquit Museum of Modern Art, OMMA. Each year an elaborate gala and auction is held to support OMMA, a local art museum that has been in existence for the past seventy-five years. Although we do not stay in Ogunquit in the winter months, we support Ogunquit's Spirit of Giving Fundraiser. This event supports over 600 needy and deserving children in Maine at Christmas time.

Each summer, Robbie and I look forward with great anticipation to the fundraiser for Camp Sunshine, hosted by our friends Steven and David. Since its inception, Camp Sunshine has offered comfort, hope, and support to over 50,000 individuals from all fifty states. Camp Sunshine is an organization that inspires hope in families affected by life-threatening illnesses. Recreational activities allow children and adults to relax and enjoy the simplicity and beauty of life on the shores of Sebago Lake in Maine.

OPPORTUNITIES TO PARTICIPATE IN CULTURAL EVENTS

In Ogunquit, there are numerous opportunities for community members to participate in a variety of performing arts.

THE OGUNQUIT PLAYHOUSE

Since the 1930s, the Ogunquit Playhouse has presented some of the country's best summer stock productions, continuing to this day to carry on its legacy as "America's Foremost Summer Theatre." The present leadership of the Playhouse continues to attract the best of Broadway, television, and film teams, productions, and performers.

OTHER NEARBY THEATERS

In addition to the Ogunquit Playhouse, there are other opportunities for theater-going in the area. In Portsmouth, New Hampshire, there is the Seacoast Repertory Theater. In Kittery, Maine, the Star Theatre. In Kennebunk Maine, the Vinegar Hill Music Theatre. Moreover, the Merrill Center in Portland, Maine is only a thirty-eight-mile drive. Productions in Boston are approximately an hour's drive. Broadway productions in New York City are a five-hour drive or bus trip away.

OGUNQUIT MUSEUM OF MODERN ART

This outstanding museum in Ogunquit is located on Shore Road, and on three acres of sculptured gardens overlooking Narrow Cove and the Atlantic Ocean. Founded in the 1950s, OMMA today displays a permanent collection of important paintings, sculptures, drawings, prints, and photographs from the late 1800s to the present. It is the only museum in Maine devoted exclusively to the exhibition, preservation, and interpretation of American art.

For two months last summer, Robbie and I attended a weekly lecture series at OMMA, called Totally Tuesday Talks. We both found this art education experience personally beneficial. Not only were the lectures most interesting and well presented, but much of the content was new and fascinating information we were acquiring for the first time.

Several noted curators, artists, and art historians spoke on an array of topics, among them the following: research on Nazi-Era Looting and Restitution at the Boston Museum of Fine Arts, to Sisters of the Brush: American Women Painters.

Most memorable this past summer, we heard the Inaugural Poet Laureate Richard Blanco read and discuss poetry from his collection. Blanco is the first immigrant, the first Latino, the first openly gay person to be a

US Inaugural Poet, having read at Barack Obama's second inauguration in January 2009.

Later in the same season, Blanco spoke about the Boundaries Project, a collaborative visual literary effort in which he participated with contemporary photographer Jacob Bond Hessler. Together, they identified poems and photographs that illustrate the visible and invisible boundaries of race, gender, class, and ethnicity in America.

AFFORDABILITY

We paid cash for our condo at the time of purchase in 1997, so our housing expenses are largely associated with our annual maintenance fees. These fees have been increasing steadily over the years but remain, as of date, both reasonable and manageable.

Housing in Ogunquit is expensive. However, there is no way I could place a price tag on Ogunquit, to choose not to live summers in this inviting town because of cost. I am more at home in Ogunquit than any other place I have lived. I especially feel connected to the town's natural beauty and proximity to the ocean, its cultural offerings, and the continuous opportunities to learn and participate in various and meaningful social activities.

There is, nevertheless, a powerful drawback to full-time living in Ogunquit—extremely cold and inconvenient winters. While many people may not be concerned about the cold—may even like cold winters—I do not.

I remember all too well my first twenty-five years of living wintertime in New England. I know well the long gray days, the difficult driving conditions, the feel of frigid outside cold, and the restrictive need to remain inside during snowbound days. Robbie and I deliberately had chosen to become snowbirds in retirement to escape the brutally cold winter weather of the north. Therefore, we continued to search for our second home somewhere in the south, somewhere in the sun.

THE DIFFICULTY IN FINDING HOME IN FLORIDA

Before we retired, Robbie and I were eager to find our second retirement home somewhere in Florida. For three years, we made many trips to different communities in the Sunshine State and explored communities on both sides, from the Gold Coast to the East Coast.

Florida, however, is a large state. During our initial visits, we did not have a specific location in mind. We spent a lot of time exploring gay-friendly neighborhoods in Ft. Lauderdale and Sarasota. After we returned to North Carolina after each trip, we seemed no further along than before.

One day, Robbie reminded me that I would not be happy living in Florida if we could not find a home close to the ocean. He was right. I was one of those people similar to George Hamilton's mother, who was reportedly quoted as once saying something like this: *If you live two blocks from the ocean in Florida, you might as well live in Georgia.* Indeed, I feel precisely the same way.

On a subsequent trip to The Sunshine State, we decided we would limit our search in three ways. First, we decided to look for a retirement home only on the East Coast. For us, there seemed to be a wider range of different people, and from all age groups, along the Eastern coastline. Next, we decided to restrict ourselves to towns and cities on the ocean in South Florida. Finally, we decided to explore only two cities, Boca Raton and Delray Beach.

During this trip, we found many lovely condos on the market, but the time was not right. It was 2003, and real estate prices were on the rise. Condos on and near the ocean were beyond the price range we were willing to pay. We did find a fine condo one mile from the ocean, on Federal Highway in Delray Beach, but Robbie said we should wait and continue to look. Again, too far from the ocean. We returned to our home in Maine, disappointed and tired.

By this time in our early retirement, we had sold our homes in North Carolina and were living full-time in Maine. I was beginning to think our intent to buy a retirement home in Florida might not happen. For the first time, I started to question if our decision to become snowbirds was financially wise. The maintenance fees, particularly in Florida and on or near the ocean, were higher than we expected. We planned to pay cash for our condo, but with the maintenance fees, we would be paying as much as a mortgage in addition to the purchase price.

Momentarily, I started to think of more practical alternatives, like buying a condo in North Carolina, close to our friend David, in Charlotte. Eventually, Robbie and I agreed no matter what our momentary obstacles, we both wanted, more than any other option, to find the right location and ideal retirement home someplace in Florida. We just had to be more persistent and patient.

Then, an extraordinary coincidence occurred one summer day, a "meant to be" moment, a moment of synchronicity, a chance meeting that played a critical role in helping Robbie and me locate our Florida retirement home.

A SYNCHRONISTIC MOMENT

Synchronistic moments happen when we find something of value when we are not looking for it. Such a gift of coincidence happened to me one day in early June 2003. I decided to take a different walking route in Ogunquit, along the Josias River, a walking path not particularly easy. The pathway was uneven, filled with rocks, and difficult to walk and maintain one's balance. I wanted to be alone that day, to sort things through, to come to terms with how best to proceed with our search for a winter home in Florida.

The day was overcast, not a sunbathing day, but a fine day for walking. It was still early in the summer, and few tourists and local people were around, particularly in this isolated area tucked behind the dunes.

During my walk, I came across an older gentleman sitting in a beach chair, reading a book. He was quite a distance away. What I noticed, even from afar, was his dark tan. He did not get that tan here in Maine, I thought. Too early in the season.

I walked over to the man, introduced myself, and asked about his tan. He introduced himself as John and informed me that he owned a condo in Delray Beach, where he lived during the winter months. He had just arrived to work as a desk clerk in a local hotel. I shared with him the events of my recent visit to Delray Beach, and the difficulty I was having finding an affordable retirement condo close to the ocean.

He listened intently, and then responded in a matter-of-fact fashion, informing me my problem was that I did not have a real estate agent. Then he volunteered additional information. A real estate friend from Florida was arriving in two weeks. If I were interested, he could arrange to have me meet with his agent friend for further advice. I gave him my telephone number, thanked him, and left to continue my walk. In a matter of minutes, I completely had forgotten about this chance meeting.

Two weeks later, however, John did call, and our progress in finding an ideal condo on the ocean in Florida changed. He asked if he and his real estate agent friend could drop by to meet with Robbie and me. Tom, the real estate agent, was young but knowledgeable about buying and selling real estate. He asked us all the right questions, and finally he made a wise recommendation.

He suggested that Robbie and I first rent a condo on the ocean in South Florida, to be sure we really wanted to relocate there in the first place. While we were leasing, Tom suggested we preview condos for sale along the coast. He could help us find a condo for rent where he lived on the ocean in South Florida, if we so wished, and in an area and community he thought we would like. We took Tom's advice and in December of 2003, we began leasing a condo in South Palm Beach, Florida.

FINDING PARADISE SOUTH: PALM BEACH, FLORIDA

The condo we rented was in the perfect location for us, right on A1A in South Palm Beach, across the street from the Atlantic Ocean. To the left of us was the Four Seasons, and to our right, the Ritz Carlton. Behind us from the condo porch was a nature preserve. Toward the end of our building, there was a large pool and the intercoastal waterway—water surrounding the complex on two sides.

I spent early mornings going for a swim in the ocean, walking and running on the A1A walking paths, sunbathing and reading by the ocean or the pool, visiting the nearby shops and restaurants at the nearby Manalapan Plaza. Within days, Robbie and I both knew we had found the neighborhood for our Florida retirement condo.

Toward the end of our first month's lease, we were fortunate to find a two-bedroom, two-bath condo for sale in the complex, directly across the street from where we were leasing. Although the condo was more expensive than we liked and in need of much renovation, we bought it anyway, thinking the renovation would be a good project for Robbie, one he would enjoy and complete with expertise. The value of this property was in its location and, like our Maine home, this condo met all eight of the criteria for our condo selection.

A GAY-FRIENDLY COMMUNITY

For the next fourteen years, we made South Palm Beach our winter residence. Unlike Ogunquit, gay life in South Palm Beach was not central to the town. Rather, it was scattered and interspersed within different condo associations and nearby communities. In time, however, we became friends with many other gay men and women living in our neighborhood and beyond in surrounding communities. As in Ogunquit, we lived a blended life within both the straight and gay worlds in Florida.

While we lived predominantly within a straight culture in South Palm Beach, we both felt, as we do in Maine, equal and included, qualities we value in our lives as a gay couple. For example, before we closed on our Florida condo in 2003, Robbie and I were to be interviewed by the Board, a traditional practice when purchasing a condo in South Florida.

When one Board member asked if Robbie was to be listed as a renter, I informed the Board that we were a gay couple, and as such, Robbie should be listed as my partner. This moment was the right time for me to let the Board know in advance we were a gay couple.

The Board President said listing us as a couple would not be a problem, and that as a gay couple, we were most welcome in the condo association. I felt pleased with myself for being honest and direct with the Board about my gay identity, my true self. At the same time, I felt Robbie and I were genuinely accepted and welcomed to the community by the President of the Board and the other homeowners present.

When we lived in South Palm Beach, if Robbie and I desired to participate more fully and actively in a gay lifestyle, we would drive thirty-five miles south on I-95 to Ft. Lauderdale, known for its beaches, bars. night clubs, and shops. In Ft. Lauderdale, there are over 100 gay-owned businesses. Many of our friends from Maine lived their winters in Ft. Lauderdale, and most of them in the mini-gay epicenter of Wilton Manors.

During different times of the winter season, we often visited Ft. Lauderdale to go to one of the beautiful beaches along a twenty-three-mile stretch and enjoy drinks and dinner later. Sometimes we visited to participate in one of the many gay events that happened yearly, like the Gay Film Festival in April, the Candlelight Vigil for World AIDS Day in November, or the Gay Pride Weekend in March.

If we wanted a more intimate gay evening out, we went to the Colony Hotel in downtown Palm Beach. Robbie enjoyed, on occasion, dressing in one of his finest jackets, and the Colony was a perfect place to go and be seen.

On Thursdays, some of Palm Beach's finest men gathered in the bar. We like the ambiance of this friendly boutique of a hotel with a British Colonial flair, just steps away from Worth Avenue. Later, we often went to The Chesterfield hotel for dinner.

AN IDEAL LOCATION

South Palm Beach is the easternmost town in Florida, located at the end of a sixteen-mile-long barrier island. The Intracoastal Waterway separates the town from the neighboring cities of West Palm Beach, Lake Worth, and Lantana.

PERFECT WINTER WEATHER

South Palm Beach has a tropical rainforest climate. The weather is wetter in the summer, from May to October. More than half of the summer days bring occasional afternoon thunderstorms and sea breezes.

As snowbirds, we lived in South Palm Beach only during the winter months, days that bring drier, sunnier, and less humid weather. Henry Flagler, the American industrialist who founded Palm Beach, built a large hotel overlooking the Atlantic Ocean, a luxury resort that was later named The Breakers. Flagler reportedly built this resort because of the inviting winter weather, for him as well as his other wealthy friends.

The average high temperatures during the winter range from 75 to 82 degrees, and the occasional cold fronts often result in cooler weather in the 50s and 60s, especially in the early mornings.

PUBLIC AND SECLUDED WALKING PATHS

The town of South Palm Beach was ideal for walking. Pathways on A1A abound in a variety of directions. Typically, I walked to the Lake Worth Pier and back to my home, a total of four miles. If I wanted to walk five miles, I crossed over the Lake Worth Bridge and walked to the center of this neighboring town, with its different art deco buildings, coffee shops, restaurants, and businesses. Sometimes, I walked along Dixie Highway back to Ocean Avenue in Lantana and then proceeded east to A1A and home, a round trip of over eight miles. My favorite times to walk were early mornings or evenings when the air is balmy and inviting.

For variation, I sometimes walked the beach to the neighboring town of Ocean Ridge and back, a total of six miles on sand. Sometimes I walked the paths in the nearby Lantana Nature Preserve, a peaceful, private, and protected parkland, with scenic hiking trails and lush tropical plant and bird life.

My walks in Florida were not as challenging as those in Maine. The land I walked in Florida was basically flat, with few hills and inclines. The weather in Florida, however, was more consistent and conducive for everyday walking than in Maine, where heavy and frequent summer rain may momentarily interfere with outdoor plans.

THE NATURAL GLAMOUR AND
BEAUTY OF PALM BEACH

Our Florida condo was located at the southernmost tip of Palm Beach Island, in its own town of South Palm Beach. On the coast, we were joined with other sections of Palm Beach by the A1A highway, with connected and continuous walking paths along well-manicured lawns with varied shrubbery and tropical plants. The township of South Palm Beach is less than a mile long and has less than a thousand year-round residents. It was a safe and serene community, however, with seven policemen who patrolled our condo residence on a regular basis.

Heading north, to the right of the highway, was the Atlantic Ocean, which seemed to change daily to different shades of blue and green. Housing in South Palm Beach was restricted primarily to condos, located in buildings that cannot be higher than six floors. Stunning homes and mansions line the ocean front on A1A after Sloan's Curve, before leading to the center of Palm Beach downtown.

To our north, approximately four miles away, was Donald Trump's residence and Club, Mar-a-Lago. Then, approximately six miles away was Worth Avenue in downtown Palm Beach, home to top-tier shops, restaurants, and hotels, among them The Breakers and The Chesterfield Hotel, with The Chesterfield being one of our favorite places to dine. This historic building, built in 1926, was in the center of downtown Palm Beach, just a few blocks from Worth Avenue in one direction and the sandy ocean beach in the other.

During one of our visits to The Chesterfield, Robbie and I stopped by the reservation desk and commented on the unusual floral arrangement on a center table. The clerk informed us that the flowers were arranged and flown in weekly from Holland. The hotel and its restaurant, the Leopard Lounge, represented elegance, old-world charm, and gilded-age sophistication.

In the 1990s, a local artist, Lino Mario, painted the ceiling of the Leopard Lounge, a task that took him, reportedly, over a year and a half to complete. The ceiling painting never fails to get our attention when we visit, for it was filled with what appears to be endless and highly suggestive figures, images, and patterns.

Since the 1920's, Worth Avenue at the center of Palm Beach has become known for its high-quality merchandise. Reflecting the lifestyle of the rich and famous, the street has approximately 250 high-end shops, boutiques, restaurants, and art galleries.

When guests came to visit, Robbie and I often took them on the Historic Walking Tour of Worth Avenue. The tour begins in the courtyard by Via Amore, and includes a detailed history of Worth Avenue, the influences on and significance of the architecture, and the development of the upper-crust social scene and fashion, from past to present.

Frequently, we traveled south from South Palm Beach along A1A through Manalapan and Ocean Ridge and then to Delray Beach and to other communities beyond, like Boca Raton. Numerous luxury homes line the highway. Sections of A1A are lined with tall and impressive palm trees, for which this area is famous.

In contrast, whereas Ogunquit possesses much natural beauty and rustic seacoast charm, Palm Beach consisted of much natural beauty and extravagant Floridian glamour.

OPPORTUNITIES FOR AN ACTIVE SOCIAL LIFE

Unlike Maine, where everything is central and compressed, our social activities and resources in Florida were scattered, frequently requiring us to drive from one town to another. Many of our social connections remained local, right in our own complex. In our Florida condo association, Robbie and I became friendly with other retirees, from many different areas of the country, from the West and Midwest to various states in New England.

Our Association consisted of six separate, two-level buildings, with eight condos to a building. In our building, our neighbors came from New York, Illinois, Massachusetts, Indiana, Rhode Island, Virginia, and California, with owners living in their Florida condos primarily only during the winter months.

Since we moved in, we became friends with most of the other owners, and in the process learned much about different regions of our country. Moreover, we enjoyed the company of our neighbors, and often joined them in a variety of social functions, from dining in their individual homes, going out with them to happy hour and later dinner, or joining them and others for dinner and entertainment at our pool. With our neighbors, we participated in many other activities, like going to lectures, the movies, plays, antique and jewelry shows, and walks and talks.

Our Florida neighbors worked in many different fields before retiring, bringing with them rich and varied backgrounds. They contributed much to our association, and they shared with each other effective problem-solving strategies. Many condo owners worked collaboratively with one another to improve our condo association by serving on different committees.

For a few years, Robbie served on the Landscaping Committee, and I served as treasurer on the Board of Directors. As owners in our condo association, we were like members of an extended family, sharing with each other, caring for each other, and learning from one another, developing in the process a genuine sense of support and community.

Beyond our friends in our condo complex, we have met numerous other friends who live along A1A in other condos in South Palm Beach and nearby towns. While there were many inviting places for Happy Hour in South Florida, one of our favorites was Basil's, a bar and restaurant nearby in Plaza Del Mar. At Basil's, we met and befriended people from all over the world with different backgrounds, from professional basketball players to international opera singers.

A considerable amount of our social life involved entertaining people who came to visit us in Florida. If the visit was a first-time experience, we enjoyed taking our friends on a tour of the area, usually down A1A to Delray Beach, up Federal Highway and back to South Palm Beach. Then we had lunch, usually at one of the fine restaurants in Manalapan Plaza Del Mar. After lunch, we usually toured downtown Palm Beach, stopping at The Breakers, Worth Avenue, and a visit to different shops, before heading home on the scenic route, along A1A and the Atlantic Ocean.

Some friends came to visit with other goals in mind, like a visit to the many fine antique shops on Dixie Highway in West Palm Beach. Other visitors just wanted to sunbathe at our pool or across the street on the beach. Two friends who visited from Maine arrived from Fort Lauderdale via Uber, just to see our condo, visit, and go to dinner before they left on a cruise.

We participated in fewer fundraising activities in Florida than in Maine. Many fundraisers in Florida were large and impersonal, like a medical fundraiser we attended for Bethesda Hospital. In Florida, we enjoyed smaller and more intimate fundraisers, like any number of them in West Palm Beach, like COMPASS, one of the largest and highly acclaimed community centers in our country, and specifically for the gay and lesbian community.

One of the missions of COMPASS was to diminish stereotypes by challenging long-standing misconceptions about the characters of the lesbian, gay, bisexual, and transgender community. Annually, COMPASS sponsored PrideFest, a series of gay pride events in nearby Lake Worth. COMPASS also offered HIV treatment and care, a safe environment and a meeting place for LGBTQ individuals. Moreover, this community provided opportunities to participate in professional groups, like the Palm Beach Human Rights Council, an organization that initiated dialogue between the culturally diverse and community leaders.

As in Ogunquit, Palm Beach is a part-time home for many who are rich and famous. It was not uncommon to see celebrities in person as we went about the business of daily living in Palm Beach. I have concluded that these accomplished people selected Palm Beach and Ogunquit as places to live or visit for some of the same reasons Robbie and I did: the natural beauty, the fine seasonal weather and accommodations, and the abundant opportunities to partake in exceptional entertainment and activities.

READILY AVAILABLE PERFORMING
AND CULTURAL ARTS

There are many outstanding museums in the Palm Beach area, among them the Flagler Museum. Moreover, there are many venues in the area for the performing arts. For fourteen years, Robbie and I enjoyed attending numerous performances at the Florida Stage, a theater first situated in Manalapan Plaza. Now called Dramaworks, and relocated in West Palm Beach, this playhouse presented top quality performances year-round and brought to the area actors of the ilk of Estelle Parsons.

Palm Beach is also the home to The Society of the Four Arts (art, music, drama, and literature). The Society, founded in 1926, offered quality cultural programs to the community. The Society made available to the public note-worthy speakers, concerts, films, educational programs, and art exhibitions. The Society is home to beautiful sculptures and botanical gardens, an adult library and children's library, and a state-of-the-art educational facility.

The Kravis Center, with its wide selection of seasonal offerings, is located in downtown West Palm Beach. The center is composed of a perfor-mance theater and a black box theater, a simple performance space painted black and designed to provide flexibility as needed in the configuration of the stage and the audience sections.

AFFORDABILITY

Like Ogunquit, Palm Beach is an expensive area in which to reside. However, with both our condos paid for in full, our largest expenses became our monthly maintenance fees and any number of needed assessments. Our other major expenses were entertainment and travel. While our yearly expenses were more than if we lived just in one place throughout the year, I acknowl-edge the importance of my snowbird lifestyle. I have found home and com-munity in both locations, my third major lesson learned in retirement.

MY THIRD LESSON LEARNED: FIND
HOME AND COMMUNITY

In my third lesson learned in retirement, I realized the importance of finding home in retirement within communities not only populated with like-kind residents, but also compatible with my wide interests and multi-dimen-sional authentic self. I value the opportunity to live year-round in warm and pleasant weather, in communities I enjoy and feel a deep sense of belonging. I escape the cold, snow, and other inconveniences of winter weather. As a friend observed, I lived outdoors all year round, and I dressed simply, in shorts most of the time.

As a snowbird, I had the best of both worlds, the warm days of Maine in summer, with crisp sweater-wearing weather in the evenings, to the bright sunlit days in Florida in the winter, with balmy mornings and evenings.

Because I lived as a snowbird predominantly outside, I increased my likelihood to be more active. I walked, biked, hiked, and swam year-round and often, keeping my blood flowing and my body moving. Therefore, I exercised more, and most likely, stayed healthier as a result, both physically and emotionally.

I did not experience the winter blues. I did not get bogged down in boring routines. I found much joy in changing my living environments twice a year, in planning refreshing, invigorating, and exciting new adventures, in discovering new places to explore, new habits to adopt, new people to meet.

I enjoyed our travels to and from one home to the other, visiting different towns, sometimes for the first time, finding new accommodations to stay in and new restaurants in which to dine. Every road trip became a new adventure full of possibilities.

In each location, I valued our opportunities to meet and befriend a wide array of people from all demographics. I appreciated and made much use of numerous resources in both locations. I treasured the opportunities within both communities to remain contributing citizens as well as active, healthy, and lifelong learners. I could not ask for much more from my snowbird lifestyle as I greeted each day in my self-chosen communities, living a quality life with financial freedom.

When friends have asked how I can afford to live so well and fully in retirement, I have shared with them another lesson I have learned along the journey: I live debt-free. Then, I find the immediate need to explain to them what I mean by this term, debt-free.

Further, if these friends are interested in becoming debt-free themselves, I have shared with them those specific financial moves I have made in retirement to become debt-free. Moreover, I also have outlined for them those financial actions I have taken to remain debt-free for my remaining years. In retirement, there is much satisfaction in living a stress-free life of financial freedom.

RETIRE DEBT-FREE

Enough

In my later career, I often studied my monthly and annual budgets, noting my biggest expenses, my mortgage payment on my primary residence and my monthly deduction for my home equity line of credit. Fortunately, I had no credit card debt.

Instead, to claim tax deductible interest, I had frequently used my home equity line of credit, particularly for large purchases. Combined, however, my mortgage and my home equity payments averaged monthly over 40% of my take-home salary. I had no car payment because I had established the habit of buying used vehicles and paying cash for them.

In my retirement years, I did not want to continue living a financial lifestyle dependent on my continuous use of home equity debt. As I explored alternative ways of living financially, I entertained often the same liberating possibility: Without my mortgage and home equity payments, I essentially could retire debt-free.

FOUR STEPS TO RETIRNG DEBT-FREE

To live debt-free in retirement, as I have done since 2003, I continuously make use of these four steps: First, I have no home mortgage payments. Second, I pay my credit card debt in full each month. Third, each month I live on less than my monthly retirement income. Fourth, each month I contribute to a separate account I call my emergency fund.

Whenever I have unexpected financial obligations, as I often do, I pay these expenses from funds in my emergency account. Without my emergency fund, I realized I could easily accumulate much debt from unanticipated but necessary expenses. My emergency fund, then, plays a critical role in the maintenance of my debt-free lifestyle.

Of course, I have regular monthly bills for both homes, like electricity, cable, telephone, and maintenance fees, and I pay them monthly as each bill comes due. Everything I spend is within my monthly and annual budgets. I both live within my means and enjoy my life in retirement without any feelings of deprivation.

Because I live debt-free, I have much more disposable monthly income to spend. Just because I have more disposable income, however, does not mean that I spend haphazardly. Nor does debt-free living mean I am frugal, rigid, and restrictive in my spending. I like to shop and spend, but I am not wasteful. Essentially, by living debt-free, I am always conscious of my spending habits and careful not to overspend, thus not living financially beyond my means.

To live debt-free in retirement may sound easy, but it is not. It requires a consciousness of what we spend and earn, a discipline not to overspend, and consistent self-honesty in our money management efforts.

For many people, a debt-free approach to retirement may not always be possible, and for other retirees with high retirement income, debt-free living may not be the best money management strategy. Also, debt is not always negative. Good debt can create future opportunities for equity building and have additional tax advantages. Thus, there is no one financial panacea that fits the retirement needs of everyone.

However, in my retirement, I chose to retire debt-free, and I absolutely have no regrets. I have less financial stress in my retirement life because of this decision and, at the same time, a stronger sense of financial freedom. Much of my retirement income is mine to spend any way I wish. However, I did not acquire a debt-free status in my life easily nor quickly.

OBSTACLES TO DEBT-FREE LIVING: SPENDING AND OVERSPENDING

For years when employed, I had to learn how to make responsible financial decisions day in and day out. Primarily, I had to learn how to be in control of my spending and on a conscious level. Most importantly, I had to learn how to keep my spending habits and practices within a budget less than my take-home salary.

For thirteen years in my early career, I did not live debt-free, nor did I save. After I became a teacher in 1960, I spent every cent I made as quickly as I received my paycheck. I financed a new car. I rented a new apartment. I moved from one teaching position to another, hoping an increase in salary would solve my money mismanagement ways. I even withdrew my previous retirement accumulations from each teaching position when I moved from one position to the next, to meet ever-occurring financial obligations. I had no net worth other than a used car and a few pieces of used furniture. My journey to debt-free living has been long and challenging.

MY LONG JOURNEY TO DEBT-FREE LIVING

In 1973, I started my career at the University of North Carolina at Chapel Hill. I was thirty-five years old. My journey to debt-free living started with the decisions to settle down, to become less of a rolling stone, and to change my reckless, carefree ways of spending. I wanted to manage my earnings and spending more consciously and productively than in my past. Time was marching on. Essentially, I wanted to overcome my reluctance to plan and save for present and long-term future needs. I started my debt-free journey by making some basic and long-term retirement decisions.

SETTING A LONG-TERM GOAL

I figured that if I worked for the next thirty years, until the then mandatory retirement age of sixty-five, I would have enough retirement accumulations over these years if I contributed long-term to a retirement plan as well as to Social Security. Initially, I naively thought this long-term retirement plan would be enough to guarantee an adequate retirement income when I reached retirement age.

SELECTING AN OPTIONAL RETIREMENT PLAN

As soon as I began my employment in North Carolina, I began one of the first components of my long-term retirement planning: a systematic contribution to a long-term retirement plan. From my salary, the university deducted monthly income and matched it with the same percentage. These monies would accumulate over the number of years of my employment, and eventually become a basic source of my future retirement.

I selected State Optional Retirement Program (State ORP) because of its flexibility in use and management. Whatever monies I accumulated could be transferred to other retirement plans, and without penalty, such as if I decided in the future to accept a new position at another university. Moreover, the total accumulations of these monies at retirement would be mine to manage and use as I saw fit. I could create my own form of a pension from a wide array of withdrawal options.

At this time in my early career, I knew so little about how best to allot my retirement contributions in relation to my investment options. With the assistance of the University's Human Resource Director, I selected initially a balanced investment approach, 50% of contributions to a stock fund, and 50% into a fixed income fund.

BUYING MY FIRST HOME: EQUITY BUILDING

I had rented apartments throughout my early teaching career. With my plans to remain long-term in my new position, I was eager to buy my first home. I wanted to experience both the pride of home ownership and the opportunity in time to increase my home equity. For my first three years of employment in North Carolina, I saved monthly for a home deposit.

I repeatedly asked different colleagues for recommendations as to where I should buy. They knew I was single at the time, did not like maintenance work, and may prefer a condo close to campus. Many kept recommending the same condo complex. I drove by it one day on my way to my office, and I knew immediately a condo in this community would be ideal for my first home purchase.

My interest was further peaked when I noticed one of the condos had a "for sale" sign in front of it. I called the listing agent and made an appointment to preview the condo the next day.

The year was 1976, and the asking price was right—$30,000. The complex was small, only eleven units. Each unit was brick and chalet-like in appearance. The location was perfect, one mile up a small hill to campus, a short walk to my office.

I liked the layout of the condo with its three levels. The entrance level had a kitchen, separate dining room, and a large and sunny living room. Two bedrooms were upstairs, joined by a bathroom, with an attic entrance for extra storage. The basement level consisted of two more bedrooms and another bathroom plus hook-ups and space for a washing and drying machine. The second bedroom in the basement had a large sliding glass door and a large patio outside. The condo was over 1600 square feet, on three levels and with four bedrooms and two bathrooms, an ideal layout for use as a rental.

I made an offer on the condo and closed on it within a month. I was starting the second component of my specific retirement planning, investing in real estate for long-term equity building.

BECOMING A LANDLORD: TAX ADVANTAGES

I asked a friend who had been sharing an apartment with me for the past three years if he would like to move into my condo and rent from me. He did, and I charged him the same as he was paying for living with me in our former apartment.

A year later, one of my doctoral students was in the process of a divorce. She was searching for a small apartment to rent near campus. I showed her the apartment I had recently created in the basement of my new home.

I had renovated one of the basement bedrooms into a combination kitchen, living room, and study area, with its own entrance and patio area. There was a large second bedroom and a bathroom down the hallway. The apartment also had its own washer and dryer under the stairwell. My student found the apartment ideal for her present needs, signed a lease and shortly moved into the apartment.

Now I was living completely rent free, and the rental income from my two tenants was paying for my mortgage, taxes, maintenance fees, and new home miscellaneous expenses. Plus, I now had two kinds of tax deductions, a mortgage plus the expenses incurred for the portion of the condo I was renting. For the first time in my life, I could claim beneficial tax deductions.

Surprisingly, I started to save some of my rental income, particularly with the intent of accumulating another down payment on a different and upgraded home somewhere closer to campus. I read regularly about new real estate projects in town and frequently perused real estate advertisements in the local paper.

BUYING A SECOND HOME: MORE EQUITY BUILDING

In early 1983, an ideal townhome became available. This home was in the historic district of Chapel Hill, in a community called Georgetown Row. The complex consisted of five luxury townhomes located only four blocks away from the University, easily within walking distance. I bought the home immediately, concerned I could lose the opportunity to purchase it if I did not act quickly. My problem now became what to do with my previously purchased condo.

GENERATING LONG-TERM RENTAL INCOME

I decided to keep my condo long-term and continue to rent it. The home was in an ideal location, close to campus, and with a perfect layout for leasing. I could rent the condo as a single home, two separate apartments, or as four room rentals to four compatible students.

I put an advertisement in the local paper and found a couple who wanted to rent the whole condo for themselves and signed a lease immediately. Thus, I began my long-term rental of this condo for the next twenty years.

PLANNING FOR A FUTURE LIFE IN RETIREMENT

In 1984, I met Robbie, one year after I had purchased my new townhome. After five years into our relationship, we both concluded we would most likely remain lifetime partners.

Assuming we did, I knew we would want a retirement lifestyle comparable to the one we were presently living: one inclusive of travel, art, theater, music, and good books and food, the continuation of our blissful lifestyle. Thus, my preference for a continued and blissful life with Robbie became a strong impetus to save more for our future lives in retirement.

TURNING FIFTY AND CALCULATING MY NET WORTH

I remember vividly my fiftieth birthday in 1988. Robbie and I had just returned to Chapel Hill from the North Carolina coast. As I lay in bed that evening, I decided by chance to peruse one of the magazines on my nightstand. On top of the heap was a financial journal with a special section that month on retirement planning.

The featured article emphasized the need for readers anticipating retirement to calculate their net worth as a starting point. The author underscored the need for readers to be as honest and as specific as possible with their estimates. In other words, the author was warning readers not to inflate these figures as was often typical of most people completing this task.

With the author's grid in hand, I jumped out of bed, went to my study, opened the file cabinet where I kept all my financial papers and records, and eagerly began this task. I was acutely aware I was halfway through my career, and I frequently questioned if I had been doing enough to save for my eventual retirement. Optimistically, I thought the calculation of my net worth would show I was on track, doing a fine job, and with a little juggling of my assets, I could retire comfortably in another fifteen years, if not sooner.

My initial optimism was based on these facts. For the past fifteen years, I had contributed systematically to a university-sponsored retirement plan. In addition, I owned at that time, three homes—one rental and two homes Robbie and I used for ourselves, one in Chapel Hill, and the other on the North Carolina coast.

After locating and noting my then university retirement accumulations and determining the most likely fair-market value of my real estate properties, I was only minimally reassured I was saving enough for retirement. My then net worth, honestly and accurately calculated, was far from what I expected it to be. Right before my eyes was the reason: large home equity debt.

CONFRONTING HOME EQUITY DEBT

Since the mid 1980's, I established with my bank a home equity line of credit, to use cautiously and with flexibility. Any interest I paid on my home equity loan was tax-deductible as well as much lower in rate than credit card interest fees.

Over the years as the value of my primary home increased, I leveraged my primary home, using my home equity loan freely and frequently. As a result, my net worth was smaller than I had anticipated. I was living a high-spending lifestyle, as I did early in my career, only this time through the generous use of my home equity line of credit.

This simple task of calculating my net worth became a personal awakening for me, a critical turning point in my life. For a second time in my working years, I realized I had to save more now, do more now, to take a more active role in planning and saving for retirement than I thought I was doing. Not only did I want to save more for a future with Robbie in retirement, but I also wanted to stop using my home equity freely and frequently. I became motivated to find ways in time to eliminate my home equity debt.

My problem of not saving enough for retirement would not go away on its own. If I did not do something soon to start saving more for retirement, the problem of not having enough funds at the time of retirement would forever remain a barrier to meeting my future financial needs.

Robbie was also ten years younger than I. If I did not do more now to save for retirement, I may not have enough accumulated for my own retirement never mind enough to share with Robbie. But how best could I begin?

LEARNING TO LIVE WITHIN MY MEANS

Instinctively, I knew my salary was not the problem. It did not matter if I were making $4000 a month or $20,000. The difficult task I had to learn and begin practicing was how to live on my net income, on my monthly take-home salary, and not on how much in addition I could borrow from my home equity loan. I calculated what amount of money I brought home each month and how much I needed to stay within my monthly budget. I also did the same for my annual budget. In addition, I carefully considered the choices I genuinely wanted in my future years in retirement, and I started to planned accordingly. Most importantly, I started to calculate how much money I could save each month, to set aside for my life ahead in retirement.

SAVING MORE

Just before I had calculated my net worth, I had just finished reading C. Scott Peck's, *The Road Less Traveled: A New Psychology of Love, Traditional Values, and Spiritual Growth*. In this classic work, Peck contends that it is only because of our problems that we grow mentally and spiritually. He informs readers of this basic premise: Life constantly presents us with a series of personal problems, and it is the whole process of meeting and solving these problems in which life has its meaning.

According to Peck, a psychiatrist, the act of solving our problems is not easy. On the contrary, the solving of problems typically is a painful experience. Therefore, many of us choose to avoid our problems rather than to suffer through them in efforts to solve them.

Peck further reminds readers that without the use of discipline in our lives, we can solve nothing. Discipline contains the basic set of tools needed to solve life's problems. The tools of discipline are techniques of suffering, how we experience the pain of problems in such a way as to work through and solve them successfully, learning and growing in the process.

The four tools of discipline Peck identifies are: the delay of gratification, the acceptance of responsibility, the adherence to truth, and balancing. While these are simple tools, the problem lies not in the complexity of the tools, but in the use of them in confronting our problems rather than avoiding them.[6]

As I read this book, I related my need to increase my savings for retirement directly to Peck's insights and advice. I first had to accept the responsibility for my problem, not saving enough money for retirement, before I could start to solve this problem. I also had to stop mindless spending beyond my means, to delay immediate gratification, as part of my problem-solving.

To delay gratification, I now willingly had to confront my problem. To solve my problem of not saving enough for retirement, I had to put something pleasant aside, the use of home-equity debt to spend for the good life now, rather than to do something more painful—delay gratification now—for something more pleasant in the future

COMMITING TO A DISCIPLINED LOVE

As Peck further notes, the use of these tools of discipline in solving problems in life is highly connected to love. The energy for the work of discipline finds its basis in love.

As I read Peck's book, I comprehended at once the relation of love and discipline. Through our commitment to each other, Robbie and I became the beneficiary of each other's sharing and caring, of each other's love, with its many positive influences. Our ongoing authentic love for each other contributed to our individual well-being. We nurtured each other unconditionally. The more our love grew, the greater the increase in our sense of worth. As we grew together, so grew our sense of joy, our daily blissful moments, ever so present and constant.

My primary motivation to save more for retirement became my disciplined love for Robbie. Not only would I be disciplining myself now to save for a more gratifying life later in retirement, but I would be doing so out of love for Robbie and myself. As Peck states, "Call it what you will, genuine love, with all the discipline that it requires, is the only path in this life to substantial joy."[7]

BECOMING MORE PROACTIVE

In summary, I learned the following from Dr. Peck after reading his book. I had to accept responsibility for saving more for retirement. To save more, I would have to make greater use of discipline than I was doing. One way I could delay gratification was by spending less now and save more for the future. My immediate goal became a personal exploration of proactive steps I could now take to reach this goal.

READING WIDELY ABOUT RETIREMENT

My first action was to gather as much printed information I could readily read about recommended strategies for planning and saving for retirement. I subscribed to financial magazines, read numerous articles in newspapers, and ordered new books. I read voraciously and started a personal file of new ideas gleaned from these references. Not only was I reading, recording, and filing notes, I was learning a wide array of new information concerned with personal actions one could use to plan and save for retirement.

I read as much as I could find on topics ranging from "how to become a lifelong saver" to "becoming your own financial planner." Ultimately, I was searching for the answer: How can I at this moment find ways to save more for retirement?

ATTENDING SEMINARS AND LECTURES

Soon, I became aware that there were numerous retirement lectures and seminars in the area where I lived, in the Research Triangle area of North Carolina. I attended as many as possible. One of the recurring themes from many of the speakers was this: There are many benefits in seeking personal and individual guidance with retirement planning and saving from reputable and established financial planners.

MEETING WITH FINANCIAL PLANNERS

I took this advice seriously and scheduled meetings with two financial planners, one who worked in nearby Raleigh and held an outstanding national reputation. The other worked directly for an insurance company associated with the university. The outcomes of my consultations with these financial advisors were insightful and beneficial, optimistic and reassuring.

As part of my first consultation with each financial planner, I was asked to complete a rather lengthy financial questionnaire, similar but more detailed than the net worth analysis I had recently completed for myself. I knew I was overusing my home equity line of credit, that I was spending more money than I was making at times. At first, I felt ashamed to share this information with both financial planners. However, neither saw my home equity use as necessarily negative. Both pointed out I had used much of the money as good debt, money I used to buy more real estate that, mostly likely, would increase in value over time. They both seemed more concerned with practical moves I could make that would increase my long-term investments. Individually, they both recommended I first take the same two actions.

CHANGING MY RETIREMENT ALLOCATIONS

First, both financial planners recommended I change the original allocations I had established fifteen years ago when I was first employed by the university. Both recommended I increase gradually my investment risk for the long-term likelihood of greater financial gain. I could accomplish this task by starting a buyback of the monies I had accumulated in my fixed income fund. I could transfer 10% of the money in my fixed account over a period of ten years, until all the money in this fund was totally transferred to a variety of equity funds.

With the increase of my equity funds being limited to 10% a year, the increase in risk would be gradual at first, minimizing any fear of loss in a sudden stock market downturn. Later, I could allot the 10% buyback amount to other less risky funds if I so chose.

With the help of a representative from the company managing my university retirement funds, I was able to start the ten-year buyback quickly, simply by completing a form, signing it, and forwarding it to the company's headquarters. The whole process was quick, easy, and painless. Moreover, it started the whole process of setting meetings with the same representative, meetings that became rich in opportunities to review and discuss annually the status of my retirement accumulations.

CONTRIBUTING TO A SUPPLEMENTAL RETIREMENT ANNUITY (SRA)

Both financial planners recommended that I consider starting a Supplemental Retirement Annuity. A Supplemental Retirement Annuity is voluntary. My contributions would be taken directly from my salary and, as both financial advisors reminded me, these contributions would reduce my taxable income until withdrawn sometime in retirement.

Moreover, in 1987, the year I started my Supplemental Retirement Annuity, I could contribute as much as $12,500 annually. As one financial planner reminded me, contributions I made to a Supplemental Retirement Annuity could grow over the years and make back for me the retirement money I had withdrawn and spent in my early career, during the first thirteen years of my teaching. I was sold. My problem was finding the money within my income to contribute to a Supplemental Retirement Annuity.

One financial planner was quick to point out something I had recorded in my questionnaire, something positive, even impressive he qualified, that I had accomplished financially, and in a relatively short period of time. I had bought my first home in Chapel Hill, a condo, and over a ten-year period, I had managed to pay off the mortgage in full, to own the condo outright, mortgage free.

During the first three years, I had saved enough down payment to pay for more than half of the purchase price. Over the next seven years, I had managed to pay off the remaining mortgage, to own the condo outright, mortgage free. I had accomplished this task primarily by turning my first home into two rentals. Subsequently, I had used the rental income to pay off the remaining mortgage in full.

Now I was living in a new home, and I was renting my condo. Eventually, both financial planners recommended the following: Why not use my rental income, or part of it, to invest in a Supplemental Retirement Annuity? Because my contributions to an SRA had to come directly from my university paycheck, I could take a comparable amount from my rental income and use to meet my monthly and annual expenses for which I was using my university salary.

This recommendation made much sense. I was already using a lot of the rental money for extra things, like entertaining more, dining out frequently, traveling, buying new clothes, books and magazines, and objects of art—the good life. I could cut back on my excessive spending. I was motivated, more than ever before, to begin planning and saving now for my future life in retirement.

In 1988, then, I started an SRA and contributed only a $150.00 deduction from my paycheck each month. I did not miss the money deducted from my earnings. The next year,1989, I increased the amount of my SRA deduction to $300.00 a month and did not feel financially strapped. By 1990, the third year, I decided to contribute the maximum amount to my SRA, $12,500 annually. By now, I had become increasing assured that I could continue to live well without a current need to use the money I was allotting to my SRA contributions.

Moreover, during tax preparation season, I could see the tax deduction benefits of the SRA contributions in my tax returns. Most important of all, I enjoyed seeing my contributions slowly and steadily grow, from $2125.13 at the end of the first year, to $9734.92 the second year, to $22,046.11 the third year. I was on my way to making back the retirement savings I had spent during the first thirteen years of my career—and much, much more. I have watched my SRA Retirement Fund grow in value over the years, before I retired, after I retired, and into the present, thirty-four years after I started this fund in 1987.

What I did not know before retirement was this: By keeping my condo as a long-term rental and by using part of the rental income to contribute to an SRA for many years before I retired, I would increase my retirement accumulations so that Robbie and I both could retire earlier rather than later in life, making us in time financially independent. We finally had accumulated a net worth twenty-five times more than our present expenses. Moreover, we could now entertain many possibilities, among them becoming debt-free and remaining debt-free in retirement.

As I review my journey to financial independence and debt-free living in retirement, I identify the personal steps that seem to have mattered the most. Even with an approach of two steps forward and one step back, I eventually managed to maintain long-term staying power: I planned and saved long-term for retirement.

I turned my first home, a condo, into a twenty-year rental property and I used that money to fund a long-term SRA. I invested in other real estate that I sold soon after retirement, and with the sale of this real estate and the purchase in cash for two subsequent retirement homes, I eventually became debt-free. I have remained debt-free in my retirement for the past fifteen years. My goal is to remain debt-free for the rest of my life. Thus, I learned the third major lesson in retirement, the many benefits of becoming and remaining debt-free.

Because I decided to participate in the Optional Retirement Program in my early career, I would not receive a predetermined and set State Pension. At the time of my retirement, my retirement accumulations would become mine to manage and use in retirement as I saw fit, and from a wide array of options, like a systematic monthly withdrawal, an annual annuity, or a combination of both.

In my retirement, I wanted to continue to live well. I had done an excellent job in my accumulation stage of retirement. In the second stage, the drawdown stage, I similarly wanted to manage my retirement funds with knowledge and skill. I wanted to learn how best to pay myself an appropriate annual salary and, at the same time, preserve enough of my retirement accumulations to guarantee both Robbie and me enough retirement funds for the rest of our lives. I needed to make choices in the managing of my retirement funds like those eventual decisions any competent CEO makes in the overseeing of a company's portfolio.

BECOMING CEO OF MY RETIREMENT FUNDS

Thus, it was now up to me to maintain a strong retirement portfolio and to manage it well for future years. It was up to me to act, make use of many investment resources and strategies, and, in the process, to monitor my asset allocations wisely and well, and hopefully, for many years to come. At the end of the day, it was up to me to determine my portfolio's future financial success or failure.

In retirement, I would have less wiggle room than I did while accumulating my retirement funds. While I was building my nest egg, I had time and opportunity on my side, to make up for mistakes or any market setbacks. Now that I was retired and beginning to withdraw money from my funds, I had less time and room for error. I understood I had to be extremely careful about my withdrawal strategies and the specific decisions I made to carry them out.

Indeed, I was the one now responsible in my retirement portfolio for making all the investment decisions. This responsibility at first was somewhat daunting, especially considering how the stock market was behaving at the time of my retirement in 2001.

However, I desired the long-term growth that investments in the stock market offered over time, so there would be no way I could completely escape the stock market turmoil. Therefore, I wanted initially to create an investment strategy that would allow me to take advantage of long-term growth of my investments. At the same time, I wanted an investment strategy that would minimize market damage to my retirement accumulations created by market volatility and other financial setbacks.

A few months before I retired, I completed what I considered some basic preliminary financial steps, among them the following.

CONSOLIDATION OF RETIREMENT FUNDS

Because I had several retirement funds with different investment companies, I decided that it would be easier for me to determine my cash flow each year and pay myself an annual salary if I consolidated all my funds into one. One large account seemed simpler to manage than several smaller ones. With the assistance of a representative from my primary investment company, I was able to roll over my funds into one, and in a relatively short period of time—less than a month.

REALLOCATING MY RETIREMENT ACCUMULATIONS

During the 1990s, the boom years on Wall Street, I had been an aggressive investor, with over 90% of my portfolio in stocks. With this aggressive approach, I was able to accumulate more money for my retirement than I had earlier imagined.

By 2000, just before I retired, I reallocated my retirement funds, assuming the long-term growth of the 1990s would not continue. I wanted to secure much of the gain I made while at the same time keeping adequate amounts invested in equities for long-term growth. I reallocated my funds to include a fixed income fund, a real estate fund, as well as an equity fund. From the fixed income fund, I would pay myself an annual income, and I would use the other funds for potential future growth.

LEARNING HOW TO PAY MYSELF AN INCOME

My asset allocation would need to be a balancing act between risk and guaranteed return. I also sensed that the way and percentage I withdrew from my retirement funds annually for my income was also a balancing act.

I did not want to withdraw so much that I would outlive my funds in later life, nor did I want to be so frugal that I sacrificed and denied myself those experiences I always envisioned in retirement. In my early retirement, I chose at first a somewhat aggressive asset allocation, 70% in equities and 30% in fixed funds.

With this allocation, I was pleased to learn that I could pay myself the same salary as I was earning in my last year of employment at the university, and that my rather low percentage of withdrawal from my total retirement accumulations did not suggest any long-term negative repercussions.

I set up an automated monthly systematic withdrawal, to be deposited directly into my checking account on the first of each month. I placed the total amount of this annual withdrawal into a fixed Money Market Fund, and I systematically withdrew and received a monthly check from the company that was—and still is—my financial service provider, the Teacher Insurance and Annuity Association of America (TIAA).

TIAA is a Fortune 100 financial service organization that is the leading provider of financial services in the academic, research, medical, cultural, and governmental fields. This systematic withdrawal from this fixed income fund became the initial way I paid myself a monthly paycheck in retirement. I continued to use this same systematic withdrawal of funds for annual income over the next seven years.

DELAYING THE PURCHASE OF AN ANNUITY

Before I retired, I agonized over whether I should purchase a fixed annuity with some of my retirement monies. In its most simple form, an annuity involves handing over a chunk of money to an insurance company in return for a guaranteed check every month for the rest of one's life.

However, in the early stages of my retirement, I wanted to retain full control over my own funds and manage them myself. Once I purchased a fixed annuity from an insurance company, I would receive a check every month for the rest of my life, but I would have to relinquish control over these funds forever in exchange for the guaranteed income.

Not knowing how long Robbie and I might live, I reasoned that the use of my retirement accumulations to buy an annuity at this stage of my life seemed somewhat premature. Furthermore, once Robbie and I both passed, the annuity monies would go directly to the insurance company.

I was also concerned about the amount of guaranteed income projected for us at this early stage of retirement. Robbie was ten years younger than I, only fifty-three at the time of our retirement. A two-life annuity income projections based on different purchase amounts yielded income figures that were too minimal at this stage of our lives.

A two-life annuity is also known as a joint and survivor annuity, an insurance annuity for two or more people. In our case, a two-life joint and survivor annuity would guarantee both Robbie and I coverage for as long as each one of us lived. Moreover, a two-life joint and survivor annuity had the advantage of providing income when people live longer than expected, just like most other annuities.

I first considered buying a one-life fixed annuity with my university retirement accumulations and leave my SRA funds in the market. If I were to die first, Robbie would receive the remaining income for the guaranteed period of my one-life annuity plus my remaining monies in the market, as well as all our real estate and savings. This move would give me more annuity income and much peace of mind. I valued the financial security that would come with a fixed life annuity.

After much internal debate, I chose to take this route: Manage my money myself, retain control of them as best I could and for as long as I could, and enjoy the benefits and flexibility that came with being the CEO of my own retirement funds.

Both Robbie and I had the potential of living long and healthy lives. Why give up a large amount of my retirement accumulations primarily for myself in a fixed annuity when we both could enjoy our total accumulations now, and at the same time, manage them as they grow in the future?

If I were to pass first, Robbie would inherit the remaining funds. This choice seemed to be the best financial decision at that time, especially at the beginning stage of retirement. Later in life when we were older, we could always choose to buy a two-life, joint and survivor fixed annuity. With less projected years to live, our projected two-life monthly amounts would increase, and significantly. Sometime in the far future, then, there may come a time to re-visit the need to purchase of a two-life, joint and survivor annuity. Many years later in retirement, that time eventually arrived.

RETIRING IN A DOWN MARKET

In 2001, just as I was in the process of retiring and early in my retirement, a stock market downturn happened rather quickly, although the collapse started earlier in 2000 as part of a large bear market. It was a stock market decline I will never forget. Several internet companies went bankrupt, followed by a few accounting scandals which forced many large corporations to restate their earnings, or report the lack-thereof. On September 11 in 2001, terrorist attacks happened, followed by two wars in Afghanistan and Iraq. Needless to say, all these domino-like events had a negative effect on the stock market and on our country's economy.

On June 7, 2001, the Dow closed at 11,090.74. Then came the explicit statement on October 31, 2001 that officially, our country was in a recession. By October 9, 2002, the Dow had dropped to 7286.27. Over approximately a three-year period, my equity stocks in my retirement funds dropped 34%.

CHOOSING TO STAY THE COURSE

I knew that this was not a time to sell, even though at times I was tempted to bail out. I also knew that after each downturn in the market, stocks rebounded and often reached new highs. Investors who sold during severe downturns rarely had much opportunity to recover their losses. If I were to sell during this downturn, I would have a most difficult time recovering my losses. I was still young and just beginning retirement. I still had time to recover much of my market loss.

Economic recovery and strong corporate earnings did help markets recover in 2003 and 2004. This Dow expansion pointed at the time to continuing expansion and stability. By October 9 in 2007, the Dow closed at 14,154. 53. By staying in the market long-term and leaving my funds to gain in value, I was able to recover the losses in my portfolio that occurred earlier in my retirement.

CHOOSING TO DOWNSIZE

For the first two years of retirement, Robbie and I owned three homes, our primary home in Chapel Hill, a condo on the ocean at Atlantic Beach, and our condo in Maine, where we lived during the summer months. One of our retirement goals was to sell both North Carolina properties and move to Florida for the winter months—to become snowbirds, living in Maine in the summers and Florida during the winters.

We decided to sell our two North Carolina properties first. Such a move seemed then, and still does today, a wise move. The beach condo in Eastern Carolina was a five- to six-hour drive from Chapel Hill, and the likelihood of our using it much in the future seemed remote. We were spending most of the year in Maine for the first two years of our retirement and returning to Chapel Hill for only a few months in the winter. By selling our home in Chapel Hill as well, we could fully eliminate my rather large home equity debt we had carried for years on this property. Most importantly, by paying off this home-equity debt, we would finally become debt-free in retirement.

I calculated that the elimination of this loan and the expense of maintaining our two homes in North Carolina would cut our annual expenses by nearly 40%. This savings would mean that I could cut the amount of my systematic withdrawals from my retirement funds by nearly half during these volatile times in the market. Essentially, I could preserve more money in my fixed account for use over a longer time, until the market rebounded and stabilized sometime in the future. Moreover, I would have cash in hand to pay outright for our Florida condo.

I sold the beach condo first in 2002. Then, in early 2003, I sold our Chapel Hill home. In December of 2003, we finally found the right condo for us in Florida and paid for it in cash. Not only were we now officially snowbirds, but we were also debt-free for the first time. We have remained debt-free throughout our retirement for the past twenty years, and we intend to remain debt-free for our remaining years.

PREPARING FOR ANOTHER MARKET DOWNTURN

For the first seven years of my retirement, I continued to take an annual salary by systematically withdrawing a set percentage from my total accumulations and placing this amount into my fixed Money Market Fund. Now that I had regained my previous loss in equity funds, I did not want to lose these funds again. We did not have the luxury of time to wait for another long-term market rebound.

In late 2007, there was much media forewarning of the potential for another stock market crash based on a high default rate in the sub-prime home mortgage sector. I had read much over the years from top financial advisors who recommended to investors the limitations of trying to time the market. Nevertheless, after many years of heeding this advice, I chose not to leave my retirement funds primarily in equity funds and at the mercy of another massive market downturn as I had done in 2001.

On October 10th in 2007, after my stock market gains had returned, I moved all my retirement money temporarily into Traditional and Fixed Funds, safe holding tanks for my retirement accumulations until I decided how best to reallocate them sometime in the future.

This financial decision was one of the best I have made in retirement, for the 2008 financial crisis did occur, also called The Crash of 2008-2009.

NAVIGATING A MARKET CRASH

On September 16, 2008, the failures of massive financial institutions in the United States rapidly devolved into a global crisis, resulting in several bank failures and sharp reductions in the value of stocks and commodities world-wide. Beginning October 6, 2008 and lasting all that week, the Dow Jones Industrial Average closed lower for all five sessions. Volume levels were also record breaking. The Dow Jones fell over 1,874 points or 18% in its worst weekly decline ever. The S&P fell more than 20%. By March 6, 2009, the DJIA had dropped 54%, to 6469 from its peak of 14,164 on October 9, 2007, over a span of seventeen months.

While all this financial turbulence was occurring, I felt relaxed because, essentially, I had taken all my retirement money out of the market and moved it for safekeeping into my fixed income accounts. While all those who remained in the market had suffered dramatically from a severe drop in the market, my fixed income account was not impacted. Rather, it was paying me a modest rate of 3.5% on my total accumulations. I knew in time I would have to put these monies to use in more productive ways, but I needed time to determine my next long-term investment plan. Eventually, I did—a plan that was two-fold: (1) buy a two-life annuity for Robbie and me, and (2) buy back into the market when it reached its apparent low.

BUYING A TWO-LIFE, JOINT AND SURVIVOR ANNUITY

In the fall of 2008, I requested several annuity projections from TIAA, the company holding my retirement funds. I chose this company primarily because it shared a long history of consistent and high national ratings, and especially for annuities.

Robbie and I were now sixty and seventy. Our two-life annuity projection, with joint survivor benefits based on my university retirement accumulations alone, was more than I previously had withdrawn in my monthly systematic payments over the past eight years.

We completed together all the necessary paperwork and financial transactions required, and since November 1, 2008, we have been collecting a guaranteed monthly annuity payment that will continue for the rest of each of our lives. When one of us dies, the other will continue to receive the annuity for the duration of his life.

Our monthly annuity payment come from my university contributions in my Optional Retirement Plan. Along with our checks from Social Security, these components of our retirement plan constitute the fixed income part of our retirement income. Since this fixed and guaranteed income is enough for us to live comfortably, we keep our total SRA accumulations invested in equity funds in the stock market for long-term growth. From these funds, I have been required, since reaching the age of seventy and a half, to take a Minimum Distribution, and I have done so for the past twelve years. Some years, I choose to spend this sum. Some years, I save this money, roll it over into other funds. Some years, I choose a combination of these two choices.

BUYING BACK INTO THE MARKET

Now that we had enough fixed income, I felt I could be somewhat more aggressive in buying back into the stock market with my SRA retirement funds. That is what I did. Knowing well no one can time the market, I waited until what appeared to me the best time to re-enter.

In March of 2009, just before the Dow Jones dropped to 6465, I placed all my remaining retirement accumulations back into the stock market, and in equity funds. As I write these words today, on the television screen behind me this Friday, January 15, 2021, the stock channel spokesperson is announcing that the Dow closed just under 31,000—unimaginable gains over the past eleven some years for my equity stocks, which I bought back in March of 2009.

MY FOURTH LESSON LEARNED: RETIRE DEBT-FREE

Since 2003, I have lived debt-free in retirement, and I intend to live debt-free for the remainder of my life. Many previous colleagues and present acquaintances have informed me that they would rather have selected the State Retirement Plan rather than to go through the work, angst, and financial uncertainty I did for so many years in retirement.

I respectively disagree with them for the following reasons. I have immensely enjoyed managing my own retirement portfolio. Moreover, I have found my total experience of becoming and remaining debt-free in retirement both joy-filled and deeply gratifying.

LIVING DEBT-FREE IN RETIREMENT: MOMENTS OF ABUNDANCE AND ONENESS

In my debt-free retirement, I spend just about any amount I want to spend, and without any financial guilt or angst. I spend monthly on discretionary items like entertainment and travel. In the process, I enjoy every moment of freedom that comes with debt-free living. Essentially, I live without financial stress. I live with peace of mind. I live with enough financial freedom to pursue all my retirement dreams and ambitions. With my financial freedom and the joy I find in debt-free living, I continue to live one with self, one with life, and in these following ways.

RECEIVING MORE RETIREMENT INCOME

By choosing to manage my retirement funds myself early in my career rather than settle for a fixed pension, I was able to guarantee a larger and ever-increasing retirement income not just for myself but also for my now spouse Robbie—for two people rather than just one. Moreover, both Robbie and I now not only have fixed income guaranteed for life, but we also have additional and substantial retirement accumulations as well—funds invested in the stock market for long-term growth.

While I earned a good salary before I retired, I make much more now in retirement. The basic reason for this increase is that I am required by federal law to take annually a Minimum Distribution Withdrawal from my Supplementary Retirement Fund. Most years after taking this deduction, I reinvest these financial gains for future growth. Sometimes I do not. When I have had substantial gains in the market during specific years, I sometimes give myself an annual salary increase in retirement, like the annual merit pay increases I received when I was employed.

HAVING MORE DISPOSABLE INCOME

Recently, I came across a copy of the last university check I received. I calculated that at present in retirement; I have 58% more disposable income than I did in my last and highest salary year when I worked. The following are the reasons why.

In retirement, I no longer pay FICA taxes. I no longer contribute monthly to my university retirement plan. Nor do I contribute any longer to my Supplementary Retirement Plan.

I also pay less taxes. One simple lesson I learned early in retirement is that for every dollar I could legitimately avoid paying in taxes is another dollar that I could spend meeting some of my other retirement living expenses. Because Florida is now my primary residence, I do not pay state income tax. Because I also have double Homestead Deductions on my home in Florida, I pay less in real estate taxes than I did when I lived in North Carolina. My combined real estate tax bills for both my Maine and my Florida residences together are today only half of what I was assessed many years ago on just my townhome in Chapel Hill. Because I no longer have a substantial home equity mortgage deduction from my check, I now have this additional amount of disposable income to use monthly any way I so wish.

Robbie and I are now legally married, and he can now claim half of the total of my Social Security. Thus, we have recently received an increase in our combined Social Security payments. We can also file our federal income taxes jointly and claim a generous standard deduction of $24,000 annually.

CONTINUING MY RETIREMENT LEARNING

Because I am an active manager of my retirement funds, I try constantly to learn something new about investment strategies. I frequently read new articles on money management strategies in retirement, attend investment lectures, and I watch and follow various investment shows on television.

ENJOYING MONEY MANAGEMENT

I also enjoy immensely the daily managing and monitoring of my retirement funds, from obtaining daily stock futures, the factors effecting the global markets, to the recording each evening of the different balances of my equity funds.

Specifically, I try to focus on what I can control within my retirement portfolio: (1) the cost of funds; (2) the right asset allocations; (3) the careful selection of diversified funds; and (4) the rebalancing of funds at least once a year.

I believe these four investment strategies are the most important I have learned and used over my past years in retirement. These four strategies account mainly for the success I have experienced in the managing of my own retirement funds.

With the managing of my funds in the future, I feel I am now somewhat on automatic pilot. My investment strategies are basically in place. I have learned my fourth lesson in retirement. I not only learned how to become debt-free in retirement, I have enough money to live a comfortable life in my remaining years.

ENOUGH

The following vignette has been around for many years. Unfortunately, I do not know its origin. Yet, I have read various accounts of this same story, and I have heard it told from a variety of different perspectives. More significantly, the essence of the story actually happened once to me. Therefore, I am going to recall my actual experience as a lived example of the vignette. It is a story that illustrates, I believe, my feelings of oneness and satisfaction with my decision to live debt-free in retirement.

In Palm Beach one winter day, Robbie and I were invited by our neighbors to attend an investment luncheon in the white and gold grand ballroom at Donald Trump's Mar-a Lago. After lunch as we engaged in light conversation, my neighbor's wife whispered in my ear, "Bill, see that man over there at the next table? He's a hedge fund manager. He makes more money than you and I will ever have."

My response to her came easily, naturally. "That may be true, Anne. But I have something that hedge fund managers most likely will never have."

"Oh? What's that?" she asked inquiringly, turning her head to look directly at me, with raised eyebrows.

I first took a bite of a chocolate with an edible gold-leaf letter T on the top of it. Then I answered her question. "Anne," I replied, "I don't have to make any more money. I finally have enough."

PURSUE PURPOSE AND PLEASURE IN EVERYDAY LIVING

Following My Retirement Path, Finding My Retirement Types

One summer morning in Maine, I was working out at a local gym, next to a young man whom I recognized as an actor at the Ogunquit Playhouse. I mentioned to him that I had seen his recent performance and enjoyed it. We engaged in more conversation about his career before the actor asked what I did for work.

I informed him I had recently retired. He paused and then continued talking, but somewhat in a more discounting and somewhat authoritative manner. "I can't imagine a life without work," he affirmed. "It's through my acting work that I find meaning in life."

After I finished my workout, I thought further about my conversation with the actor. At one time in my life, I felt similarly as the actor about work and purpose in life. I once thought the identity of self with meaningful work was the primary route to purposeful living. I also once believed that a life spent in retirement did not result in the leading of a meaningful life at the same level of significance as a life spent in meaningful work.

I recalled a visit some years ago to the home of one of my newly retired colleagues. As I sat with him and his wife in their sunroom, they both took turns explaining to me the new and expanded construction on their home. Later, they showed me plans for a new outside garden. After more conversation, my former colleague asked if I had seen his new electronic piano, which I had not, and I did not care to see it. Nevertheless, he quickly escorted me to an area of the home where the piano was located and proceeded to play many show-tune medleys.

Both my former colleague and his wife were obviously happy, productive, and active in their retirement. They both appeared to find much purpose and pleasure in retirement as they went about planning new projects, completing new tasks, and developing new interests.

However, at this time in my life, I could not accept my colleague's life in retirement as comparable in purpose and pleasure as my life spent in meaningful work. Silently, I concluded that my world of work was more important, more purposeful, more of value to myself and society than my former colleague's casual and free-flowing retirement activities. At an earlier stage in my life, then, I believed a life of meaningful work was more purposeful living than a life without work in retirement.

Now, after nearly two decades lived in retirement, I know for certain my life during my academic career and my life during retirement have been two distinct stages, with different foci, contexts, and environments. One stage has not been more purposeful or less purposeful than the other. Each stage has been uniquely purposeful, each in its own special way. Therefore, neither stage has been the only way—nor the ultimate way—of finding purpose and pleasure in life.

THE PURSUIT OF PURPOSE IN RETIREMENT

When I retired, I understood I would be leaving behind many resources in academia in which I previously found much meaning (like teaching), a professional identity and title, and essentially, a long and prestigious career. However, I also knew I would be bringing with me into a yet unknown life in retirement some of the same resources for finding meaning I had already acquired and used frequently, not only in my daily work, but in everyday living. Essentially, there were four primary sources of purpose I would bring with me into retirement.

A SHARED LIFE WITH ROBBIE

My shared life with Robbie is the centerpiece of my identity and fundamental to my feelings of purpose and fulfillment in life. Robbie is my immediate family. His well-being, support, and care matter profoundly to me, as does our relationship and our journey together in life.

We love each other unconditionally. We communicate well with one another. We solve problems and make major decisions jointly. We treat each other with respect and share openly with each other our individual concerns. Robbie would become my retirement companion, and together we hoped to share many more years of continued happiness.

Robbie and I live fulfilling lives. We engage in many novel and challenging activities. We spend quality time together, even while completing mundane household tasks. We approach life with zest in our hobbies, interests, even in our politics. We share numerous moments filled with joy and laughter.

We planned on finding much shared purpose in retirement, but also individually. We are two distinct individuals, each of us with his own interests and perspectives, and personal agendas. We had learned over time how to give each other his own space, his own sense of autonomy.

REMAINING AUTHENTIC

A second resource I would bring with me into retirement would be a strong inner desire to stay true to self, to act and make decisions congruent with my authentic self. I wanted to use and integrate into everyday living my unique skills, abilities, and interests. Specifically, I would be bringing with me into retirement my rare gift of joy and my deep desire to participate fully in daily creative endeavors.

THE USE OF JOY

In order to live an authentic life in retirement, I needed to make daily use of my natural and rare gift of abundant joy. This gift of joy, an intrinsic desire to find immense pleasure in everyday living, was a personal and vital source of strength and power. Joy was a personal gift of resiliency, intellectual searching, and creativity.

THE USE OF CREATIVITY

I would also be bringing with me into retirement a strong desire and need to engage in many moments of creativity and imagination. I needed to live artfully, with a life filled with time for creative and imaginative endeavors. Creativity expanded my perceptions, and with expanded perceptions, I often found new ways of solving problems. Creativity allowed me to expand my mind by doing new and exciting things, engaging myself in ways that allowed me to reach new and higher levels of performance and achievement.

Often, joy seemed to work hand in hand with, or become part of, my different creative undertakings. My continuous and increasing use of joy and creativity in retirement would contribute significantly to the likelihood of my living a happy and productive life.

AN ACTIVE LIFE OF CONTINUOUS INQUIRY

By nature, I am a curious person and self-motivated to learn. I would be bringing with me into retirement a mindset of continuous inquiry and a need for lifelong learning experiences.

Although retired, I would still want to learn new skills and knowledge, explore new resources, and participate in new cultural experiences. My wide participation in self-initiating activities could also lead to rewarding social inclusion and continuous personal development. These aspects of a life of the mind were basic everyday needs for me, as well as potential sources of purpose to explore and use in retirement.

THE ABILITY TO COMMUNICATE
WELL AND SOLVE PROBLEMS

In addition, I would be bringing with me into retirement good communication and problem-solving skills acquired and used in my past career and everyday life. To solve problems in retirement, as I had done well in former stages of my life, I would be choosing to experience the difficulty of working through my problems before eventually solving them, thus learning and growing throughout the process.

For these reasons and others, I viewed my impending retirement not as an end but a beginning. Retirement was now my time and opportunity to experience a new life, one in which I built upon my past accomplishments and individual resources. Now was also a time in my life to continue growing and learning, hopefully discovering in the process new sources of purpose and pleasure.

FINDING MY RETIREMENT PATH

During my early years in retirement, I soon discovered a new and powerful source of purpose: my individual retirement path. In a most general sense, I understood different retirees take different paths as they structure their lives in retirement. I knew the basic retirement path I would choose to follow in retirement would influence significantly how I found much purpose and pleasure in everyday living. However, I knew little more. I had not read nor conversed with others any established research on retirement paths and types.

One day before officially retiring, I happened to peruse a university publication listing the names and addresses of retired professors from my professional school. I was surprised to find that only three out of twenty-three professors listed had moved away from Chapel Hill. I immediately wondered why so few had moved away and why so many had decided to stay.

I assumed that most of these retirees stayed living in Chapel Hill because of the university's many fine attributes and offerings. I also assumed that many of these same retirees wanted to maintain their previous ties with the university and ongoing university-sponsored activities.

PRESSURES TO REMAIN "OTHER THAN" BEFORE RETIRING

For a short period of time, I started to question my intent to move away from Chapel Hill, a town which I called home for the past thirty years. I started to feel somewhat guilty about my decision to leave and begin a whole new life as a snowbird. I started to challenge my individual and personal goals and to re-evaluate the logic behind my intentions. These feelings of doubt and guilt were the subtle and direct results of an array of different pressures on me to remain *other than* who I authentically wanted to become in my retirement.

From family members, both Robbie and I were criticized for choosing not to remain living nearby. We were, in their minds, leaving them behind, forgetting about them and the place they should be playing in our retirement lives.

From many colleagues, I was faced with comments of concern about my retirement decision-making ability. They reminded me by moving away I would be choosing to sell my home and all my acquisitions for which I had worked so hard and for so long. Plus, I would be leaving behind my established friendships and relationships, with them and their families and other acquaintances. From community members, I was reminded that I would be moving away from Chapel Hill, a town recently named as one of the top places to retire.

In time, I discovered a major distinction between myself and many of the retirees who stayed living in Chapel Hill. Their choice of retirement path, to remain living a quality life in a prominent university town, was fine and appropriate—for them. They were colleagues who continued in retirement with a life similar to the one they had led in work.

Soon, it became easier for me to recognize the responses from family members, friends and colleagues, and community members as subtle and direct pressures to behave *other than* what I genuinely wanted for myself.

The retirement path many others were suggesting to me was not the one I wanted to follow. I wanted a different retirement path, that of a snowbird. I wanted to travel, live in other places, meet new people, and contribute to new communities. As a good friend kept reminding me, I wanted a whole new journey in life, a whole new adventure.

As soon as I understood and acknowledged that I was on a different retirement path than my former colleagues, my feelings of guilt disappeared. I could accept that different retirees make different retirement choices. One choice was not more right nor more wrong than the other. They were just different choices made by different retirees on a variety of similar and different retirement paths. As soon as I comprehended this distinction, I continued with my plans, to become a snowbird.

DISCOVERING MY RETIREMENT TYPES

In my retirement, it was also important for me to live a life compatible with the needs of my authentic self. I needed to follow a retirement path that allowed for much freedom and unscheduled time, the exploration of new opportunities, and the participation in joy-filled and creative activities.

Nearly a decade later in my retirement, I read Nancy Schlossberg's book *Retire Smart, Retire Happy: Finding Your True Path in Life.* In this insightful book, Schlossberg identifies and describes five different retirement paths and types of retirees.

After reading this book, I understood more clearly how I differed from many of my former and retired colleagues who remained living in Chapel Hill. I also understood more fully how I was both similar to and different from other retirees.

Many of my former colleagues who stayed connected to the university basically were the type of retirees Schlossberg identifies as Continuers: retirees who stayed on their academic path, attended professional meetings, staying in touch with colleagues who still worked at the university, and attended professional meetings.

In addition, Schlossberg further reminds readers most retirees are different combinations of the five types of retirees she identifies and describes. While we tend to be a dominant retirement type, we are likely, over time, to change our combinations of retirement types.

I could relate well to Schlossberg's preceding statements and observations. Early in my retirement, I was a combination of two types of retirees. Once I became more settled in my retirement journey, I became a third retirement type. Initially, however, I was a combination of Adventurers and Searchers, two retirement types Schlossberg identifies and describes.

As an Adventurer, I wanted to explore a life filled with new options, a life that moved beyond my previous academic work. I wanted to become my own itinerary and use my self-chosen activities as the basic structure to each day. As a Searcher, I was separating from my past, but I had not yet found a basic routine nor sense of home or place.

Until Robbie and I finally found our new homes as snowbirds, I was a combination of Adventurer and Searcher. As I settled into later life as a snowbird, I became a different type of retiree. The dominate kind of retirement type I had become, and still remain, had a name: Easy Glider, and I fit Schlossberg's definition extremely well:

> Easy Gliders ...*enjoy unscheduled time, select activities that appeal to them, and pace themselves according to my newfound freedom. They want to relax and enjoy the whole retirement ride— sometime meandering, sometimes working, and sometimes involved with family and friends. Easy Gliders are open to anything but are still in control.*[8]

In another and subsequent publication, *Revitalizing Retirement: Reshaping Your Identity, Relationships, and Purpose,* Schlossberg warns readers of a downside to being an Easy Glider:

> *Easy Gliding is not necessarily a perpetual vacation. Once you've had a chance to drift for a while, the result of having so much unstructured time can lead to boredom, which can make you feel you no longer matter.*[9]

This warning gave me pause. Why was it that I rarely felt throughout my retirement life that I was bored or drifting? How was it that I felt, on the contrary, that I was living a worthy and meaningful life? What was I doing differently, or in addition to, my basic and dominant Easy Glider retirement type?

Eventually, I concluded that not all Easy Gliders glide in the same way. While I was an Easy Glider is a general way, open to almost anything, I was also an Easy Glider who had to remain in control, to set boundaries on my Easy Glider lifestyle. Over time, these boundaries have resulted in many moments of active, engaged, and purposeful living.

BECOMING AN EASY GLIDER: SETTING BOUNDARIES

The three major boundaries I have used as an Easy Glider are as follows: (1) I assume responsibility for short- and long-term problem solving; (2) I impose a personal order on unstructured daily living; and (3) I participate in a wide array of treasured activities. These boundaries have helped me determine the way I live in retirement, with purpose as an Easy Glider, and with control over my Easy Glider lifestyle.

TAKING RESPONSIBILITY FOR PROBLEM-SOLVING

To illustrate, my decision to become an Easy Glider with newfound freedoms and unscheduled time in retirement did not mean I was being undisciplined in retirement, or lacking in responsibility, or setting myself up for an empty and meaningless life during my golden years. I still needed to set some personal boundaries for finding new purposes and pleasures in life.

One of my boundaries as an Easy Glider was choosing not to ignore my major responsibilities in life. Just like all retirement types, Easy Gliders complete necessary daily tasks and confront and solve problems. Most retirees, Easy Gliders or not, will experience circumstances daily that invoke the use of skills, accumulated knowledge, and resources that are available for use in solving problems and side-stepping obstacles. Since life in retirement poses an endless series of problems, Easy Gliders, likewise, have numerous opportunities to solve these problems and thereby gain resulting meaning in our lives.

PLACING ORDER ON AN UNSTRUCTURED LIFE

As an Easy Glider, I sometimes live a free-wheeling, somewhat unstructured, and spontaneous life. However, my choice to live a meandering life in retirement does not mean I am lost in my direction or faltering in my usefulness. Each day I still write down a daily agenda, my personal itinerary. I still set short- and long-term goals in writing, and I monitor the meeting of them by marking them off once completed. In other words, I anchor myself in purpose and direction even in my unstructured, dominant Easy Glider lifestyle. At other times, my creative abilities and retirement projects typically require me to remain spontaneous and free, open to new and fresh insights, possibilities, and projects.

Finally, because I participate daily in activities that keep me continuously active and engaged, I feel I matter, that my life is of value. These activities have resulted in increased personal interests and developments, and from multiple dimensions of myself, from spiritual awareness and enhancement to physical, creative, social, and lifelong learning experiences. Moreover, these treasured activities often provide me with a framework for finding and developing new and different levels and layers of meaning in life.

PURSUING TREASURED ACTIVITIES: INTROSPECTIVE MOMENTS OF ONENESS

As an Easy Glider, I select activities that appeal to me. I like the exploration of new and different interests and opportunities. I pace myself through each day as I participate in many treasured activities, many times meandering and relaxed, remaining open to most anything, but still in charge, still in control.

MORNING MEDITATIONS

My morning life on my porch transcends the stereotypical image of an elderly person rocking away in a chair with nothing better to do. On the contrary, my private time each morning on my porch appears to assist me in my use of different types and levels of reflective thought.

I start each morning by embracing the beauty of each day. Mornings are golden on my porch, with bright sunlight and expansive skies. Daily I observe the beauty and varied colors of clouds, trees, ocean, and buildings. The time I spend in the mornings on my porch has become what I call my personal sacred time, time to reflect, to become one with self, become one with nature, one with life.

JOURNAL WRITING

During my morning hours on my porch, I often complete various forms of journal writing, using a variety of writing techniques to help me discover content deep within.

In the early 1990s, I read Julia Cameron's book, *The Artist's Way: A Spiritual Path to Higher Creativity*. In this magnificent work, Cameron recommends two basic tools for readers interested in freeing themselves from writing and other creative blocks. One writing tool Cameron recommends is the writing of morning pages.

MORNING PAGES

The writing of morning pages involves recording whatever comes to mind until you have written three pages. That is all that is required of morning pages—except Cameron stipulates we must write our morning pages every day, that writing morning pages is nonnegotiable.

Her rationale makes sense, as does her payoff. We write morning pages to help silence our internal censors, to dissolve our writing and other creative blocks, those negative messages we send ourselves that often prevent us from leading productive and creative lives. Overtime, the continuous act of writing three morning pages each day will get us on the other side of our inner censor.

Writing morning pages became another form of writing I used daily during my meditation and reflection time on the porch. Through meditation combined with my writing of morning pages, I have discovered new and creative insights for making positive changes in my life. For lasting creative recovery and discovery, Cameron also recommends the use of a second tool: the artist date.

ARTIST DATES

Cameron defines an artist date as a block of time, like two hours or more a week, spent nurturing our creative consciousness, our inner artist. An artist date is time we set aside for ourselves, to partake in any number of self-chosen events, sacred moments of play and imagination our inner artist requires, a process Cameron describes in part as "filling the well."

> If we do not give some attention to upkeep, our well is apt to become depleted, stagnant, or blocked...... As artists, we must learn to be self-nurturing. We must become alert enough to consciously replenish our creative resources as we draw on them--to restock the trout pond, so to speak. I call this process filling the well.[10]

The following are some artist dates I have taken alone over the past two months to fill the well: a visit and long stroll through a botanical garden;

a visit to a whitewater rafting center; a tour of a winery; a long hike up and down one side of a mountain; and a day trip to Lincolnton, a nearby city. I also have attended a lecture by a local author; a jazz festival concert; and a grand opening of a new grocery store.

By taking these and other artist dates, I have learned that self-nurturing takes many forms. I have gained confidence in doing tasks alone that I never thought possible, from water rafting to climbing rock walls. Through greater observation of nature, I have learned to honor my often ignored or forgotten elements of surprise and wonder within. I have learned much new information from spontaneous conversations with strangers.

Most of all, artist dates have helped me become "unstuck," both in my thinking and my planning. Typically, I have come away from many of my artist dates with a greater awareness of these insights and a renewed sense of confidence. I have more options available than I previously thought possible.

SHOPPING, GATHERING, AND CREATING

Daily shopping is another activity I enjoy. Typically, I shop for something every day at different local markets, and I look forward to these shopping experiences. I specifically enjoy the meandering nature of shopping, going up and down the aisles and seeing items I may or may not have intended to purchase.

Because Robbie and I eat lots of fresh fruits and vegetables, I shop for them daily. Starting on Thursdays in our area of South Florida, some stores offer many Buy One, Get One Free specials. Both Robbie and I have developed the habit of studying the grocery store ads in the local paper before these sales, and we make a list weekly of the Buy One, Get One Free bargains we want to purchase each week. This week, for example, our favorite coffee Gevalia is on sale. My favorite Italian water has been reduced to $1.25 a bottle. Light English Muffins are Buy One, get One Free, as is fresh, chopped pineapple. We stock up primarily with food items that we use on a regular basis.

COOKING

In addition to shopping daily, I enjoy cooking and the creative nature of cooking. I even enjoy the physical act of chopping in preparation for a meal. Robbie is a master at making a variety of salads. One of my favorites is his fresh fruit, avocado, and shrimp salad with black walnuts. I especially enjoy making soups. Last night I made a butternut squash soup with chicken broth, celery and carrots—simple, healthy, and delicious.

We both enjoy not only the creativity involved in cooking but also the artistry and beauty in the presentation of food. We often invite friends to our home just to cook for them in new and special ways.

Recently, we learned that two friends from Maine were coming to visit us. When Robbie and I were married, these particular friends, a husband and wife, had taken Robbie and me to a twelve-course dinner and wine-pairing at an outstanding restaurant in Kennebunkport. For almost four hours that evening, we dined, drank, and shared exhilarating conversation. Not only were these friends generous and supportive, but they were also connoisseurs of fine food and drink.

When they visited us in Florida, I decided I could create my own twelve-course dinner of small bites and match each one with a suitable wine. Robbie knew wines well. I could be the chef, and Robbie could be the sommelier.

I created a menu of small bits, ranging from lobster tails and dill sauce to pear, prosciutto, and blue cheese wraps. Robbie selected a fine wine for each of the small bites. Together, we selected the dinnerware that complemented each bite. The dinner was a success and fun. More importantly, the event became a way to use some creativity. The planning for and preparation of the dinner were creative and imaginative extensions of self.

Robbie and I cook for ourselves on a regular basis in retirement, and with no less care or creativity. Moreover, we enjoy dining at fine restaurants at least once a week, and more frequently during holidays. From these culinary experiences, we always learn something, from new spices and sauces, to new recipes and food combinations.

FINDING BEAUTY IN HOME AND NATURE

Our homes reflect our souls. Both Robbie and I like to be surrounded by beauty in our homes, both inside and out. Throughout our shared life, we have purchased condos, townhomes and houses based on the property location and surrounding beauty outside. Inside, we like space and flow. We also like to collect all kinds of objects of art to enhance the beauty of our homes.

SEARCHING FOR OBJECTS OF DESIRE

We spend much leisure time exploring various venues, from antique shops to flea markets, for what we call "objects of desire." We enjoy immensely the search for just the right object to purchase, and for just the right spot.

During our visits to different shops, we do not always make a purchase. Nevertheless, we still enjoy visiting and perusing antique malls and galleries, searching and wondering if we will find that rare and just-right new object of art.

We like visiting Boca for lunch and visiting the Z Gallery. We have found in this shop some rare and beautiful Christmas ornaments we use each season. In Lake Worth and West Palm Beach, there are several antique shops along Antique Alley. We have purchased a few select objects of desire in these shops, from an early Stephen White painting to unusual pieces of English garden statuary.

I enjoy the feelings of surprise and spontaneity that accompany my everyday basic creative and imaginative efforts, from completing morning papers, taking artist dates, shopping, cooking, entertaining, to the search for objects of desire. In addition, I extend the use of creative nature and efforts to other daily activities, like exercise.

PHYSICAL ACTIVITY AND MENTAL WELL-BEING

I find much additional purpose and pleasure in retirement by keeping both my body and my mind working as I age. I complete some form of exercise each day. When I worked, I exercised when I found free time. In retirement, I find time every day to engage in some physical activity, from running and walking to lifting light weights, or various combinations of these same activities.

As I write today, I have just finished a vigorous four-mile walk along Lake Worth. Tomorrow I plan to do the same walk again. The next day I plan to swim at my fitness center for an hour or so, and the following day, I plan to lift some weights and swim afterwards.

WALKING

Of all exercise, I enjoy walking the most. Since retiring, I have participated in several 5K runs throughout New England, North Carolina, and Florida. I have even come in first in my age category in a few of these races. I enjoy participating in these races and always meet new and interesting entrants of all ages.

There are many benefits to walking daily. Walking is a low-impact exercise and can be done for long periods of time. Walking regularly can lower blood pressure and cholesterol levels. Walking also improves overall fitness, cardiac health, mood, endurance, circulation, posture, and contributes to weight loss. Daily walking can also reduce the risk of stroke.

Walking also provides a sense of mental well-being. Walking triggers the creative flow of ideas to use in problem-solving, and improves joviality, vigor, attentiveness, and self-confidence. Walking regularly has the further potential for relieving the symptoms of anxiety, depression, and negative thinking.[11]

WEEKLY MASSAGE

Each week I reward myself with another activity, a massage. My longtime masseuses in Maine (David) and in Florida (Kim) both know how to eliminate my body's many places of pain, the result of stress, tension, and muscle strain, typically acquired from frequent exercise and long driving trips. I appreciate and value their services and afterward feel rejuvenated, realigned, and relaxed.

Massage is generally considered today part of integrative medicine. Studies of the benefits of massage conclude that massage is an effective treatment for reducing stress and anxiety, pain, and muscle tension. I usually request what is called a Trigger Point Massage. During this massage, the masseuse focuses on areas of the body with tight muscle fibers that form after injury or overuse.

One observation I have made during my massages is that during the process, my body and mind both seem to benefit from the healing and cleansing results of massage. I have noticed that as soon as I am in the process of being massaged, I start talking at random and my random talk is either something that quickly and unexpectedly pops into consciousness, or it is conversation with the masseuse about a personal dilemma I may be experiencing at the time and I start verbalizing possible resolutions.

During my massages, my random talk seems to happen automatically, without control and self-censoring. Years ago, I read a study about the written composing processes. In this study, the researcher speculated upon the roles the hand, eye, and brain shared in the writing process. One intriguing insight she shared with readers postulated that the eye and hand were reinforced in the writing process by the brain's left hemisphere.

I have often wondered during my weekly massages if a similar process could happen when we compose orally. During my massages, I noticed I have strong inclinations to talk aloud. Could my body and the masseuse's touch similarly be activating the left hemisphere of my brain, resulting in involvement with and reinforcement of my oral composing process during massage, and in a similar way to the hand, eye, and brain in the written composing process? For me, there seems to be such a connection.

Most of all, my massages frequently become both a physical and a mental healing experience. As with my daily walking and exercise regimen, I cannot imagine my life in retirement without massage therapy.

DAILY SOCIAL CONNECTEDNESS

Robbie and I value our many social connections. Our old and new friends and community connections are all important in our retirement lives. The many social activities in which we participate provide us with a sense of purpose and belonging. We communicate with others daily, either by emails, texts, telephone calls, or in person.

We surround ourselves with positive friends we value, friends balanced in disposition and wise in judgment. We enjoy our lively and rigorous conversations with our friends and the many opportunities they provide us to learn new and interesting information. During our many varied social events, we laugh a lot and learn a lot, two major benefits for us from many of our social engagements.

We also enjoy helping our friends in ways that we can, to serve them and our communities in ways we find helpful and satisfying. For example, I like giving books to friends whom I think will benefit from reading the book's content, and Robbie, a music buff, enjoys making CDs for friends who enjoy music as much as he does.

LIFELONG LEARNING

Both Robbie and I are lifelong learners. If I were asked to identify the one aspect of my retirement I value the most, it would be lifelong learning, especially the pursuit of these specific activities: reading, writing, listening, and viewing.

A strong pull in my life is constantly the need to learn new information, no matter how seemingly small or insignificant. Most times, the information I am learning is of much consequence to the world at large. For example, at present I am trying to comprehend how Russia could have interfered with our 2016 Presidential Election. I am fascinated with so much new learning about how Russia paid internet trolls and botnets to disseminate fake news via social media to influence American voters.

I want this information in order to know how I can be best informed to make judgments based on facts and common sense. I want our democracy to stay strong, to not become vulnerable to further and similar acts from any country or groups of individuals. Therefore, I am presently learning all kinds of new information, particularly about trolls and bots—sometimes called multifaceted information warfare.

I am also reading Kurt Andersen's recent book, *Fantasyland*. This author demonstrates through a review of 500 years of American history what is presently happening in our country, the "fake news" movement. Through his research, Andersen shows us this movement is not something new. But it is our present path, one of make-believe or fantasy, of both a post-truth and post-fact way of viewing the world.

Literally, I read throughout the day and evening. In the morning, I enjoy pacing myself slowly through all sections of *The Palm Beach Post* and *Boston Globe*. In the afternoon, if I have a lull moment, I like to sit in my favorite living room chair and read one or more of our current magazines. Most evenings after I go to bed, I read late into the night, often until 2 AM. Right now, on my nightstand, I am reading three books intermittently—Augustus Burrows' *A Wolf at the Table*; Patricia Cornwell's most recent book, *Chaos*; and Richard Russo's *Everybody's Fool*. Two books I plan to read soon arrived today in the mail, Walter Isaacson's *Leonardo Da Vinci* and Sarah Bakewell's *At the Existentialist Café: Freedom, Being, and Apricot Cocktails*.

I read for many reasons. Sometimes, I read for pleasure. Many times, for therapeutic value, what some people call bibliotherapy. Other times, I read to gain new information. Reading is a primary mode for me to be and remain a lifetime learner. So is writing.

I write every day, often with myself as my primary reader, such as when I do my journal writing. Often, I keep my written thoughts and ideas in notebooks and file them away for further work and later completion. Some days, my writing includes numerous email responses and the writing of letters. I still enjoy writing and sending handwritten letters and, even more, receiving them.

I look forward to various kinds and forms of written composition each day, from making lists, writing for self, sending email messages, writing to friends, writing business letters, to capturing and writing content for this book and other written works in progress.

There is no end to the enjoyment of and benefits from composing daily in a wide array of written forms. I develop and hone my communication skills. I clear my mind, recall momentarily forgotten memories, activate and use a number of cognitive activities, develop a sense of accomplishment, and unleash personal content and creativity on paper.

I also attend intriguing lectures. In our retirement communities, we have town lectures, hospital lectures, university lectures, investment lectures, and lectures in a variety of cultural settings, from museums to the performing arts. This coming Wednesday, for example, Robbie and I will be attending a lecture by the actor, Rob Donahue, following his performance in TRU. A few weeks earlier, we attended an after-performance discussion given by Estelle Parsons. We also take a variety of different classes to gain new knowledge and self-growth and improvement. We are always trying to learn new information and experience new and exciting experiences and meeting new and interesting people in the process.

As ongoing patrons of the arts, we participate often in diverse and inspiring cultural experiences. We attend plays, community discussions, intellectual book talks, opera and the ballet, films, art exhibits in various museums, and concerts—all cultural arts that spark our imagination and challenge our minds. By attending these events, we gain much knowledge, about society as well as ourselves. We learn much new knowledge about current conditions in our present time and history.

We make efforts throughout the year to see recommended movies. We try to analyze and capture the intent of different films as well as the filmic elements used by different directors. We enjoy the movie theater experience, as it involves the use of our sensorial skills in interpretation, and on many different levels of response, hearing, viewing, listening, with the use of color, movement, and setting. From January through February each year, we try to see all the Oscar-nominated films, and afterward, engage in much after-viewing discussion and response.

By my wide participation in these kinds of daily experiences, I stay informed, learn new content from a wide array of rich resources, enhance my use of critical thought, and live daily, as best as we can, a life of the mind, a life of lifelong learning.

MY FIFTH LESSON LEARNED: PURSUE PURPOSE AND PLEASURE IN DAILY LIVING

Essentially, by my regular participation in my treasured activities, I had learned the fifth major lesson in my retirement: the importance of pursuing purpose and pleasure in daily living.

As an Easy Glider, my itinerary for any given day may take this basic structure: Wake up, drink morning coffee on the porch, meditate and write, go to the gym, shop for dinner, visit friends for Happy Hour, return home for dinner, watch some television, then go to bed and read. Indeed, if that were all I did each day, then my life as an Easy Glider could become quickly one of boredom.

Within my activity outline, however, I do so much more. I become connected with my treasured activities; I become one with this basic itinerary. I explore daily how best I can find deeper purpose and meaning within each time category I have scheduled as part of my daily structure. I deliberately set out each day to use a form of personal mindfulness.

For example, while waking up on my porch, I complete my morning pages, meditate, and reflect. I view these personal choices and opportunities as powerful self-chosen activities to continuously evaluate events in my life, to learn and grow, personal mental efforts for monitoring and committing to an array of different daily contributions.

I do more than go to the gym. I do specific exercises, and through my completing of these exercises, I gain both joy and many physical and mental benefits. While shopping for dinner and cooking dinner, I participate in many creative activities. Through daily contact with friends, I gain more than support but often new knowledge and personal insights. Through my daily participation in a variety of lifelong learning activities, I am constantly acquiring new knowledge, new information for present and future use.

MANY AVENUES TO PURPOSEFUL LIVING

Throughout my retirement, I have learned there are numerous ways of finding purpose in life. The identity of purpose through work is only one way, but an important one. Individually, however, each of us has numerous and additional sources of purpose within, as well as many other ways we find purpose outside our lives in our environment. Sometimes, we want to matter to others. Other times, we want to matter more to ourselves.

By partaking in a wide range and array of interests and activities, I have found in retirement much purpose and pleasure in everyday living. I also have found much meaning and personal growth through facing necessary

problem-solving tasks. Further, I have found purpose and meaning at different stages of aging by following my individual retirement path and making
it congruent with my retirement types and my authentic self.

Thus, in my fifth lesson learned in retirement, I have experienced much
happiness and fulfillment, and often through the pursuit of self-initiated
interests and activities. These interests and activities have been multifaceted
in nature, inclusive of physical, mental, social, and educational dimensions.

At times, many of my activities were unstructured and spontaneous,
and others planned with greater detail. I especially enjoyed being socially
active, meeting new and interesting people, and participating in an array of
conversations, whether at a social function or just talking with someone in
line while checking out in a grocery store. Robbie reminds me constantly
that I never met a stranger.

Friends and acquaintances also have noticed my self-satisfaction and
enjoyment. Frequently, many have commented upon my active outdoor and
year-round life in the sun and described my retirement activities as exciting
and productive. To them, I seemed to have it all, and often I felt similarly.
I was content and happy with my snowbird lifestyle, with little desire for
anything else. I was living the good life, making conscious efforts to mesh
my authentic self with my daily tasks and responsibilities. Because no two
retirement days were ever the same, I remained true to self with different
degrees of frequency and intensity.

For this meaningful and charmed life during my first decade in retirement, I felt both blessed and grateful. Nothing should ever interrupt such a
powerful way of living, I often thought silently as I went about experiencing
a life of bliss, a life of oneness in my pursuit of treasured activities. I saw no
need to change nor possessed any desire to change. My retirement life was
good just as it was.

THE BEGINNING OF BEVAVIORAL CHANGE
AND DEVELOPMENTAL GROWTH

Therefore, I did not envision nor entertain any kind of changes likely to occur in my retirement life anytime soon, especially any changes involving a declining interest and participation in any of my present and preferred activities. These activities were the kind I would always value, the activities in which I would continue to participate, and for as long as I remained physically and mentally capable of accomplishing them.

There was nothing more I wanted from life--until I entered my next stage of developmental aging in retirement. Then, the direction of my life began to change, and with this change came unexpected new challenges and opportunities.

I was beginning a major transition in my retirement. Gradually, I was moving away from a life focused on freedom and adventure to one with a growing desire for the cultivation of more contemplative dimensions within myself. I was entering my Reflection and Review stage of developmental aging, one in which I would reach new and higher levels of transcendent awareness and growth, levels of consciousness I had not previously experienced nor realized.

PART TWO:

REFLECTION AND REVIEW

SEARCH FOR DEEPER PURPOSE AND MEANING

Recognizing and Accepting Transcendent Growth

Quite by surprise one day, I made a personal observation, and one of significance. I had been spending more time than usual, particularly in the mornings, on my Florida porch, engulfed in deep reflective thought. These contemplative moments occurred day after day, week after week, month after month.

Eventually, I realized I was engaging in deeper self-examination and self-evaluation, noting how certain aspects of my retirement life over the past years, while exciting and fulfilling, now had become somewhat routine and predictable, excessive, shallow, even self-limiting. Essentially, I seemed to be questioning if the present status of my life in retirement was all there was going to be in my remaining years.

At this same time, I was becoming conscious of a strong inner desire to do more with my life in retirement, to contribute more, to find the good within, whatever it may be, and let this goodness emerge, naturally and freely. Ever so slowly, I was beginning an inner search to find deeper meaning and purpose in my remaining years.

Ironically, as new insights emerged, I initially resisted these feelings because they suggested a need for me to change my present ways of living. For over ten years in retirement, I had been busy, happy, and active. Why was I suddenly questioning and re-evaluating certain aspects of my past lifestyle? Why was I now feeling I was not living my life in retirement to its fullest?

I recalled Schlossberg's earlier reminder to retirees that sometimes we become a combination of different retirement types. While we may begin retirement as one dominant type, over time in retirement, we could change to another or become a new combination of types.[12]

What suddenly became clearer was the possibility I may be extending my Easy Glider lifestyle and combining it now with another retirement type, that of a Searcher.

BECOMING BOTH AN EASY GLIDER AND A SEARCHER

Although I considered myself predominately an Easy Glider as a retiree, I was now becoming both an Easy Glider and a Searcher. As a Searcher, I could separate from some of my present behaviors and activities in my Easy Glider lifestyle that now possessed diminished meaning. At the same time, I could experience and explore new, different, and more fulfilling behaviors and activities.

LESSENING THE FIRM GRIP OF MY EGO

One morning after meditating, I realized I had become part of my own present problem in retirement. In my early retirement years, I often thought and behaved in strong ego and self-centered ways, socially-driven and consistently engaged in the pursuit of excessive pleasures, hedonic living. While in this powerful grip of my ego, I had been unknowingly, and for some time, restricting myself in retirement from finding and exploring a more complete sense of self.

This personal observation became a moment of greater self-awareness, and as such, facilitated my lessening the firm grip of my ego. As Tolle notes, when we become aware of the ego within us, we become aware of the person we truly are beyond our ego--"The recognition of the false is already the arising of the real."[13]

I also expanded my consciousness of a new inner desire. More than in my past years in retirement, I now desired to evolve and grow, to transform my present life, to reach different and deeper levels of meaning in my remaining years. I could make better uses of my ego along my retirement journey, rather than continuing to pursue restrictive and self-limiting behaviors.

As I spent more time in self-reflection and contemplation, many new questions surfaced, but most frequently the following three: What did I believe were some of the limitations to my present retirement lifestyle? Why was my interest in attending social events suddenly declining? Why was I now suddenly spending more time than usual in deeper reflection and meditation?

A MAJOR LIMITATION TO MY PRESENT LIFESTYLE: HEDONIC LIVING

Frequently, I found myself questioning the nature of my social life. Was I being too excessive in my retirement lifestyle and activities? Was I living a too hedonic lifestyle? Was I being too self-indulgent and lenient?

While being socially active had been a high priority in my early retirement years, I now seemed to be searching for something beyond an ever-increasing social existence of excessive pleasures. Was I, essentially, omitting the inclusion and use of other dimensions of self in my retirement, especially opportunities for personal change and growth?

THE WOMAN AT THE COCKTAIL PARTY

One evening, Robbie and I were invited to an afternoon cocktail party, given by a friend in honor of her mother, who was visiting Palm Beach after spending a year touring Europe. The mother, in her eighties, appeared attractive, energetic, and gracious as she circulated around the room introducing herself to other guests.

Eventually, she joined my small group, and one by one we introduced ourselves. The members of this group were presently engaged in a lively discussion of all the fine restaurants and dining experiences available to retirees in South Florida.

After introductions, the guests in my group continued discussing the many fine dining options available to retirees in our area, even citing different menu items and specialty drinks at different venues, with members appearing at times to impress and outdo one another in their verbal contributions and recommendations.

Suddenly the woman interrupted our conversation. "Surely," she said, "you must do more than eat and drink your lives away. Tell me about yourselves, who you are and what you do to learn, grow, and contribute to society? What books have you recently read? What unusual places have you visited?"

At first, the members of the group appeared stunned, caught off guard, and became momentarily quiet. Then a woman in the group politely responded.

"We all lead interesting and purposeful lives," she informed the guest. "We read, travel, and learn all the time. But we also enjoy dining out at different fine restaurants in the area. We enrich our lives as well through fine and varied dining experiences."

A man in the group spoke next, in an affirming and positive manner. "Yes, we are all Epicureans of one kind or another. As we learn through reading and travel, we also learn from sharing exceptional dining experiences. That is what we are doing right now. Please join us."

The guest of honor snapped back, sharply informing the group that she was more interested in sharing the experiences of her recent travels abroad instead of a discussion of food, and quickly left our group for another, apparently in search of more challenging conversation.

Immediately, I thought of the famous quote often attributed to Eleanor Roosevelt: "Great minds discuss ideas; average minds discuss events; and small minds discuss people." Were we as a group talking about low-level pleasures rather than more elevated ideas? In talking about our favorite foods and restaurants, were we interacting with small minds by discussing people over ideas? Then, I recalled one of Shakespeare's quotes *in Hamlet:* "What is man, if his chief good and market of his time be but to sleep and feed? A beast, no more."

While this guest of honor appeared rude and judgmental, she did, nevertheless, trigger a critical question I had been privately ruminating for some time. Was I, in my retirement, eating, drinking, and socializing so excessively that I was living predominately a hedonistic lifestyle in retirement? While keeping busy and active, was I also living a socially satisfying but somewhat shallow life? Was I now in retirement fast becoming "a beast, no more"?

QUESTIONING A DECLINING INTEREST IN EXCESSIVE SOCIALIZING

For numerous seasons in Maine, Robbie and I attended weekly on Sunday evenings a local disco show. At the disco show, we met and connected with many friends and acquaintances in town, enjoyed brief conversations, watched the disco show, and sang along with the performers, before returning home for the remainder of the evening.

THE DISCO SHOW

The space for the disco show in the club was relatively small, without enough space and seats to accommodate all who wanted to attend. To guarantee us a table and seats for the show, we often arrived at the club around 6 PM, ordered drinks, then dinner, and stayed later for the show, keeping the same table we reserved earlier. Those who came later and could not get a table often circulated around and among the tables, greeting friends and exchanging conversation, seemingly content to watch the show by standing in the aisles.

Robbie and I both found much personal value in the opportunity to visit with friends and acquaintances we had known for the past twenty-four years. As we waited for the disco show to begin, numerous people came by our table, greeted us for a few moments, and later moved on to visit with people at other tables. Other people followed in their place, friends from town, the beach, nearby communities, and tourists from other states near and far away, many who summered in Maine at different times of the season.

The disco show finished at 9:15 PM. By the time we left the premises for home, it was usually around 10 PM—four hours spent at a local club most Sunday evenings for the past two summer seasons. Was the meeting and conversing with numerous friends at this weekly disco show worth the investment of four hours a week?

One Sunday evening late in the summer season, I remember questioning my decision to be present at the disco show for another four hours. I constantly looked at my watch, waiting for the show to end.

As the evening passed, I grew tired and irritated with the audience, who was no longer listening to the performers but talking and singing and yelling along in their own worlds, as they lifted their glasses in the air, sloppily spilling drinks on one another and themselves.

While the disco show was a great opportunity to meet and socialize with friends and acquaintances, I ended my regular attendance at the disco show that night. The whole experience had become too repetitive, too time-consuming, too confining, too self-limiting.

EMERGING MOMENTS OF CHANGE AND ONENESS

Slowly, I began limiting many of my previous social activities, especially the ones I now found superfluous and ego-driven, for more personal, private, and subtle ones. On Sunday evenings, Robbie and I now began to engage in new and different activities. Often, we attended a local movie theatre, to view a current film. Or we participated in even more simple activities, like a walk in the evening to the center of town, where we sometimes bought and enjoyed a scoop of our favorite homemade ice cream as we sat on a bench in front of the local market, "people-watching" and "people-reading."

LETTING GO, SURRENDERING

With my changing behaviors, I was not deliberately ignoring or rejecting my friends and past activities. Rather, I was letting go of my previous ego-based needs. I was developing and acting upon new activities, the result of a strong inner desire to evolve and grow as I aged.

Most of these new activities reflected my personal efforts to let go, to surrender to a strong inner desire to participate more fully in alone and quiet time, in those self-chosen activities I now was pursuing but also preferring in this new stage of my retirement life.

My personal surrendering was both a time of hanging on and letting go of my past excessive activities. I would always enjoy food, drink, and socializing. However, now I was no longer as ego-based and excessive in the pursuit of theses pleasures.

SEEKING SOLITUDE AND SILENCE

I now preferred more peaceful, quiet time in my life, quality time spent alone, often in silence, with more time to reflect and meditate—to stay present, in the moment, just being, a time for inner peace. I was doing a better job of discerning and selecting those activities that mattered the most to me, those events and people who enriched my life and gave it deeper meaning.

Soon, I was living a calmer, more peaceful life. I had pulled away from many surface and insignificant social activities to spend more time with a handful of meaningful friends, or at home reading, writing, or quietly engaged in one of my enjoyable and lifelong learning activities.

I no longer desired the same level of involvement in activities that provided me in the past with much immediate gratification and pleasure. I no longer possessed the same feelings of urgency and involvement in the meeting of social demands. I found myself retreating from noise, crowds, and often needless chatter. I started to enjoy staying home more frequently, enjoying more time alone.

When July 4th weekend arrived in Maine, Robbie and I typically headed for the beach in the evening to watch the fireworks. Rather than attend and fight the crowds on their way to and from the beach, I decided to watch the fireworks from our deck, or finish reading a book, or catch up on desk work.

On Saturday nights, rather than go out to the dance clubs with Robbie as I had done so often in the past, I now preferred to catch up on my phone calls, finish reading a book, or watch one of my favorite mystery shows. I also transferred my desire for alone and quiet time to other settings as well.

I no longer desired to spend long periods of time sitting every beach day surrounded by large crowds, and for hour after hour. Instead, I began the practice of moving further down the beach to more isolated areas, to relax alone in the sun, enjoying being alone to read, write, think, and observe, surrounded by the natural beauty of the ocean and dunes.

I also began enjoying long and solitary beach walks, nature walks, and hikes. I looked forward to the many moments of peace and serenity that typically accompanied these adventures. Soon, I began walking meditations as part of my daily exercise. I started to spend more time alone in lovely natural settings, and for extended periods of time. I was going within, reflecting more, as I reexamined my present life.

QUESTIONING WHY I WAS SPENDING MORE TIME IN REFLECTION AND MEDITATION

When I first awoke, I typically retreated to my porch to enjoy a cup of my favorite Brazilian coffee. Morning was a convenient and ideal time for me to be alone, surround by nature and beauty, to reflect and meditate, activities in which I found much personal enjoyment and moments of peace.

I loved my morning ritual of sitting on my porch, attempting to go deeper within, to engage in a greater sense of presence. As I greeted each day, I found myself searching for deeper spiritual meaning and a greater alignment with my spiritual past.

While I followed no regimented pattern of behavior, I began each morning with reflection and meditation on a variety of topics. Essentially, I was preoccupied with how I best could become more aware and present, more connected to nature, more engaged in private forms of prayer, and more contemplative about how best to serve a greater good.

INCREASING AWARENESS AND THE PRACTICE OF PRESENCE

However, the practice of staying present did not come easily to me. I found the act of quieting my mind at first extremely difficult to do. I was always thinking about things in my past, or jumping ahead, thinking about things I wanted to accomplish for the day, to planning for events in the distant future. I soon realized I have spent most of my life living primarily in the past and future, and the act of staying present, in the moment, needed much more practice.

I began by first slowing down my thoughts and physical behavior. In this slowing down, I learned how to become quiet, calm, and still, more centered, more conscious of things both inside and outside, more one with the present moment. When I was present, I felt more peaceful and relaxed.

By becoming more present, I also was attempting to reach a higher level of consciousness. I was making strong efforts to become more connected to my true and inner essence, my authentic self, that core part of me now in need of greater spiritual development.

CONNECTING WITH NATURE

From my porch, I often observed the natural beauty and various colors of the sky, clouds, palm trees, and Mediterranean-style buildings. During my morning meditations, I often contemplated my connections to nature, the relatedness of all living things, the universe, and my relationship to a powerful force beyond myself, a Higher Being many called God.

My yearning for greater spiritual connections and experience, however, were not limited to morning time spent meditating on my porch. For example, one spring evening in Florida, as I was returning home from a walk around a nearby lake, I witnessed the sky ablaze with one of the most spectacular sunsets I have ever seen, a mixture of vibrant colors, breathtaking to behold.

When I reached the outside of our condo, I yelled to Robbie to come outside to experience with me the beauty of this sunset. He did, and we walked to our pool near the lake and observed the sunset until it disappeared just after dusk.

Surely, I must have enjoyed other spectacular sunsets in my life over past years. Why was I now suddenly responding to the beauty and wonder of this particular sunset with such deep intensity and awe? I concluded I was now at a stage of life where I was becoming more aware, of myself, nature, and my surroundings.

ENGAGING IN PRIVATE FORMS OF PRAYER

On many occasions, I thought my morning meditations and reflections might be my personal and private attempts to pray, a morning communion of sorts with a Higher Being, for daily direction and guidance.

Although I rarely verbalized it, I did greet each day by silently reciting Psalm 118:24, words I had memorized years ago. Somehow, this small action of silently praying each morning helped me to set in gear numerous opportunities for daily positive action: *"This is the day the Lord has made. Let us rejoice and be glad in it."*

CONTEMPLATING HOW BEST TO
SERVE A GREATER GOOD

Of late, however, I found myself during my morning meditations seeking guidance from a Higher Power as to how best to proceed daily, to how best I could serve a greater good. I began praying silently and privately each morning, and primarily for greater guidance and direction in my life.

The following I knew for sure: After ten years in retirement, I had limited time left, and with that time, I wanted to do more with my life, to be a good and better person than in the past, to serve a greater good, to become a higher self. My whole experience of searching for a greater good was complicated, for I first had to determine what serving a greater good was not, and reject those efforts as viable options.

Over my lifetime, I knew too many people who falsely claimed to be altruistic in nature, but who were artificially serving a greater good. From fellow educators, politicians, friends, and community members, I had formed acquaintances with people over my lifetime who sought to appear good in their actions, but who were engaged in these acts primarily for self-gain or reward, for enhanced self-image. This false kind of serving a greater good was not the kind for which I was searching.

In contrast, I was searching to serve a greater good in ways that would make my end years in my retirement genuinely more meaningful. Intuitively, I knew connecting with people, helping other people, especially those in need, giving unconditionally, and practicing simple acts of kindness were among the immediate ways I could serve a greater good.

ANOTHER SYNCHRONISTIC MEETING:
THE WOMAN ON THE AIRPLANE

One day, I gained greater insight into the reasons behind my recent behavioral changes in retirement and my desire to serve a greater good. I experienced an unusual coincidence, a moment of synchronicity, the uncanny and fortuitous timing of an event in my life that seemed to go beyond pure chance. The incident happened one spring day in May, while on a flight from Charlotte, North Carolina to Portland, Maine, after engaging in a conversation with a woman sitting next to me.

The woman, an attractive and sophisticated-looking older person, interrupted her reading, smiled, and returned to reading what appeared to be an academic journal. She continued to read intently until the flight attendant interrupted her to ask if she would like a beverage.

While she was momentarily interrupted, she introduced herself and we began a general conversation. She informed me that she was retired, lived in Asheville, North Carolina, and often took weekend trips to Portland, to visit family and friends, and sometimes just to spend the weekend dining at the many fine restaurants in the area.

I asked about her reading material. In her past career, she informed me, she worked for a national organization on aging, was a member of the American Society on Aging, and that she was reading an article in this organization's quarterly journal.

Sensing that she may know much about the aging process, I cautiously shared with her my increasing awareness, but lack of full understanding, of my recent desire and apparent need for change as I aged. I mentioned my increased use of contemplation, my desire for aloneness and silence, hoping she would not find my comments too personal, evasive, or far-fetched.

To the contrary, she smiled knowingly, bobbing her head slightly in agreement as I spoke, and casually informed me of the following: What I was describing to her was called transcendence by gerontologists, researchers, and specialists who study older adults and various dimensions of the aging processes.

TRANSCENDENCE

Many people as they grow older, she explained, tend to engage in greater self-evaluation and the examination of their relationships with others. They begin to integrate their past with the present, often in search for deeper meaning. As individuals increase in age, she assured me, many prefer a quieter lifestyle with increased opportunities for deeper contemplation.

Many adults, she continued, discover as they age the typical ways of finding meaning in life, like accumulating possessions and achieving social success, no longer met their needs. Instead, they begin to experience a new stage of adult development typically called transcendence.

Transcendence, she further elaborated, refers to a person's change in perspective with age. A transcendent adult often chooses to become a new and evolving self with different values and beliefs, with new world views and behaviors, all indicative of individual developmental growth, and overall well-being.

She quickly reminded me that not all older and aging adults experience transcendence. Many aging adults remain vital and involved with lives based on firmly established and automatic behaviors. Thus, they devote little time to improving self-awareness. Often these same people are so firm in their habits of thinking and behaving that there is little chance for them to accept the kind of openness a transcendent experience requires.

Then, she bent forward and unlatched a travel bag, fetched a pen and piece of notepaper, and wrote a name before giving me the slip of paper, commenting that she thought I might find the works by this researcher both interesting and personally helpful. Later that evening, at my condo in Maine, I found the article online and read it immediately, and with great interest.

The research article was written by Dr. Lars Tornstam, a Swedish sociologist. In the research article, Tornstam found that as people age, many naturally transcend the boundaries of ordinary and everyday living by developing new and positive ways of living. Tornstam thus defined aging differently than many researchers interested in the topic, in terms of psychological well-being instead of physiological function.

RECOGNIZING AND ACCEPTING TRANSCENDENT MOMENTS OF GROWTH

After reading this article, I immediately recognized myself as an older retiree with a new and different focus on life from the one I used and enjoyed in previous years. I had been experiencing, and was continuing to experience, a different kind of retirement life by transcending the boundaries of my previous everyday living patterns and behaviors. I was now aging with new and different preferences and improved psychological well-being.

In my changing self, I had been participating, often unknowingly, in a stage of adult development Tornstam identified as gerotranscendence. In his research, Tornstam further identified three levels of age-related change: (1) the Level of Self; (2) the Social Level, and (3) the Cosmic Level.

THE REDEFINITION OF SELF LEVEL

At the redefinition of self level, Tornstam found older adults experience much self- confrontation, and in the process often discover new and other aspects of self that were previously hidden. They often became less self-centered and developed an increase need for solitude.

I could relate to this level and definition. I had been functioning at the redefinition of self level when I confronted myself, privately questioning whether I was living a too hedonistic lifestyle in retirement, being too self-indulgent and lenient. I had been participating at the redefinition of self level when, by personal choice, I sought to spend more time alone, inside my home and outside in nature.

THE SOCIAL LEVEL

At the social level, Tornstam described how older adults as they age become less interested in participating in frequent social events and relationships but have an increased need for more solitude. Moreover, older adults often shed those activities that now hold limited meaning for them. They become more selective. They often prefer reading or listening to music or spending time with only a few good friends, not because of the lack of possibility but by personal choice. The need for solitude became a self-imposed choice, a necessary developmental change.

Tornstam also noted that older adults often become less self-centered and more selective in their choice of activities. They decrease their interest in the superficial, like excessive social interactions and the need for continued accumulation of possessions. They often learn to live effectively, spending more time alone. Solitude becomes more important to them than in the past. They have a greater need for introspection and meditation. These behaviors often lead to increased and positive transformations in personal and developmental growth.

My recent transcendent behaviors were consistent with Tornstam's research findings. My social interactions eventually changed in value and importance by self-choice, not lack of opportunity. I similarly had experienced a declining interest in superfluous social contacts, becoming more focused and selective in my choice of social activities.

I experienced diminished interest and desire to remain as self-centered, hedonistic, and socially active as in my earlier years in retirement. More than ever before in my life, I was experiencing a preference for more moments alone, being quiet, enjoying solitude, and appreciating silence.

THE COSMIC LEVEL

At the cosmic level, Tornstam found nature became increasingly important to older adults as they view themselves as an integrated part of the universe. Older adults at the cosmic level tend to accept more willingly the unknowns and mysteries in life. Also, at this stage, sources of happiness in many older individuals changed, shifting from interest and participation in complex and grand events to partaking in more simple and subtle experiences.

Tornstam also underscored the strong correlation between gerotranscendence and spirituality at the cosmic level, leading him to conclude that spiritual transcendence as one ages is naturally occurring, along and throughout the adult lifespan.[14]

Here it was, at Tornstam's cosmic level, a justification for my altruistic desire to contribute toward a greater good that transcended my individual needs. While functioning unknowingly at the cosmic level, I had devoted an increasing amount of time to reflection and meditation. I spent much increased time, particularly during mornings, reflecting and meditating on a wide range of topics, as I enjoyed the beauty of nature surrounding me.

In addition, as I continued to experience aging at the Cosmic Level of gerotranscendence, I found myself also engaging, if only in fleeting and momentary ways, in more opportunities to connect with spirituality. Beyond finding beauty in nature, I was now making new efforts to comprehend the relatedness of all life, and often by contemplating how my individual worth must come from being part of a larger entity.

As I progressed in my retirement, I gradually was becoming a different retiree than earlier, one with new and transcendent qualities. With a gradual naturalness and seeming life of its own, my new and transcending self slowly emerged, in search of a life in retirement with deeper meaning.

My gerotranscendent experiences all brought with them opportunities for me to evolve, transcend my former self, and become in the process a retiree with new personal traits and behaviors indicative of personal change, growth, and psychological well-being. My natural and evolving participation in all three levels of gerotranscendence was one course I was taking in my search for deeper purpose and meaning.

A CHANGE IN VALUES

I had not only experienced all three levels of Tornstam's gerotranscendence, but I had also determined what was and was not any longer important to me. As I changed, my values changed.

While I had by choice lessened my need to be socially active much of the time, I had also learned to let go, to spend more time alone, quiet and restorative time, sometimes at home and other times outside of home, such as in and with nature, staying present in the moment. I now preferred greater solitude, autonomy, reflection, and meditation in my life, more rest and relaxation.

With my new values and developmental changes, my present retirement life was not less than before but different from the way I chose to live it in past years. *I had evolved into a different retiree as I aged, not declined into one, a most important distinction.*

MY SIXTH LESSON LEARNED: SEARCH FOR DEEPER PURPOSE AND MEANING

I had learned, and was continuing to learn, my sixth major lesson in retirement, to search for deeper purpose and meaning along the retirement journey As I entered my third stage of developmental aging, I was beginning to examining my past and present life in retirement, going more deeply within, questioning my relationships with myself, other people, even nature, the universe, a Higher Being.

I had entered a new stage of adult development called transcendence, a time of deep self-confrontation as I explored new aspects of myself previously hidden. I was becoming a new and evolving self, with new values and beliefs, indicative of much personal developmental growth.

Most importantly, I had learned to accept my transcendent changes as I aged as natural and positive indicators of positive change. I was experiencing a calmer mind, a more peaceful self, a simpler daily life. I was becoming more selective in my personal choices, less self-centered, with new desires to become more altruistic, to serve a greater good, to reconnect with my spiritual past, an aspect of my life I had ignored and neglected for far too long.

SPIRITUAL TRANSCENDENCE

For most of my adult life, I had remained detached from my past spiritual life, even somewhat guarded, ashamed, and embarrassed by my beliefs, unwilling to openly share them with others, including Robbie.

Most of the people I knew had a stable set of religious beliefs and practices. My faith-based beliefs and practices were of the spiritual kind, many of my own making since my early childhood days. Moreover, they were untrained, happening only on occasion, undeveloped, incomplete. Thus, I feared those with more formal, extensive, and religious backgrounds and training would dismiss my spiritual experiences as not worthy or acceptable.

Moreover, my spiritual beliefs were too personal, too private, too individualistic to share. They were too unbelievable, too incredible. For most of my adult life, then, I chose to keep my spiritual life and experiences to myself.

I was typical of many of the people Hopcke described after he interviewed them about their spiritual lives:

> What I didn't expect, however, in talking with people about their spiritual lives, was how few people had ever told anyone else the story of their spiritual awakening, a sign, in my opinion, of just how devalued, or perhaps protective, people have become about these sacred stories which, in other cultures, have a central place in human relationships. I felt very privileged, for this reason, as I listened to tale after tale unfold of how, through sheer chance, people found themselves on the road to higher consciousness.[15]

MY PAST SPIRITUAL LIFE: DECIDING
NOT TO REMAIN *OTHER THAN*

As I debated whether to include the next chapter in this book, I found my *Other Than* censor encouraging me strongly: *Don't. Don't go there. No one will ever believe you. No one will believe your past experiences and practices, nor their continuing and powerful influence on your life today.*

As I listened to my inner censor, I knew I had no choice now but to write and include the next chapter. If I continued in life to submit to *Other Than* messages, I would continue to allow them to block me from being and becoming my authentic self.

Often, I have associated moments of my past spiritual development with the ongoing occurrence of unusual events in my life, surprising and sometimes startling coincidences of different kinds and levels of meaning. Since my early childhood days, many of these coincidences appeared spiritually-related in nature, some even miraculous, as if sent by a Higher Force, a Higher Power, God.

As I aged and matured in life, I realized my belief in many of these coincidences as spiritually influenced seemed not much different from a prevalent belief used frequently today in much religious dogma: *God exists and mysteriously finds ways into our lives.*

EMBRACE SPIRITUALITY AND SYNCHRONICITY

Reconnecting with My Spiritual Past

Recently, a minister friend defined spirituality to me as the deepest values and sense of meaning we individually ascribe to our spiritual beliefs and truths. I was reassured by his spiritual perspective, for it both captured and validated how privately I had gone about practicing and nurturing my own spiritual experiences.

As a child, I had only my family and my subjective spiritual experiences, and I paid close attention to these experiences. Regardless of my lack of formal religious training, I considered myself then, and I still do today, a deeply spiritual person.

MY SPIRITUAL BEGINNINGS

I grew up with a handful of informal spiritual practices, like learning to pray, communing with nature, and meditating. Throughout my lifetime, I have made much use of these natural if simple spiritual activities.

Since age five, I have learned to trust my heart, intuitions, and instincts, wherever they may lead. For years, I have acted on these inner resources by doing what seemed right, for myself and others. Today, I believe my strong spiritual beliefs and practices have been rooted primarily in two personal and influential childhood incidences: learning to pray and determining the role of God in my life.

My first spiritual experience involved learning to pray at home. At night before going to bed, my mother or older siblings frequently knelt at the side of my bed with me, and we would recite this nighttime prayer, until over time, I had memorized it.

It was the standard childhood prayer, long in existence, its original source being a prayer John Adams reportedly recited each night, even in his adulthood: *Now I lay me down to sleep, I pray my soul for you to keep. If I should die before I wake, I pray my soul for you to take.*

This prayer was my introduction to God. From the reciting of this prayer each night, I concluded that God had special powers that humans did not, and he was a good God because he could take care of me and my soul should I die in my sleep.

My second spiritual incident involved the questioning of the role of God in my life. This incident was not so typical as my first—learning to pray—for it was one that began my spiritual journey in my childhood outside the context of home.

My family lived on a small farm, far in the New Hampshire countryside, isolated from other families, with our neighbors, schools, and local town and businesses many miles away. As a result, I had no one my age with whom to play before my school years. Since I was a self-initiating and somewhat independent child, I soon found a solitary activity to occupy some of my time.

Our home in the country was surrounded by rolling pastures, lots of trees, and numerous paths leading into the woods that all appeared to me, as a young and curious child, inviting and never ending. Thus, I began my early childhood exploration of life beyond the paths into the woods.

At first, I filled much of my time each day venturing down the main path, a dirt road leading from the left side of our home into a deeply wooded area. The forest beyond the entrance fascinated me the most. Eventually, I journeyed further into the woods, cautiously at first so I would not become lost. During each visit, I noted as best as I could markers for the way home— the path itself, a fallen tree branch across the path, a wooden and unfinished fence.

Just beyond the fence on a small knoll was a large rock with lots of edges, ideal for a young boy to climb and pause, to sit for a moment, and take in the beauty, wonder, and enchantment of the spot.

The knoll and large rock were surrounded by tall trees, so high they appeared to go on forever into the sky. Lots of sunlight poured through the top of the trees which grew around the rock in a circular pattern, with the top of the trees framing an expansive and typically clear, blue sky. On windy days, the top of the trees swayed and rustled in the breeze, sometimes forcefully.

I never ventured beyond this rock. This spot in the woods was all I really needed at this time in my young life. Soon this spot became my spot, my own private place in the woods to sit, think, marvel, and wonder about how things like the sky, trees, plants, and rocks came to be and were connected.

THE FEELING OF PRESENCE

Today, I believe this moment in my young life was the beginning of the feeling of "presence," my emerging awareness of being somehow related to other forms of life.

On returning home, I had numerous questions for my parents. How far away is the sky? Is there something beyond the sky? Can trees talk? Are trees alive? Do trees begin as plants and later grow? Where do rocks come from? I was struggling to make sense of the universe.

My parents did their best to answer these questions. They never answered my questions specifically, choosing instead to respond typically in this way: "God. God created everything."

EARLY FEELINGS OF CONNECTEDNESS

Even as a young and questioning child, while visiting my special place in the woods, I was experiencing new and unusual feelings and insights. As I noticed the crevices in the rock, the different kinds of trees with different barks, and turned to gaze upward toward the sky and light, I felt a connectedness to all these elements. Beyond my feelings of being related in yet unknown ways to other forms of life, I was also searching for a deeper and direct connection with God.

As I looked up at the trees toward the vast and typically blue sky, I felt for the first time in my young life a strange and strong inner connection, what to this day still feels like an inner pull, as if I were in the presence of a Higher Force, a Higher Being, God. God was somewhere beyond the trees and sky, and he was looking down over me, God whom I could not see, but a God who could see and hear me. God, a good God, who would guide and protect me in life.

These early memories of being connected to all forms of life and being guided and protected by a Higher Power became the foundation for my undeveloped and spiritually evolving self. Since my early childhood days to my present aging self, I have believed I am and have been connected to a Higher Being, a powerful force many call God.

Was my desire for a relationship with God nothing more than what Jung described as a religious instinct, nothing more than a young boy's desire for a connection with God? I believe not, because I have never wavered from these beliefs over my lifetime. I formed my belief that there was a God who would guide and protect me in life at age six, and I accept it today, as I have done throughout all the intermittent years.

After I started first grade and became busy in all kinds of school and after-school activities, I did not return to my special spot in the woods. I moved on to other experiences and stages in my young life. In time, the memories of my special spot in the woods, my spiritual feelings, and God popped into my conscious mind in unusual and often unexplainable circumstances. When they did, these thoughts were often short-lived and fleeting but related in some strange and then unknown ways to new occurrences in my young life, the continuous receiving of unexpected and unexplainable gifts of coincidence.

EARLY GIFTS OF COINCIDENCE

My earliest recollections of receiving special gifts of coincidence also occurred when I was about age six. Even as a young child, I understood not all of these coincidences were of the same kind or at the same levels of meaning and importance. Some of my coincidences were memorable, but just coincidences. Nothing more. Nothing exceptional.

For example, I remember one of my older sisters had recently married and moved away. As I was playing alone outside one day, I missed her and hoped she would come home to visit us soon. At another time on the same day, I remember wishing for something totally unrelated to this previous wish. I wished I had a coloring book.

Both thoughts disappeared as quickly as they happened. Nor had I shared them with anyone else that day. The next day, however, my sister did come visit us, and she brought me a gift, a coloring book.

From this first memory of experiencing a pleasant and desirable coincidence, the receiving of things for which I previously and deliberately wished, other similar coincidences followed.

THE RED BIKE

Just before my tenth birthday, I secretly wished for a gift of a bicycle. As I fantasized about my new bike, I didn't want any kind of bike. I wanted a red bike.

I distinctly remember not mentioning this wish to anyone, because I knew a new bike would be expensive and a financial hardship for my parents. I do not know why I wanted a red bike, but I strongly recall my desire for a new and red bike. On the evening of my tenth birthday, my father brought me home a birthday gift, a new bicycle, and it was red.

On the other hand, many of my coincidences were truly extraordinary. Even startling. They demanded my further attention and consideration. They felt as if my spiritual growth was being assisted by a force other than my conscious will, by a force with the potential to provide me with unbelievable and unexplainable beneficial outcomes.

One day, a different and much more startling and dramatic coincidence also happened when I was age ten-- the arrival of a person in my life when I needed him the most, and both of my parents were present, to experience and share with me this extraordinary coincidence.

AN AFTERNOON TRIP TO THE BEACH

One warm September afternoon in 1948, my father and mother took me swimming. We drove to a remote beach at the end of a long road in nearby Kittery, Maine, to an area called Kittery Point. During this beach trip, my first of a series of new and extraordinary coincidences happened.

The beach was isolated and private, with no homes nearby, surrounded instead with numerous and large sand dunes on three sides. No one else was on the beach that late afternoon, nor were any other cars in the parking lot. In front of us, the Atlantic Ocean glistened, filled with numerous large and inviting waves that came one after another, crashing onto the shore.

My father helped my mother to a folding chair he first placed down on the sandy beach. Recently, my mother had suffered a serious stroke. She was now paralyzed on the left side with limited power of speech. She could say one or two words on occasion, but with much difficulty.

While my father fetched a blanket from the car, I grabbed an inner tube on which to float. I did not know how to swim and neither did my father, who immediately warned me to stay near the shore, to not go out into the water over my head.

Soon, I was on the inner tube in the ocean, waving to my parents, enjoying riding into shore on the end of waves. Then, I grew more coura- geous and adventuresome. I stayed on the inner tube and started to float out to sea as far as I could, sailing up and over big waves, excited after reaching the other side, until the unexpected happened. A large wave hit me firmly in the back, knocking me off the tube into the water.

I bobbed up and down, realizing I could not touch bottom. My father, looking terrified, ran into the ocean as far as he could, but I was still a distance from him. He could not reach me without being able to swim. I kept bobbing up and down, swallowing lots of water.

After surfacing and resurfacing for air a few times more, I felt as if I no longer had the energy nor ability to stay afloat. Panic set in as I realized I might be drowning.

When I surfaced again, I looked at my mother, whose face was white with fear. From a distance, I heard her yell "Help." Then again and again. "Help. Help."

My father joined in, and the two of them were loudly yelling in unison, "Help. Help."

Within seconds a young man came running over one of the large dunes, dove into the ocean fully dressed, swam swiftly to where I was bobbing, lifted me up above the waves, and carried me safely to shore. My father thanked the young man profusely.

"No problem, "the young man said. "Now gotta go." And as soon as he had appeared, he had left, leaping over the same dunes out of sight.

When we were driving out of the beach parking lot immediately after this incident, my parents and I looked behind the dunes from where the young man had appeared. No signs of anyone. No vehicle parked nearby. No visible homes. Just the long road ahead, leading away from the beach.

How strange a coincidence that this young man should be nearby and hear my parents' cries for help at the precise time they and I needed his assistance the most.

"Miracle," my mother said. "Meant to be," my father replied.

A LIFETIME FILLED WITH GIFTS OF COINCIDENCE

Since my childhood days, these unusual coincidences continued to happen in my life, spontaneously, unplanned, unsought moments occurring in unknown and mysterious ways. As the years passed, I learned to take them for granted, to expect them, to experience and accept them, and with interest and openness.

I have never intentionally denied nor ignored these coincidences, nor felt frightened of or overwhelmed by them, and primarily for one simple reason. My coincidences were all of one kind: fortuitous, of much personal value. In addition, they brought with them different kinds and levels of meaning and in a variety of different circumstances.

Many times, my gifts of coincidence interacted and overlapped. Ultimately, they all have assisted me in pursuing personal growth and deeper meaning at different stages of my life. I met the people I was supposed to meet, and at the right time. Doors opened when I least expected them. I found unsought for gifts of immediate value. I experienced events too extraordinary to readily dismiss.

Often, throughout my life, I thought much about how these coincidences happened.

I frequently asked myself with uncertainty if these unusual coincidences occurring in my life were sent to me in unknown and unexplainable ways by God, working in mysterious ways. Was God guiding and protecting me, bestowing on me divine gifts of grace, free and unmerited favor? What I do know with certainty today is that my gifts of coincidence have another explanation and name: synchronicity.

SYNCHRONICITY

In the 1920s, C. K. Jung defined synchronicity as meaningful coincidences of two or more events where something other than the probability of chance was involved.[16] To Jung, then, synchronistic events had no causal relationship.

These events were acausal in the sense their physical cause could not be determined. No one knew what caused these synchronistic moments.

How these synchronistic events happened, then, was unexplainable because they existed outside of known and natural law, thus remaining scientifically incapable of being explained.

Nevertheless, moments of synchronicity can significantly influence our individual lives. In his book, *There Are No Accidents: Synchronicity and the Stories of Our Lives,* Robert H. Hopcke, a Jungian psychologist, contends synchronistic events have not only subjective meaning for the person involved, but "they bring about a different way of seeing ourselves, a broader perspective on our lives, or a deeper understanding of others or the world."[17]

Hopcke reminds readers that not all kinds of coincidences are the same, that they can differ in kind and levels of randomness. Some synchronistic events may be simple, ordinary, and unexplainable occurrence in everyday life, while other acts of synchronicity may be dramatic. Some may appear as premonitions and within dreams. Some even may be embedded within numerology and paranormal experiences.

Many of these coincidences, Hopcke notes, we soon forget because they serve little importance in our lives. However, other coincidences are more extraordinary and readily catch our attention:

> *The moment such a coincidence occurs we know something quite important, something very meaningful, is happening to us. We can see and feel a significance in the randomness.*[18]

In this detailed and insightful book, Hoepke leaves little doubt that extraordinary synchronistic moments do and can occur in all of our lives. He has extensively documented stories of numerous moments of synchronicity in the lives of different people at different ages and with different backgrounds, people nearby like his clients and of other people living far away. Moreover, the contexts for the recollection of these stories also varied widely, from stories of love, work, and everyday living experiences, to dreams and spiritual encounters.

Chris Mackey, in another and more recent book, *Synchronicity: Empower Your Life with the Gifts of Coincidence*, likewise distinguishes between ordinary and unusual circumstances. Mackey defines ordinary coincidences of mere happenstance as serendipitous events, such as the discovering of something of value but nothing particularly astonishing. My childhood recollection of my desire for my sister to come visit, which she did the next day, would be an example of a serendipitous coincidence.

Synchronicity, on the other hand, goes well beyond mere coincidence or happenstance and brings with it another layer of meaning. Like Hopcke, Mackey contends unusual coincidences are not just lucky but charged with meaning because of the likelihood of the incident having special meaning and connections to the recipient's own individual life. My previous recollection of being saved when nearly drowning is an example of a synchronistic coincidence.

Mackey, an Australian psychologist, writes from personal experience, not only as a practitioner but also as a patient. He defines synchronicity as the uncanny and fortuitous timing of events which seems to go beyond pure chance, but this timing is much more than coincidence. Synchronistic events are most valuable gifts from the universe, because they affirm that we are going in the right direction in life.[19]

THE MANIFESTATION OF SYNCHRONICITY

What is especially noteworthy about Mackey's book are his perspectives on how synchronicity manifests itself and how we can tap into this powerful source of potential for personal transformation, thus reaping the many benefits of intuitive and holistic thinking beyond rational and linear thought. In addition, beyond the inclusion of synchronistic stories in the lives of other people, Mackey draws upon synchronistic patterns reoccurring in his own life over time, and how they have influenced his own life path.

SYNCHRONICITY AND SCIENCE

Further noteworthy in Mackey's book are his discussions about the relationships between science and synchronicity. Mackey clarifies how logical reasoning and intuition overlap in quantum physics, concluding there was no such thing as an objective external world separate from the observer's consciousness.

In a later chapter on synchronicity and brain science, Mackey also contends the study of synchronicity is not counter to rational or even scientific understanding. Mackey presents evidence to show how we individually possess the ability to alter our brain and mental processes as well as our genes, especially our DRD4 gene, what he refers to as the synchronicity gene.

Not only do we possess receptor genes that open and close and thus allow some kind of internal control over the number of neurotransmitters we produce, but some of these genes contribute to novel and luminous experiences that affect deliberate changes in our consciousness. Mackey's point is that we may have more power over the brain's ability to generate synchronistic moments than we previously thought.

SYNCHRONICITY AND SPIRITUALITY

Mackey also contends that synchronicity plays a key role in helping us individually tap into our intuitive mind and our altered states of consciousness, and may represent profound transformation and interconnectedness in some individuals, especially as they experience powerful feelings of spiritual interconnectedness.

These moments of transformation, interconnectedness, and invisible consciousness as captured by Mackey are moments consistent with my feelings of authenticity, moments when I have felt one with self, one with life, one with other people, nature, the universe, even at times, one with a higher power.

Mackey underscores synchronicity, with its many mysterious and miraculous spiritual qualities, is often perceived only as intellectual intuition as opposed to logical or rational thinking. Instead, Mackey argues for a shift toward an expanded worldview, one with greater acknowledgment of the relevance of intuition and spiritual phenomena as legitimate content for inclusion and study in the sciences.[20]

DOUBTING SEREDIPITOUS AND SYNCHRONISTIC COINCIDENCES

Even with growing evidence of synchronistic events, many people still do not accept the possibility of synchronistic events happening in their lives. Rather, they argue that these incidences happen only by coincidence, nothing more. They do not give credence to mystical phenomena not rooted in science, often concluding such experiences are suspect, superstitious and biased, held by people unduly suggestible.

They do not and cannot find any meaning or purpose in things not sought because they do not recognize the synchronistic nature of events that do happen in their lives. Thus, many people, especially those who typically display a total disregard for spiritual and subjective thoughts and feelings, do not accept synchronicity as unexplainable occurrences that are often miraculous in nature. Instead, they consider these events questionable and suspect since they are not supported by science. Therefore, they do not take advantage of synchronistic acts as having the potential for human and spiritual growth.

Hopcke, however, warns we must not blind ourselves to synchronistic events in our lives because the line between objectivity and subjectivity, as Mackey has similarly stated, may not be as precise as we have come to believe. As Hopcke notes:

Used to thinking in cause-and-effect terms, we are called by synchronistic events to acknowledge that the line between objective reality and subjective experience is not as neat as we have been given to think. If this realization is sometimes befuddling and scary, it also enriches our experience of the world and restores to us a sense of wholeness and belonging. Likewise, synchronistic events, with their emotional and synchronistic levels of meaning, serve to remind modern people of two very valuable and uniquely human qualities: our ability to feel and our ability to imagine, fundamental aspects of our humanity which have unfortunately been misplaced in a world increasingly obsessed with rationality.[21]

EMBRACING GIFTS OF COINCIDENCE IN RETIREMENT

As in all stages of life, retirement is filled with many turning points, moments of change, new transitions, new decisions to make, and opportunities for more self-discovery. By welcoming and embracing synchronistic moments when they happen, we can use these moments to illuminate new insights and other options along our individual retirement journey. We can use these extraordinary experiences to enrich and enhance deeper meaning and purpose in life.

These unusual kinds of synchronistic events appear in our individual lives with uncanny timing. We find things of value, things unsought, when we are not looking for them, unusual events too extraordinary to dismiss as merely coincidence. Often, we immediately grasp a connection with something within us and the coincidence that has just happened.

SOME FORTUITOUS GIFTS OF ONENESS IN RETIREMENT

I share the following accounts of some gifts of synchronicity I received in my retirement for specific reasons. They illustrate how, in my retirement, I was guided to the right place at the right time. I found something for which I had been searching. I met the people I was supposed to meet. I was guided to the right people, choices, and received the answers to complex questions. I found something of value I had previously discarded.

I chose the first example because of its relative simplicity. This synchronistic event shows how I was guided to the right place at the right time and found something of value for which I had been searching.

A WALK DOWN LAKE AVENUE

In November of 2011, our beloved dog, Zsa Zsa, died unexpectedly in Robbie's arms. We had inherited Zsa Zsa four years earlier, from a Florida neighbor who herself had recently passed. Zsa Zsa, a small Maltese, changed both our lives in so many positive ways.

I had never had a dog, so Zsa Zsa initiated me into the daily world of a small dog's life. She lived up to her name, barking until her demands were met, prancing around the house until she positioned herself perfectly on a floor or on a small piece of furniture, then posing, looking up at us, as if to say, "Look how beautiful I am." And she was, both in appearance and personality.

When I returned home from the gym, I waited for her greeting. When I watched the late news on television, I looked forward to my snuggles with Zsa Zsa on the sofa. When I went to bed to read, I knew it would be only a matter of minutes before Zsa Zsa would follow me into the bedroom, waiting to be picked up and placed in bed, and cuddle right next to me. Yet, she basically remained Robbie's dog for the four years she was with us.

Robbie referred to Zsa Zsa as an extension of his physical self. Zsa Zsa was a small and needy dog. Robbie carried her everywhere. He bought her food, fed her regularly, walked her many times during the day—her favorite activity—and took her regularly with him whenever he traveled.

When Zsa Zsa died unexpectedly, we were both devastated. We knew she had a heart murmur. We knew she had recently developed fluid in her lungs and now was taking prescribed medication daily. Nevertheless, when Zsa Zsa died, our lives changed, particularly Robbie's.

In the morning, he would sleep longer. He became silent. He lost interest in our daily social activities. He withdrew. I knew he was suffering from a low level of depression, but I thought it would soon pass. It did not.

Two months later, I knew I had to get another dog for Robbie. We sat on our porch and discussed it. "I don't want another dog. No other dog can replace Zsa Zsa," he continuously replied.

"We have to give another dog a try," I repeatedly suggested.

One Sunday, we decided at the spur of the moment to go for breakfast at one of our favorite restaurants in Lake Worth, a place we often frequented. After our brunch this particular day, we decided to walk along Lake Avenue, moving down the street from the restaurant, into the center of town. We enjoyed looking into the windows of various shops, and stopping and talking to other people we knew, like friends or neighbors dining outside at other sidewalk restaurants.

Sometimes we walked Lake Avenue just to experience the beauty and magic of the street. Robbie enjoyed this ritual as much as I, the simple act of walking down one side of the street, crossing to the other side, and walking back up the other side of the street to our car, typically parked on another side street.

As we were about halfway down the right side of Lake Avenue going toward A1A, I stopped suddenly. Across the street, a woman was holding a small white dog on a leash, and the dog seemed to be begging for food, sitting at times on its hind legs. After the woman gave the dog something to eat, the dog lapped her face in appreciation.

"Look at that beautiful dog across the street," I commented to Robbie. "Let's ask the woman what kind it is."

Robbie was nonplussed and uncooperative. "Let's just keep walking," he retorted, as we reached the center of town and crossed to the other side of Lake Avenue. By the time we reached the spot where I first saw the cute white dog, I had completely forgotten about the incident until I turned and spotted her again just a few steps from us, still on a leash, still begging for food, still giving sloppy kisses.

I immediately walked up to the woman and asked her the breed of her dog.

"I don't know," the woman informed me, and then told this story:

Two young women heading back to Ohio just dropped off the dog with her while she was standing on the corner. The women apparently could not provide for the dog anymore, and asked this woman if she could take the dog to an animal shelter somewhere close by. She also informed me she already owned five dogs and did not want another.

I immediately wanted this dog. I reached down and picked her up. She licked my face until I turned away. I passed her to Robbie, and he held her. Then I told the woman about the passing of our former dog some two months ago, and that we now were looking for a little dog.

"You can have her if you want her," the woman replied.

"Should we take this dog home with us?" I asked Robbie. I wanted his approval in the decision-making.

He responded, "I suppose we can give her a try," he said, somewhat smiling down at the dog in his arms.

"Lucky dog," a man standing nearby and overhearing our transaction commented.

"No, we are the lucky ones," I responded.

And we were. From that moment when Eva first came into our lives, Robbie's mood changed: He was back to his old self, nurturing Eva, caring for her every need.

Soon, he was walking Eva up and down our condo complex and along the lake and beach on the A1A promenade, introducing Eva to other neighbors and their dogs. From our porch one day, I heard Robbie inform a neighbor, "This is Eva, my new dog."

The preceding random coincidence happened when I was searching for something of value, a small dog to replace the recent loss of another. Through the synchronistic event of meeting Eva, I was guided to the right place at the right time.

Was this incident coincidence? Or was it meant to be?

A SERIES OF RELATED COINCIDENCES

I chose the next series of coincidences to share because they represent more complexity and interrelatedness than the occurrence of an isolated synchronistic event. The following story includes a series of five coincidental happenings, all random but all fortuitous events occurring one after the other, in a timely and purposeful sequence.

Together, all five of these coincidences happened in my life when I was in much need of information, personal assistance, and direction. Together, they guided me toward the right information, people and resources, and at the right time, illustrating how synchronistic events can facilitate the meeting of people we are supposed to meet.

These five examples, however, do not equal one another in degree of synchronicity but they are related to one another and in a sequence. Two of the following synchronistic events are more unusual than the others in their randomness of fate.

AN UNEXPECTED DIAGNOSIS: KIDNEY CANCER

When I turned seventy-three in 2011, all seemed to be going remarkably well in my day-to-day life. I was at my best self, participating in numerous daily events, with many new and valued friends and relationships in my life. I felt blessed for the smooth unfolding of each day. Quite quickly and unexpectedly, I experienced my first major retirement dilemma.

Over a series of months, I noticed that I started to bloat frequently, with lots of gas and fluid retention, accompanied by a large, grotesquely distended stomach. Today, I know I had been experiencing a series of bouts with gastritis, most likely caused by drinking too much strong Brazilian coffee in the mornings and too many glasses of wine at "happy hour" in the early evenings. However, these bloating symptoms, then new to me, became more frequent and increasingly worrisome. I first sought the advice of my family doctor in Florida, who ordered a CT scan of my abdomen.

AN INCIDENTAL FINDING

Soon, I received the results. The CT scan did not find anything related to my bouts of bloating, but what the CT scan did find, and incidentally, was both personally important and alarming:

> *"A 4.5 cm in diameter heterogeneous enhancing mass arising from the right kidney, consistent with renal cell cancer. No discrete evidence of metastasis disease at present time."*

I had kidney cancer. The diagnosis was my first major obstacle to an otherwise healthy, smooth, and pleasant retirement. Initially, I processed this startling finding in these ways. I acknowledged I had kidney cancer and this diagnosis was serious, even life-threatening. I also knew, in contrast, I felt overall quite healthy and fit regardless of this diagnosis. Thus, I remained optimistic that I would find in time the best surgical option and medical doctors for successfully treating my kidney cancer.

The first of a major sequence of synchronistic coincidences had occurred. While searching for a cause for my gastritis, I discovered my kidney cancer, and early enough to do something surgically about it.

I started my cancer treatment inquiries by seeking the advice of many different urologists and specialists in renal cell carcinoma. The first urologist I visited was helpful and reassuring. He further told me the size of my tumor was still somewhat small, just at the beginning of stage two.

However, this same doctor also informed me that my kidney cancer could not be treated with chemotherapy because of its location. The gold standard, the doctor explained, would be for me to have my right kidney totally removed, a full nephrectomy, noting in addition that lots of people live well with only one kidney. Since I was on my way back to New England to spend the summer, he suggested I have the operation somewhere there.

I immediately called several urologists in New England and set up appointments prior to my return. My goal was to gather as much information about treatment options for renal cell carcinoma before making a final decision.

Prior to our departure for Maine, Robbie and I often sat on our Florida porch and talked constantly about my kidney cancer treatment options. We both, on several occasions, verbalized the same feelings: It seemed a shame to have my kidney completely removed just because a relatively small tumor was cancerous, just because a total nephrectomy was the gold standard. We both, nevertheless, acknowledged the potential danger of the cancer metastasizing.

THE UROLOGIST AT THE GYM

Then, while dressing in the men's room at the gym, I started a conversation with a man standing next to me about his Garmin watch. After a few minutes, the man informed me he had to get back to work, that he was a urologist, and had afternoon meetings lined up, back-to-back.

Before he left, I informed him of my kidney cancer diagnosis and difficulty deciding on a surgery procedure. He asked me about the location and size of my kidney tumor and if it were an isolated growth. Based on the information I shared with him, he recommended that I take my time in deciding on my treatment option, reminding me that it was important for me to be comfortable with my final decision. I had some time before making a final decision, he reassured me.

This chance meeting with a urologist at the gym was my second coincidental event in this series of synchronistic events. Through this random meeting, I was reassured that I should take time to decide my treatment option and that I had time. My tumor was still an isolated growth. I needed to be comfortable with my final decision, he emphasized, important information I needed to hear and heed, with my tendency to be impulsive, to act too quickly, especially while making important decisions.

Previously, I had read online about laparoscopic treatment for kidney cancer, and I momentarily started to favor this option over the gold standard, the total removal of my kidney. I expressed this tentative preference with my family doctors, one in Florida and another in Maine.

Both doctors mentioned to me the downside to laparoscopic kidney surgery, warning me that this option could be rather "messy," implying that sometimes with laparoscopic surgery the cancer later returned, or spread to other parts of the body, if the cancerous growth was not completely removed at the time of the laparoscopic procedure.

In essence, they both were warning me about the limitations of laparoscopic surgery over nephrectomy, the gold standard, the full removal of the total kidney.

I did not want a full nephrectomy, but I wanted less the likelihood of my cancer later returning with laparoscopic surgery. For the moment, I remained undecided between what seemed like my only two options.

THE MAN AT THE GAS PUMP

I was still leaning toward laparoscopic surgery until, one day, after returning to Maine, I stopped to buy gas for my car while shopping in a nearby town. A man on the other side of the pump was talking loudly and nervously on his cell phone. I heard him say, "My kidney cancer has come back and has spread to my lungs. I need another operation."

After he ended his telephone conversation, I told him I also had recently been diagnosed with kidney cancer. He asked what kind of surgery I intended to have for treatment, and I told him I did not know but was leaning toward a laparoscopic procedure. Then he told me that he wished now that he had pursued the gold standard because his cancer had spread to his lungs. He wished me luck, got in his car, and drove away.

Thus occurred the third synchronistic event in the series, and while pumping gas into my car at a randomly selected gas station: unsought feedback from a man who had kidney cancer, laparoscopic surgery, and now his cancer had spread to other parts of his body.

I quickly concluded the outcome of this man's laparoscopic kidney surgery did not represent the results of all such operations. Nevertheless, I also recognized his present situation was an example of what my family doctors had pointed out to me earlier as limitations of laparoscopic surgery.

I also knew in this wide and large world there were many fine laparoscopic surgeons that could successfully treat my kidney cancer with long-term success. I just had to find such a surgeon, someone with whom I had trust and confidence in.

Bubbling in my mind, however, was this nagging question: Was laparoscopic surgery really the better choice for me? I had two choices: a complete nephrectomy—the gold standard—or laparoscopic surgery. Based on the feedback from my doctors and the feedback from the man at the gas pump, I knew I should decide on a full nephrectomy, the gold standard. In my heart, however, I wanted neither procedure.

THE UNSOUGHT FOR NEWSPAPER

That same evening while driving home, I stopped at a convenience store to buy some creamer for my morning coffee. While I was waiting in line to pay, I noticed a copy of a newspaper on a nearby stand. I rarely bought newspapers anymore and when I did, it was just to read about the real estate being sold in the area or local entertainment.

I knew I really did not need this paper, but I bought it on impulse anyway, and forgot all about it until later that same evening. After watching the evening news on television, I was getting ready for bed when I noticed the unread paper on my kitchen counter, where I had left it once I returned home. I decided to browse through it before retiring for the evening.

I quickly surveyed the front page, local news, theater and entertainment news before coming to the health and fitness section. And there it was, the article I was meant to read, the article with information for which I was searching, the fourth of the synchronistic events in this series, an Associated Press release titled : "Renal Cell Cryoablation: A Viable Option for the Treatment of Kidney Cancer."

The article was about a vascular and interventional radiologist at John Hopkins University and his recent research findings. This researcher, identified as Dr. Christos Georgiades, had just presented the results of a three-year study on percutaneous cryoablation at a national medical convention. His major conclusion was that renal cell cryoablation was a viable option for the treatment of kidney cancer.

In this study, Dr. Georgiades found that the cancer-specific survival rate for renal cell cryoablation was 100% and the 5-year recurrence free survival rate was 97%. He reported also an overall significant complication rate of 6%, lower than other surgical options. These results were comparable to the gold standard in terms of efficacy, and better in terms of safety.

Furthermore, the article described the surgical procedure for renal cell cryoablation as not necessarily complicated. Renal cell cryoablation, a somewhat new method of treating kidney cancers depending on the location of the tumor, was a minimally invasive procedure.

With percutaneous cryoablation, no incisions are made. The surgeon inserts cryoablation needles and sensors through the skin on the back, using extremely cold temperatures and precise targeting skill to destroy the cancer tumor cells while at the same time keeping the remaining healthy kidney tissue intact and functional. Moreover, image-guided percutaneous cryoablation could be performed with conscious sedation.

As I read further about the surgical procedure and its possibilities, I became filled with hope and promise. Cryoablation for renal cell carcinoma appeared to be the viable option for which I was seeking for my kidney cancer treatment.

A RESPONSE, REASSURANCE, AND RECOMMENDATION

I found Dr. Georgiades's email address at John Hopkins and wrote him that same evening, informing him about my recent diagnosis of renal cell carcinoma, and asking him if he thought I might be a good candidate for percutaneous cryoablation. He immediately emailed me back the next day, requesting that I send him a disk of my most recent CT scan.

A few days later, he emailed me again, informing me that my tumor was in a good location for percutaneous cryoablation, adding that the treatment of my tumor would require more probes than usual. He could do the surgery for me if I so chose to travel to Maryland.

However, if I chose to have the surgery in Maine, Dr. Georgiades recommended a former student and colleague, now a skilled and well-established interventional radiologist who could perform the surgery, at the Maine Medical Center in nearby Portland.

The fifth synchronistic event in this series had just occurred. Through my email follow-up messages with Dr. Georgiades, I finally decided on the procedure and surgeon for my cancer treatment.

On June 16, 2011, now nearly ten years ago, I underwent percutaneous cryoablation surgery at Maine Medical Center. After having numerous follow-up CT scans over a five-year period, I am most happy to be alive, cancer-free, with both kidneys still functioning.

In reflection, I view this series of five coincidental events leading to my kidney cancer diagnosis, treatment procedure, and surgery, as all blessings in disguise.

Coincidences or meant-to-be moments? How strange I should seek medical help for gastritis and end up finding out incidentally I had kidney cancer. How strange I should meet a urologist at the gym who urged me to take my time before making a final choice of treatment procedure. How strange at a gas pump I should hold a brief conversation with a man who had chosen laparoscopic surgery for his kidney cancer and his cancer had returned, causing me to consider further if laparoscopic surgery was the right choice for me. How strange I should buy on impulse a newspaper and learn about a new and viable option for treating my kidney cancer. How strange, within an email response from a doctor I previously had not known, I was guided to the right surgical procedure, surgeon, and treatment center at the right time in my life.

THE GLIDING CHAISE LOUNGE

I chose to include the next story because it illustrates how a synchronistic event can assist us in the miraculous return of a possession of great personal value previously discarded.

When Robbie and I moved from Palm Beach back to North Carolina in 2017, we left behind for the new owners much of the furniture we wanted to replace in our new home. There was one piece of porch furniture I wanted to take with us, a gliding chaise lounge we had kept on our Florida porch, but Robbie kept reminding me there just was not room for it in a U-Pack, the method we choose for the transporting of the personal items we planned to take with us. The piece of furniture was too large and too awkward in shape, too space-consuming to transport.

I relented, but I still regretted that we somehow did not find a way to bring the chaise lounge with us. I continued to remind Robbie of this disappointment in a matter of fact, non-critical manner.

"What is so important about that chaise lounge?" Robbie asked one day. "We can get another one."

Could we really, I thought. There was something special and different about this chaise lounge, but I did not discern its significance in my life until many months later.

Most mornings when we lived in Florida, I would rise, go to the porch, sit on this chaise lounge, and do my morning reflections and meditations. I enjoyed the lounge because it was of a glider kind. In other words, I could rock my body back and forth in it as I completed my morning meditations. The glider was made of iron, strong, and it held me in a comfortable and solid fashion as I rocked back and forth.

As I participated in my morning reflective rituals, I felt the glider somehow was assisting my meditative processes through this gliding movement. My body movement of swinging in the chaise lounge seemed to assist my brain in these two ways: with the surfacing of subconscious thought and with my awareness of it during my moments of deep reflection.

In addition, the gliding movement of the chaise lounge seemed to facilitate my finding and use of deeper understanding and use of these meditative thoughts. In specific ways then, the chaise lounge had become not only a place for me to sit and conduct my meditations, but a facilitating vehicle for the discovery and use of many thoughts not previously entertained.

After we had moved back to North Carolina, I reminded Robbie that I found a perfect place on our new patio for my morning meditations. I showed the spot to him, reminding him again that if we had kept the chaise lounge, this spot on the patio would be the ideal place for it.

"We'll find another one," he responded, reassuringly.

And so, I stopped verbalizing my regret about leaving the chaise lounge behind in Florida when we moved to North Carolina.

A year later at the spur of the moment, Robbie and I planned a trip back to Palm Beach for a short winter respite. We also wanted to visit with our former neighbors and friends we came to know over the past fourteen years. Unfortunately, I had waited way too long to reserve a place to stay, and finding an accommodation that would accept pets was not an easy task.

Two weeks later after our original departure date, I found a two-week rental cancellation of a small home in downtown Lake Worth in what is known as the Cottage District. The home was perfect for us in every respect, especially its location. It also included an enclosed tropical backyard for our pets.

One late afternoon after we had arrived for our vacation in Florida, I decided to go for a long walk on A1A, a route I walked many times before when we lived in Palm Beach. On this route, I walked past our former condo and noticed the porch seemed dark and empty.

I noticed a light in the condo next door, a unit owned by a neighbor from Indiana. How wonderful it would be to see and visit with her for a while, and so I did.

During my visit, my neighbor informed me the owners who bought my former condo had just left to return to Europe because the husband needed an operation and preferred to have his surgery performed abroad. She also informed me that her new neighbors had recently renovated my old condo including the porch. After a pleasant if brief meeting, I left to continue my walk.

As I walked down the stairs to the first level, I noticed what appeared to be a park bench in front of a gazebo that hid our former garbage cans. The bench looked so attractive, so right, placed there for homeowners to use, to sit and relax, while out for a walk. But why would it be placed in front of the garbage dumpsters? No one could have direct access to the use of the dumpster with this bench in front of the entrance.

Then I walked closer to the bench for a better look. To my amazement, it was not a bench at all but my former gliding chaise lounge. Now it made sense. The new owners had discarded it in the completion of their renovation project, and they had left it by the garbage area for maintenance to carry away.

My next-door neighbor saw me looking at the old chaise lounge and yelled down to me, informing me the new neighbors threw away the chaise lounge when they left this morning. She also said a number of people have driven by and looked at it, but no one has taken it so far.

I quickly went to get my vehicle and Robbie. We returned to our former condo premises, placed the chaise lounge in the back of our SUV, and drove it back with us when we returned to our new home in North Carolina. It now resides in the new spot I found for it on our North Carolina patio.

Each morning during my ongoing meditations, I drink my morning coffee, write my morning papers, meditate, and glide happily away as I continue to search each day with the glider's help, for daily guidance and direction.

Coincidence or meant to be? How unusual to discover and retrieve my former and much valued chaise lounge on the same day it was discarded a year or so later after leaving it behind when I moved. How strange I happened to be in the right place at the right time, and two weeks later than when I originally planned to return to Florida. Was it a coincidence no one else had taken this piece of furniture before I arrived? Was it just waiting there for me, another gift of coincidence?

Synchronistic moments do happen in our lives, and when they do, they provide us with much meaning. My preceding three stories of synchronicity in retirement illustrate the power and different levels of meaning these unusual events bring with them. When I was in need of a new dog, one found its way into my life. After being diagnosed with kidney cancer, a series of fortuitous coincidences occurred, and in a timely and purposeful sequence, and when I needed them to happen. An unplanned trip to Florida led to the fortuitous repossession of a valued piece of furniture formerly discarded. All three of these random acts guided me to the places, people, information, and objects, and at the right time in my life.

NO LONGER WILLING TO LEAVE THE GIFT UNWRAPPED

In retirement, we have ample opportunities to make much powerful use of these synchronistic moments; these uncanny coincidences have much meaning for us. Synchronicity is related to our inner subjective experiences and the meaning behind them. If we miss or do not see this meaning, we do what Markey previously has warned: We leave the gifts unwrapped.

Many of my synchronistic events in my life sometimes brought with them, and out of randomness, a desire to search for new ways to develop my spirituality. As I examine and analyze my past moments of synchronicity, I unwrapped most of my gifts of coincidences but I did not make as much full use of them at the time of occurrence as I could have chosen.

For example, as I aged into adulthood, I left my childhood moments of synchronicity scattered and only partially used. Further, while I later allowed moments of synchronicity freely into my life, I did not make full use of them to advance other dimensions of my spiritual development. Amazingly, until just recently, I had left partially unwrapped a powerful and spiritually-related synchronistic gift of coincidence I had received over fifty-four years ago.

A TRAIN TRIP ACROSS THE AUSTRALIAN DESERT

When I was age fifteen, I began making greater use of my hometown library, especially in the completion of new and more demanding high school assignments. The librarian, a woman named Miss Dorothy Vaughn, provided much assistance with the location of books and other resources as I requested them.

Ms. Vaughn was a tall, formidable woman with two distinct facial features, somewhat bulging eyes and protruding teeth. While many may have found her unattractive, her kind consideration and assistance were what I remember most about her.

When I asked Ms. Vaughn for a specific book, she not only helped me locate the book, but she found me at least four more on the topic, and later asked if she could be of further help before she left. Her kindness and willingness to be of assistance and service were impressive and memorable.

One evening, while still a student in high school, I read in our local paper that Ms. Vaughn, also an accomplished organist, would be playing sacred music on the coming Sunday at a local church in the center of town, and interested community members were invited to attend. I had never been in a church before, but my desire to hear Ms. Vaughn play sacred music became so strong I decided to go to church for the first time.

When I arrived at the church that Sunday, the doors were open and most of the congregation already had been seated. I could not see from the back any available seats. I sat off to the side of the church on the top cement step, hoping the doors would remain open during the service so I could hear Ms. Vaughn play sacred music.

She played the organ only three times, at the beginning of the service, in the middle of the service, and at the end. When I was walking home after the service, I was pleased that I heard Ms. Vaughn play the organ, but I did not know why the selections she chose were considered examples of sacred music. I intended to ask her when I saw her again at the library, but I never did.

I saw Ms. Vaughn in the library only on a few occasions during my remaining high school years and when I did, she was always busy with other students and community members, always giving her outstanding attention and service to everyone present.

In time, my need for follow-up discussion with Ms. Vaughn about the meaning of sacred music diminished. Soon, the incident passed and I moved on in life.

Eventually, I left my hometown, attended college, moved away to begin my teaching career, and traveled widely throughout Europe during summer vacations. Since my early high school days, then, I did not have any further contact with Ms. Vaughn, until twelve years later.

When I was age twenty-seven, I was completing a three-year teaching assignment halfway around the world in Melbourne, Australia. Before I returned to the States, I decided to take a five-day train tour across the Australian dessert, starting in New South Wales and ending in Western Australia. The year was 1967, and there were few Americans living in or visiting Australia at that time. During my three years of teaching and living in Australia, I had not met another American.

On the third day of my train trip, I was sitting in a passenger seat next to a window, taking in all the outside scenes of expansive Australian desert with its rich brown, gray, and green colors, marveling in the beauty of the terrain. Behind me to my left were two women, talking somewhat excitedly and loudly, in anticipation of dinner that evening on the train, to be followed by a production of *The Sound of Music*. The cast from the show was on board, traveling from Sidney to Perth.

One woman's voice was distinctive, an American, most likely a New Englander. Another American on board, I thought to myself with excitement. I turned to look.

The woman sitting on the aisle chair was dressed in a heavy coat and looked too large for the seat, but it was her bulging eyes and protruding teeth along with her accent that caught my attention and triggered my memory. Could this woman be Ms. Vaughn, the librarian from my hometown, a person over 3000 miles away from home, a person whom I had not seen in the past twelve years?

At first, I was doubtful. Often in my early travels, particularly in London, I would pass people quickly on the street, and as I did, I would think to myself that the person was so and so from another place and time in my life, and later realize the person was only someone else who looked like another person I had previously known.

As the woman continued to talk, I knew she had to be Ms. Vaughn, the librarian from my hometown. Eventually, I turned toward the woman, introduced myself, and asked her directly if she was Ms. Vaughn from Portsmouth, New Hampshire.

She looked surprised and startled. She paused for what seemed like a longer than usual time to respond, and finally said yes, and asked immediately how I knew her.

I explained to Ms. Vaughn our past student-librarian relationship. In turn, she informed me she had recently retired from this position and was taking the train trip across Australia as part of her retirement celebration. She had not remembered me as a student, nor had I expected her to. I further shared with Ms. Vaughn that I had heard her play the organ in church when I was a high school student, and so many people attended the service that Sunday that I could not get a seat inside. I explained that I had stayed to listen anyway, sitting outside on the top step of the church's entrance.

She remembered her organ recital that Sunday because it was one devoted just to sacred church music. When I asked her what sacred music was, she explained sacred music can vary widely, but the term in her case was used to denote the traditional music of her church.

Music was an important part of her church's worship service, she elaborated, because it speaks to the soul deeply and powerfully, often creating strong moments of beauty and reflection within those in attendance.

Before she and her companion left for dinner, she informed me that although she retired from her librarian position, she still served as the organist at her church. Then, she invited me to come hear her play any time I was in my hometown.

"Come earlier next time and come sit inside. Let the music speak to your soul."

As she was leaving to go to dinner, she turned in the aisle and remarked how unusual a coincidence it was for us to meet on a train tour crossing the central Australian desert, so far away from home, so many years later in our individual lives. I responded I similarly found the experience unusual.

UNWRAPPING THE GIFT

Since this chance coincidence of many years ago, my unusual meeting with Ms. Vaughn while crossing the Australian desert has popped into my mind only periodically. In those moments, I made few efforts to determine symbolically the meaning behind this unusual occurrence. Obviously, it had to do with an invitation of sorts, but an invitation to what? Now, finally, after all these years, I have unwrapped this gift. I finally know the meaning behind this unusual gift of coincidence. As the adage goes, "When the student is ready, the teacher will appear."

AN INVITATION

Ms. Vaughn's invitation for me to visit her church again to listen to her play sacred music was also a symbolic invitation for me to pursue my spiritual development, to not delay or dismiss this dimension of myself any longer, to overcome and conquer the foreboding and earlier warnings to do otherwise, to reflect and find the beauty and peace in the present moment, to let the sacredness of my spirituality speak directly to my soul.

ACCEPTING THE INVITATION

Finally, in my late retirement years, I am ready to accept this invitation. I want new opportunities to reconnect with my childhood spiritual past and to expand my spiritual development. I want to make greater use of my intuitive awareness. I want to become more conscious of my connectedness and oneness with all forms of life. Most importantly, in my exploration of a deeper and transcending spiritual self, I want to discover and begin practicing what I have not yet found nor clearly understand, my elusive yet deep need within to serve a greater good.

MY SEVENTH LESSON LEARNED:
EMBRACE SPIRITUALITY AND SYNCHRONICITY

As I reconnected with my spiritual past, I learned my seventh major lesson in retirement. I embraced with greater awareness and use my spirituality and continuing gifts of synchronicity. I reexamined and confirmed the powerful role of a Higher Being in my life, a force that has and continues to guide and protect me in life.

Today, I continue to await unusual moments of synchronicity in my retirement, moments capable of bringing with them many different levels and kinds of personal meaning, many spiritually related. Many of my spiritual gifts of coincidence are capable of guiding me toward a greater sense of interconnections and feelings on oneness, with self and with others, and the tapping into my intuitive mind as I go about my remaining years in search of deeper purpose and meaning.

In today's society, there is increasing recognition and acceptance of the need for broader notions of spirituality, inclusive of synchronistic moments. In the fields of physical and mental health today, many doctors and therapists are now drawn to Eastern disciplines and practices like yoga, meditation, and mindfulness techniques, because they often result in feelings of happiness and well-being.

An important point we must remember, however, is one Hopcke underscores: spirituality and synchronicity "need not be single, dramatic incidents but can also take the form of a slow process of emerging wholeness in a person's life story."[22]

As I age in retirement, I want to continuously align my authentic self with new dimensions of my evolving spirituality and new gifts of synchronicity. From these new alignments, I hope to become in my remaining years more spiritually aware and awake, more harmonious and balanced, more whole and complete.

MASTER MAJOR LIFE TRANSITIONS

Changing Directions in Retirement: Resolving Dilemmas,
Meeting Obligations, and Exploring New Opportunities

At age sixty-three, I retired and naively assumed that my life ahead, with lots of personal freedom of choice, would basically remain much the same over the years—uncomplicated, unchanged, uninterrupted. Of course, it did not. Too many new and unanticipated life transitions occurred, bringing with them much change in the direction and focus of my retirement journey.

Many of my transitions happened immediately, as natural outcomes of the retirement transition itself. Other transitions occurred later, after the passage of much time lived in retirement. Many of these latter transitions resulted in a personal need to re-examine my sense of self and my current beliefs and values. By taking responsibility to address these transitions, to master them, to act on them rather than ignore or fight them, I eventually was able in my retirement to move forward with my pleasant life.

SIX MAJOR RETIREMENT TRANSITIONS

Fifteen years into my retirement, when I turned age seventy-eight, a series of related transitions required my immediate attention, and some of them simultaneously. Specifically, these six major transitions involved (1) resolving present retirement dilemmas; (2) meeting an unexpected family obligation; (3) relocating to another area of the country; (4) purchasing a new home; (5) assuming a new role as a part-time caregiver; and (6) witnessing positive characteristics of aging while engaged myself in advanced aging.

RESOLVING SOME PRESENT RETIREMENT DILEMMAS

For fourteen years in retirement, Robbie and I had lived a continuous snow-bird lifestyle—five months in Maine, and seven months in South Florida. As years passed, the demands of being a snowbird gradually took its toll on the both of us.

Each year we had to plan and prepare for leaving and arriving at each property. The required cleaning and packing became increasingly time-consuming, complex, even complicated. Although we had sufficient personal belongings in each home, we continued to take our favorite clothing, foods, and books from one location to the other. We also had to pack and find room in the car for the pets, their food bowls, and the litter box.

With Robbie's impaired vision from a recent eye stroke, I did all the driving to and from each home, each way over 1500 miles. Because we had pets, a cat and a dog, driving each way to each home became our basic and preferred mode of travel. In time, the long October drive from north to south and the May return trip south to north became increasingly more difficult and stressful. I had to attend more, and for longer periods of driving time, to the many vehicles whizzing by, particularly the transport trucks.

The hotels, restaurants, and places we typically frequented during these travels eventually lost their excitement of newness and novelty. Our sense of adventure was not as pronounced as in earlier days and, instead, we were now finding our long-term retirement lives as snowbirds becoming too much work, too much effort.

Robbie and I talked frequently about the possibility of downsizing to one home. But where? We presently had the best of both worlds. We enjoyed the seasonal weather in each location. Maine after October was way too cold for full-time living, and summer months in Florida after May were too hot.

Because we were not willing to downsize to either one of these two locations, we continued with our snowbird lives, just complaining more than usual about the long increasingly difficult drive to and from each home.

For most of our early condo living in South Florida, Robbie and I have many positive memories. We reaped the benefits of the location, on A1A in South Palm Beach, a spot with water on two sides. Most of our neighbors, like us, were seasonal residents.

After we moved into our Florida condo, we quickly became friendly with other residents. Soon, we were part of a friendly, supportive, well-managed, and proactive homeowners' association. Basically, many of the other condo owners were like extended family. Each fall, we looked forward to our return and reunions with our neighbors and friends, to our winter home in our sun-filled condo with its southern exposure.

As active members of our condo association, we contributed willingly to community-building, from partaking in social activities to assuming leadership roles on our volunteer board. Moreover, we appreciated the professional way in which our current board members assumed association responsibility, typically with positive leadership, honesty, and integrity. We were pleased to be owners in a condo association that worked together as a community, and, as a result, we experienced much pride in our condo ownership.

For many years, we remained pleased with our decision to retire as snowbirds, pleased with our purchase of our Florida condo and its location in Palm Beach, pleased with our home in the sun we fondly called "Paradise South.

CONDO MANAGEMENT DISSATIFICATION

Then, the downturn in the real estate market in Florida happened as the 2008 recession brought with it many unanticipated changes. The value and sale prices on the condos in our association plummeted overnight and remained low for several years. Gradually, new owners bought into our association, and living conditions changed, and not for the better.

Many of the new owners possessed little prior knowledge and experience with Florida condo living, especially an understanding of the association's bylaws and governing documents, and the need to adhere to these requirements to assure appropriate management conditions and, at the same time, to maintain quality living conditions.

In just over a few months, all owners were faced with a slew of new everyday living and management problems, like illegal parking and noise violations. Frequently, neighbors engaged in loud verbal disagreements and arguments over governing issues with one another and board members. On many occasions, local police were called to mediate and resolve condo owner conflicts.

Many of the previous efforts by previous owners to foster good community behaviors and boundaries quickly began to erode and disappear. As former board members became disenchanted with deteriorating condo living conditions, they resigned, sold their units, and moved elsewhere.

Eventually, their vacant board positions became filled by a group of new owners. More frequently than not, the new board members dismissed the association's bylaws and governing documents and, instead, made up their own rules and imposed them on other owners. Further, they made deliberate efforts to hold board meetings privately, isolating themselves from other owners and their concerns, choosing instead, a dictatorial leadership style, one in which they openly discouraged owner attendance at board meetings. When other owners did attend board meetings, they were told they could not speak.

Consequently, many owners viewed the new board with much distrust, disapproval, suspicion, and criticism. Especially, I resented living in an unpleasant and undemocratic environment. Most of all, I missed the feeling of community and community-building efforts, and my former pride in condo ownership.

Initially, I decided to give things time, in the hope that the present leadership of our association would improve, but it did not. Frequently, Robbie and I discussed whether we should sell our condo and move elsewhere and, if so, where and when. We had no special place to move, no alternative potential home in mind, either in or outside Florida.

Moreover, we liked many aspects about our condo life in Florida, from its layout to its location, and all the nearby amenities. We did not want to move to an unknown area just because we did not approve of the new board members and their management behaviors. I did want, just the same, a more honest and open board of directors.

Then, quite by surprise, we were presented with a sudden family obligation, and in the process of meeting this family obligation, we were confronted with the need to meet a new and unforeseen retirement transition, one involving a request from Robbie's mother, Mrs. Franklin.

MRS. FRANKLIN

Since I first met Mrs. Franklin in 1984, I avoided her as much as possible. To Mrs. Franklin, everything seemed to fall into two categories, right or wrong, and regardless of the circumstances, Mrs. Franklin was always right. Without question, she was one of the most inflexible, controlling, and manipulative people I had ever met.

She refused to listen to or entertain counter arguments or viewpoints, typically cutting off other conversations by talking over the conversation in a louder voice, and often marching out of the room to curb the continuation of the conversation.

Mrs. Franklin also has this habit of criticizing her adult son, Tony, who lived with her before his death, and in front of other family members. I was amazed how Tony's other siblings, living independent lives away from their mother, typically sat quietly and passively when visiting while Mrs. Franklin frequently demeaned Tony.

Once, when I privately expressed to Tony my objections to the way his mother treated him, he looked directly at me and said, "You don't know the half of it. She can be as mean as a snake."

As Robbie and I left at the end of each family visit, Mrs. Franklin admonished Robbie with the same message, "Come back and stay longer next time. You only have one mother," an effort to both criticize and level guilt.

When I asked Robbie why his mother was consistently rigid and inflexible, he responded that she acted this same way ever since he was a child, ever since he could remember. Whenever we visited her, I was always ready to leave, and could not imagine returning for any future visit, but I did, because of my loyalty to and support of Robbie.

One day during one of our visits with Mrs. Franklin, I came across this quote while reading a local paper in her home: "Entertain infinite flexibility in your thinking and experience amazing results." What a wonderful expression, I thought to myself, and what an appropriate statement to share with Mrs. Franklin.

After I read the quotation to her, she turned her head and looked away, out the living room window next to the chair in which she was sitting. Then, she turned, looked directly at me and said, "Things are either right or wrong in life, and I choose to do what's right."

She was not only rigid in her thinking, I thought, but also self-righteous, completely incapable of seeing that in her arrogance, in her insistence that for every situation there was a right or a wrong, there was also much ignorance.

Essentially, things were to be done her way and her way only. She was in control all the time, allowed no alcohol in her home, eating food only prepared by her and in her way, and even controlling who could talk and when. On holidays, her relatives and guests in attendance sat quietly at the dining room table and listened to Mrs. Franklin as she dominated the conversation, talking on and on, about the weather, a neighbor, or someone from her church.

However, during one holiday, Mrs. Franklin lost control over the conversation and became visibly upset. One of her adult relatives she invited this particular holiday began talking naturally and spontaneously, about a trip she had recently taken, and other adults at the table started to asked questions, make comments freely, as they laughed and enjoyed sharing their own stories. Soon, most everyone at the dining room appeared happy and animated, except Mrs. Franklin.

I observed Mrs. Franklin carefully, witnessing her reaction. She was beside herself, visibly annoyed, obviously shaken. Her face contorted in anger. She said nothing, but soon rose from her chair at the head of the table, moved to the kitchen seemingly to calm herself, sat in a kitchen chair alone, while other family members continued to engage in a rich and enjoyable conversation.

I did not like nor respect Mrs. Franklin. One of the few things I did not want now, especially in my smooth and enjoyable life in retirement, was to spend any more time than necessary in Mrs. Franklin's company.

MEETING AN UNEXPECTED FAMILY OBLIGATION

Robbie and I had just celebrated our thirtieth anniversary of living together as life partners, and our second year of being legally married, when Robbie received a call from his mother. She informed Robbie that his brother was ill and she needed him to come home and live with her, to help take care of his brother.

I was so pleased with Robbie's response. He said, "Mother, I have my own family to care for." This response was not what his mother wanted to hear.

Upon a subsequent trip to visit his ill brother, we were asked by Mrs. Franklin if were married. We both said yes. She wanted to know why we had not told her before. I informed her I did not think she would approve.

From that time on, Mrs. Franklin seemed to accept the idea that Robbie was not going to come home and live with her. I resented her even more. She knew Robbie and I had been partners for over thirty years, and by insisting

Robbie come home to live with her, she was discounting our long relationship and its significance to us.

Yet, I also believed she had respect for the institution of marriage, regardless if we were gay. Whether she approved or not, she did seem to accept and consider Robbie and me as a married couple with responsibilities and commitment to one another.

Then, two years later, in 2015, both of Robbie's only siblings died from two different kinds of cancer. Robbie's brother, Tony, had lived with Robbie's mother until his death. With the passing of both his brother and his sister a few months later, Robbie was the only remaining sibling left to help care for his aging mother, who, at age ninety-two, had been recently diagnosed with aortic stenosis.

One winter day, Robbie's mother called again, but asking this time if Robbie would move back to North Carolina, to be of greater assistance to her as she aged. Robbie and I gave much thought to this request before making any final decisions. We spent many hours reviewing our options and obligations openly and honestly.

CONFRONTING CONTRADICTORY FEELINGS

I expressed to Robbie two conflicting feelings. On one hand, I was at a stage of retirement where I was in pursuit of ways to serve a greater good, in search of those best ways to put the needs of others even beyond my own, like the request his mother was making. On the other hand, I was feeling just the opposite about Robbie's mother regardless of her aging and care needs, less charitable feelings of frustration, irritation, disapproval, and immediate rejection.

THE CRITICAL CONCERNS

However, I was most concerned that Robbie and I would be relinquishing our own retirement lives and activities if we met Mrs. Franklin's request.

Essentially, we might be putting on hold our own lives to assume caregiving roles.

In addition, Mrs. Franklin, although she was age ninety-two and had aortic stenosis, had the potential to live a number of years longer, into her 100's, as had many of her siblings, perhaps even outliving both Robbie and me.

Potentially, then, there may be a likelihood we could end up living our remaining years in artificial and diminished ways, at the will and mercy of a woman I found unpleasant, rigid and controlling, unlikable. Essentially, we could be choosing to become less than who we truly were and genuinely wanted to be and become *other than,* as we complied with Mrs. Franklin's rigid standards and mandates.

For the first time in our long relationship, Robbie and I were faced with a major and critical family-related decision. Should we move back to North Carolina and assume, even part-time, caregiving roles for Robbie's mother? Or should we explore other ways of assisting Mrs. Franklin with her present home and healthcare needs? We both decided first to have an important discussion with Mrs. Franklin about her expectations of our caregiving roles.

A FAMILY DISCUSSION

The following weekend, we drove to North Carolina to meet with Mrs. Franklin. I was most concerned that she may expect Robbie to live full-time with her, to move into her home full-time and care for her, as her now deceased son, Tony, previously had done. I believed she did not care at all about Robbie's and my long relationship, nor what happened to me. To her, I was only getting in her way. She and her needs came first, and everything else was irrelevant.

Surprisingly, Mrs. Franklin made it clear she did not want us or anyone else living with her, just living nearby. She had her own living habits and rituals, and she did not want anyone invading her space. She wanted to remain independent, living at home for as long as possible, and remain in charge of her own life.

What she did want was for us to move closer to her, to be able to reach her and help her should there be an emergency in her life, and to be of some help and assistance to her with some of her home management tasks. She further clarified she was now capable of living independently, but soon may need regular assistance and support, and would want our help in finding her reliable home care resources.

A CHANGE IN PERSPECTIVE

On our return drive to Florida, Robbie and I both found ourselves responding more positively to Mrs. Franklin's request. We both agreed we could keep intact the priorities in our own lives while at the same time living somewhere nearby Mrs. Franklin. Her request was manageable, even somewhat necessary.

After all these years of living together, I knew Robbie well. I knew he would feel as if he were betraying his mother if he did not move home to help care for her. Also, I would not be pleased with myself if I did not honor his feelings and support him. At the same time, Robbie and I both saw an opportunity for us in the meeting of this family obligation, an opportunity for a new home in our retirement, and in a new location and community.

AN OPPORTUNITY FOR A NEW HOME

Here was an opportunity for us to begin a new retirement life free of past snowbird lifestyle and Florida condo living restraints and unpleasantness. We could maintain our own lives together, buy a new and desired home for us in a community close to where Mrs. Franklin lived, and, at the same time, be of help and assistance to her.

During further discussions, Robbie and I discovered many benefits of moving back to North Carolina. Our drive to and from Maine would be less. Instead of snowbirds, we would become half-back retirees, cutting our driving time approximately in half. We would have the four seasons in our lives again.

In addition, the weather in North Carolina was moderate in winters. Rather than continue to live in a relatively small condo in Florida with questionable board governance, we could buy a home, one with the potential for a more peaceful and satisfactory quality of life.

We could even purchase a new home, our dream home, one with lots of space and flow. We had previously discussed the possibility of downsizing to one home as we aged. We could buy that home now rather than later and lease in Florida during winter months.

Besides Robbie's mother, our best friend, David, lived in the Charlotte area. Moreover, because we lived in Chapel Hill for over thirty years during our careers, we were well-acquainted with the State, the Charlotte area, and the many advantages of living in this part of the South.

We could choose to live in the University Park area, near our friend David, a professor at the nearby University of North Carolina at Charlotte. I liked the whole idea of being close to the university and taking advantage of its many cultural offerings.

Robbie, however, had some reservations. The drive to his mother's home would be much further, and the university area was more populated with traffic, more congestion. With his impaired vision, he saw the University Park area, basically, as not our best choice.

Charlotte was Robbie's home. He grew up in the area. As southern New England was my provenance, the Charlotte area was Robbie's provenance. Here was an opportunity to find a home for Robbie. His final decision as to where we should purchase became a high priority.

After visiting and researching communities within a ten-mile radius from where Robbie's mother lived, eventually we found an ideal community for us—Belmont, North Carolina.

BELMONT, NORTH CAROLINA

Belmont, a small community with a population just over 11,000, became our first choice as the place for us to relocate. The downtown area had been carefully restored and renovated. Numerous restaurants lined Main Street. Near to downtown, there was a college, Belmont Abbey. Many new residential communities were being planned and developed.

Recently, we had watched a CNN Special about Belmont, one in which the television commentator discussed the recent revival efforts made, with the downtown restoration becoming a small mecca of fine restaurants for the Charlotte area.

During dinner downtown one evening, Robbie and I were informed by a waiter that Belmont really had not changed much with the renovation. "Belmont is still just like Mayberry," he informed us, "only now with bars."

We found the ideal community for us to live in Belmont, in a planned site with a series of homes being built along the Catawba River. If we were ever going to buy our dream home, we wanted one newly constructed, a home with space and flow.

PURCHASING A NEW HOME

Eventually, we found the ideal home, one with an exceptional design, and we bought it pre-construction. The home had an ideal location, just a few blocks off the major interstate I-85 in Belmont, a quick drive to Gastonia, where Robbie's mother lived. The home was close to downtown Belmont, a short drive to downtown Charlotte, located close to top-tier medical resources, and just five miles away from a major airport.

In addition, our home was situated in a beautiful natural setting nestled among hills and trees, with a large community pool and numerous walking and running paths. The individual homes included land for homeowners interested in gardening and a large patio for entertaining and relaxing.

Our new home was the very first building at the entrance to our community, with lots of privacy, situated on a large lot with no buildings on the right side. The front of our home faced a large pasture rather than the street, with a view that took advantage of the lovely tall trees that lined the perimeter of the field. While additional homes were planned to be built beyond us, we would be able to maintain our privacy because of our ideal location and zoning restrictions. No one could build to the left of our home and obstruct our exceptional view.

The home included three bedrooms, three bathrooms, and a two-car garage. Downstairs, the home had much space and flow, an open-concept home, with nine-foot walls, cathedral ceilings, and ten floor-to-ceiling windows that took full advantage of the morning sunlight.

The floor plan was open, with a large kitchen, sitting area, dining area, guest bathroom, and lovely back patio. To the back of the home was a large master bedroom with a large walk-in bathroom and attached walk-in closet. A two-car garage was in front, joined to the kitchen by a utility room.

The space upstairs was large with good flow, filled with more windows and light, and two large bedrooms with walk-in closets and a large bathroom. There was a large hallway with a sitting area at one end with a floor-to-ceiling window. A large storage room was located at the other end of the hallway. From all windows, upstairs and downstairs, the views were unobstructed and breathtaking.

In our new home, we had space, flow, an open-design, and a prime and safe location.

Moreover, we have many amenities nearby. At the bottom of our entrance, there is a community gym. Because our home is located on a series of hills, we have many rigorous walking paths in the neighborhood. With a moderate winter climate, we are able to walk outside continuously for most of the year. When raining or too cold outside, we go to the gym and walk on the treadmill or swim in the inside pool.

A large shopping area is located conveniently a few blocks away, inclusive of pharmacies, medical facilities, and grocery stores. We appreciate the convenience of these facilities and, at the same time, enjoy the privacy of our nearby home.

We own our home outright and thus find our monthly expenses and upkeep minimal. Surprisingly, our new association fees include water, sewer, garbage pick-up, external insurance, landscaping, pool maintenance, and management company fees, all under $200.00 a month.

In Florida, by comparison, our hurricane insurance by itself was comparable to a mortgage payment, and was included within a much larger and ever-increasing monthly maintenance fee. We now save considerably more money monthly with our lower maintenance fees.

Furthermore, in Florida, there were limited ways to increase home equity if you lived and owned a condo on the ocean. If any equity gains were made from year to year, these sums were offset by larger and ever-increasing maintenance fees and assessments. In contrast, and just within six months, our new home in North Carolina has increased considerably in value and, more likely than not, will continue to increase.

While Robbie and I daily find something positive to say about our new home, our cat, Morris, and our dogs, Eva and Tripp, likewise seem to enjoy it. Like us, they love the space.

They run up and down the stairs daily, excellent exercise for all of them. They enjoy our fenced patio area, and stay outside for hours at a time, especially in warm weather.

While many of our friends and former colleagues have passed, and others have moved into independent and assisted care facilities, Robbie and I have chosen to buy a lovely new home, and at ages seventy and eighty, respectively. We believe for us and for now, we have made the right decision.

Our new home, however, was more than a new place to live. Our new home became, and rather quickly after we moved in, a powerful source of a new and personal adventure, a place ideal for furthering my spiritual development.

NEW MOMENTS OF SPIRITUAL CONNECTEDNESS AND ONENESS

Before we moved from Florida, I was already aware I was living and experiencing a different stage of adult development than when I first retired, one I call Reflection and Review.

In this new stage, I had begun to explore new and transcendent ways of finding deeper meaning in retirement by engaging in more contemplation, solitude, and spiritual practices, dimensions of self previously ignored, undeveloped.

Could features of our new home, I now questioned, somehow assist and enhance new spiritual dimensions of myself? Could our spacious new home, with its high walls and cathedral ceilings, help shape and expand my fundamental habit of self-reflection? Could more space influence somehow my spiritual experiences and ultimately, how I made sense of these experiences?

Three specific features of our new home in North Carolina seemed to facilitate, even encourage, many moments of introspection and reflection.

LIGHT AND REFLECTION

From early morning until dusk, our patio and new home becomes ablaze with light, light brighter than even in Florida. This light may only appear to be brighter. It may really be that we have more windows as sources for morning light, nothing more.

However, this abundance of light in our new home has become an automatic invitation for me to engage in much meditation and reflection, for long periods of time, and at deep levels. Previously in Florida and Maine, I had greeted each day in awe of the beauty around me and a short morning prayer.

Now in North Carolina, the light in our new home seems to encourage a more personal search for ways to become more spiritually conscious, to find, through the increased use of awareness, a greater sense of peace, of being, of becoming one with self, one with the moment, one with life.

SPACE AND NESTING

In our new home, we have more space and privacy than in our previous Florida condo. We are now living primarily alone, rather than connected by building structure to other owners, to other lives, to noise other than our own.

As we live in our new home, I am beginning to prefer staying more at home than going out during the days and evenings. By staying home for longer periods of time, we are using and enjoying living with more space not previously available.

For the past fourteen years in our retirement, we lived as snowbirds in small and somewhat confined condos. During this time, we typically lived outside our condos and in the sun, always on the go, often engaging in outside activities, both outside of home and away from home.

Now in our new home, suddenly we are doing the opposite. We are pulling away from a busier, more active outside life. Now, we are starting to nest more, and for longer periods of time, increasingly enjoying being alone for long periods of time.

After our move to our new home, I have become more reflective and content, more centered and focused. Both Robbie and I have started to garden, building an outside walkway garden, two other gardens on the out-side patio, and more recently, a solarium inside.

In addition to gardening, Robbie enjoys bird-watching and feeding, the exploration of new dog-walking paths, conversations with other dog walkers, and being home in his own provenance, in our lovely new home with its exceptional space and flow.

LAYOUT AND FLOW

The upstairs of our new home has become predominantly my area. We set up the front bedroom as my office. Robbie later built a wall-to-wall bookcase, and we placed my desk in front of the window. From the window, I have an extraordinary view of rolling hills and tall trees.

The room has a large walk-in closet that I use to store office supplies. Along the entrance wall, we have placed a small sofa, to sit occasionally and read comfortably. On the wall opposite the bookcase, we have placed a large television, to monitor the news and the daily fluctuation of the stock market. This room has become the perfect location for my office, for it is an ideal space for activating flow.

In his book, *Flow,* Mihaly Csikszentmihalyi defines flow as a state of optimal functioning, creative thinking, and seemingly effortless productiv-ity. People experience flow when they pursue a goal with deep involvement and enjoyment, and when in flow, they often forget about time and place.[23]

Similarly, when I taught many of my classes in my past career, I became momentarily lost in flow. For the past year, I have been similarly experiencing many moments of flow in our new home office. Many mornings after my meditations, I go to my office and work, sometimes all day, until it is time for my evening walk before dark.

During this long period of time, I experience many moments of flow, moments in which I seem to transcend time as I write, read, research a topic, and talk on the phone. Rarely in my past have I found this amount of flow in my life in any of my former homes. What is it about this new home that now encourages my use of flow?

I believe the light, space, and layout of the home contribute greatly to the feeling of flow, especially as I pursue daily activities with deep involvement and enjoyment, and to the degree that I frequently become oblivious to time and place. In my moments of flow, I find joy and satisfaction wherever I am and whatever I am doing. These moments of joy and flow are also related to synchronicity.

FLOW AND SYNCHRONICITY

In his book, *Living in Flow: The Science of Synchronicity and How Your Choices Shape Your World*, Nelson-Isaacs states the concepts of flow and synchronicity are mutually dependent. When we align with circumstances, Nelson-Issacs claims, circumstances align with us.

We align with circumstances when we get in a state of flow, what Csikszentmihalyi calls getting "in the zone." Our circumstances aligned with us in moments of synchronicity, what Jung described as meaningful events related to one another but that happen without any possibility of proving the relationship is a causal one.

These connections bring with them many "nuggets of joy." Nelson-Issacs urges readers to look for those little nuggets of joy in life wherever we are, and in whatever we do.

Every moment in flow and synchronicity can bring us useful information, Nelson-Isaacs contends, but how we respond to these nuggets of joy that show up randomly makes a huge difference in what happens next. In other words, not only is it important to find meaning in moments of flow and synchronicity, but also in the choices we make as a result of these unusual experiences.[24]

Beyond my feelings of flow and random feelings of joy in and with our new home, I was hopeful and optimistic that I would find "nuggets of joy" in random ways in other aspects of my new life in North Carolina. In particular, I wanted to find much joy from our choice to assumed new roles and responsibilities as caregivers in retirement.

BECOMING CAREGIVERS: ASSUMING A NEW ROLE IN RETIREMENT

After Robbie and I returned to North Carolina, we became caregivers to his mother, each in different ways. Robbie visited his mother almost daily, and if he could not for any reason, he always called her. During his visits, he would do errands for her, like grocery shopping, picking up her prescriptions, completing home repairs as needed, and driving Mrs. Franklin to her different appointments.

My role as caregiver was somewhat different. While I did do much of the driving for Mrs. Franklin to and from her doctor's appointments, my role was to sit and socialize with her, to be company while Robbie went about completing other tasks. At first, this simple task was most difficult for me to do, especially for any length of time.

At first, I found little joy in my visits with Mrs. Franklin. In short, she refused to engage in most conversations. I typically sat on her living room sofa while she sat in her chair next to the window. The fan churned and hummed loudly in the silence. When I made a statement or asked a question, she would simply smile, turn away, look out the window, sometimes commenting on something totally unrelated, like what she saw outside. This behavior appeared to be her way of telling me what I was saying or asking was not of interest or meaning to her.

In time, I began to drive Mrs. Franklin to her doctor appointments. Robbie's compromised eyesight was a concern to the both of us, so I volunteered. Mrs. Franklin did not approve of this change.

While she sat next to me in the front passenger seat, she repeatedly tapped her index finger on the side window for the duration of the trip, a visible and audible sign of disapproval. In a strong voice with a critical edge, she informed me I was not driving at the right speed, or I was not in the right lane. She preferred I drive in the left lane because all of the turns eventually to be made were on the left side of the highway. She was giving her commands, and I was doing my best to follow them, with my patience growing thin.

Within a few months after we moved back to North Carolina, one of Mrs. Franklin's close friends died unexpectedly. He was also a fellow church member with whom Mrs. Franklin previously and regularly joined for lunch each Sunday. Robbie and I, knowing how much Mrs. Franklin enjoyed these luncheons, decided to continue the custom with her ourselves, by joining her or taking her for lunch each Sunday. Ever so slowly, these weekly luncheons improved my relationship with Mrs. Franklin.

THE SUNDAY LUNCHEONS

One day a friend connected to a nearby community inquired if I knew anyone over the age of ninety who might like to contribute to a book she was writing on aging. I shared this information with Mrs. Franklin, and she immediately rejected the idea, firmly stating her life was not noteworthy.

I told her I thought it was, mentioning how she managed money well and took care of all household and family expenses by working long hours at hard work after her husband died.

She let me know she had no intentions of contributing to the book. I volunteered to listen and write her memories down if she so wished. She did not, she informed me bluntly, and that was the end of that conversation.

I noticed, however, from that day on, each Sunday after lunch, Mrs. Franklin began to engage in more conversation with me. I believe I had validated to her in some small way that her life had meaning. She, in turn, started to trust me more, and with that trust, she felt comfortable, even willing, to share with me small but detailed stories about her past and present life, not much at any one time, but small glimpses of events she seemed to find both meaningful and memorable. In time, I became comfortable enough with her to ask her lots of questions, and she began to answer them.

For the first time in thirty-five years, I started to listen more carefully, more deeply to Mrs. Franklin. While she was often repetitive, I gathered after a few Sunday visits, she was trying to share with me those moments which gave her a sense of personal accomplishment, of meaning in her life, and I began to enjoy my visits with Mrs. Franklin more, to even look forward to them.

Mrs. Franklin was born in 1924, the daughter of mill workers. Her early conversations focused on the difficulty of life during the Great Depression. Everyone was poor then, and she and her family were no different. She often repeated how difficult it was for people to survive with few opportunities to make money.

She told stories of living near her grandparents, who rented a mill home in the neighborhood. All family members worked together, took care of each other, gardened together, and shared food together during those financially challenging and historic times.

On other Sundays, she talked more about herself, how she graduated from high school in 1942 and began herself working in the mills. In her second year of work, she met her future husband, Gaines, and they married a few years later.

Each Sunday, she added more detail, sharing with me her move with her husband to Gastonia, North Carolina, the homes they rented, bought or later built, and stories about her three children, when they were born, how they were different, and what they did while growing up.

In her stories, I heard how difficult it must have been to both work and raise children. Mrs. Franklin worked in the mill from 6:00 AM until 2:00 PM, then came home, cleaned the house and did the wash, and later cooked dinner for her family.

She saw her ability to be frugal as one of her best attributes, the ability "to twist as much out of a penny as she could." She succeeded in part by making use of budgeting with the help of envelopes, each marked with a name of a utility company, her church for weekly tithing and mission donations, food allotment, and other weekly bills. She was not only frugal out of necessity but seemed to enjoy the whole process of living frugally and within her means.

Near age seventy, she retired from the mill, made and sold quilts for a few years, and later found a part-time job cooking in a child daycare center. She worked this job until she retired in full around age eighty-six.

From our Sunday conversations, I learned much about Mrs. Franklin from listening to her stories. Essentially, her life was a story of survival. She and her family had survived the Great Depression by working hard, staying together, living close together, taking care of one another, and sharing the same beliefs and values.

AGING ON AUTOPILOT

While she was practical and self-sufficient, Mrs. Franklin lived basically on autopilot throughout her long life, set in her thinking and behavior, with little interest in changing, or developing other dimensions of her total self.

As I listened to Mrs. Franklin, I realized the person she became in her advanced age was the product of the way she thought and behaved since her childhood. She accepted the lot she was given in life. She aspired for little more and possessed little interest in further learning or expanding her thinking.

As she aged, she became more controlling and less flexible, more closed and restricted in her thoughts and behaviors than open and curious, more critical and demeaning than accepting and caring. She saw herself as doing the right thing by doing what was known and familiar to her—a predictable, practical, and routine life.

Rarely did she engage in reflective thought, in inner exploration of fresh discoveries of new options, or in new ways of responding to her everyday situations. Thus, she chose to live her life on autopilot, completing her daily tasks automatically, with little conscious consideration of other possibilities.

Like Mrs. Franklin, many people choose to age less conscious of how they are aging. They tend to restrict themselves in the process of aging. They limit and restrict their use of personal awareness and different levels of functioning, other options and alternatives available to them.

However, there is nothing wrong with the choice to age on autopilot. While the options available may be more restrictive than necessary, many people who choose to age on autopilot, like Mrs. Franklin, still find much purpose and satisfaction in life. Moreover, many people who live on autopilot still exhibit many positive characteristics of aging positively, as did Mrs. Franklin.

As I learned about her past life living on autopilot, I also observed and witnessed Mrs. Franklin's life at age ninety-five, filled with multiple characteristics of aging positively in her final years. As I observed and noted these behaviors, I changed many of my previous feelings about her. I started to gain more respect for her. I started to like her, to care for her, and more deeply than I once ever thought possible.

WITNESSING CHARACTERISTICS OF POSITIVE AGING

Within the memories Mrs. Franklin shared with me, I found buckets of joy by witnessing firsthand many of her powerful characteristics of positive aging while I also was in the process of advanced aging myself. Thus, Mrs. Franklin became in many ways a good role model for me to follow in my desire to age positively in my remaining years.

GOOD SELF CARE

Upon rising, usually around 8 AM, Mrs. Franklin made her own bed before eating breakfast. Then she would take her morning bath or shower before dressing herself appropriately for the events she had planned for that particular day.

A DAILY PLAN

She spent her days cleaning house, connecting with friends by talking on the phone with them or receiving them at home when they came to visit, or going to appointments. For exercise, she walked to her mailbox and back, down a hill and back up a hill, taking her time and monitoring her breathing,

On most Sundays, she enjoyed going to church followed by lunch with some friends. On other days, she enjoyed going shopping with Robbie or another relative, cooking, paying her bills, and watching her regular television shows.

She engaged in her daily interests, such as watching televised baseball games, church services, and specials. She enjoyed keeping up with the daily weather and completing crossword puzzles.

SELF-SUFFICIENCY

Mrs. Franklin was a person determined to be self-sufficient and responsible. She was proud to tell others, "I paid off a thirty-year mortgage on this home, put on two roofs, painted it four times, and recently replaced all the windows."

FRUGALITY

Before she paid someone to complete a necessary household task, she first considered who she could ask to complete the work free or at a lowest cost. Who could come and put a new battery in her car, check her furnace before turning it on in the fall, or replace a few pieces of siding blown off her home during a recent storm? Similarly, when it came time to roll over her CDs, she always researched which local bank would give her the best interest rates.

INVENTIVENESS

One day, Mrs. Franklin informed Robbie and me that she wanted a walker with a chair, a light-weight walker that she could use to walk in grocery stores and in her walks to the mailbox and back. With the help of the walker, she could walk so far and, if she became tired or her breathing became too difficult, she could unfold the chair, sit and rest awhile, until her breathing improved.

She informed us that she got the idea for a walker with a seat after observing an older neighbor using one as he walked to the end of her drive, unfolded the seat on his walker, before he sat for some time, watching the deer graze in a nearby pasture.

When she turned ninety-two, her family doctor sent her to a heart specialist, who discovered Mrs. Franklin had severe aortic stenosis. After he explained to her all her options, she refused to have any surgery, choosing instead to be treated with medications. Her solution to her heart problem had become this: "Work a little, sit a little, and catch my breath. Work some more, rest some more."

INDEPENDENCE

At age ninety-five, Mrs. Franklin lived at home alone, and desired to remain living independently for as long as possible. She still insisted on cooking her own meals, doing her own laundry, cleaning, and meeting her inside and outside household responsibilities.

Now at her advanced age, these tasks became increasingly difficult for her to complete with skill and ease. The outside work of mowing the lawn, pruning the bushes, picking up twigs and debris, washing her car, painting the outside house trim became too difficult for her, particularly with her increasing breathing problems. Rather than ignore these tasks, she found other people and resources to get these tasks done.

ADJUSTING TO AGING

At age ninety, she had stopped driving. Neighbors and church members volunteered to take her shopping, and she reluctantly let them. With her advanced osteoarthritis, she took more time to walk from the car to the store and back. Her breathing and standing for any length of time became increasingly difficult.

Because of her aortic stenosis, she now coughed and spit up fluid frequently, so she stopped going to church. Her church was a big part of her life. Both Robbie and I were concerned and encouraged her to go, to take a cup with her and spit in the cup when necessary. She would not have any part of this suggestion. "I've been going to that church for forty years now. It's time for the church to come to me."

The church members did come, often and on a weekly basis, bringing her copies of the church service and food, spent much time visiting, even carrying away her garbage and recyclables with them as they left.

EXCEPTIONAL MEMORY AND MENTAL ACUITY

Mrs. Franklin, even at ninety-five, had maintained her excellent memory and cognitive functioning. She was always sharing with Robbie and me ways of staying active and independent. For every day, she had a plan, a list of things to get done. She wrote her own checks and paid her bills on time. She kept a calendar with daily things to do.

DETERMINATION

On our visits with her, Mrs. Franklin often informed Robbie and me that she had no intention of giving up, that she intended to stay active right up to the moment "the good Lord called her." She was never going to give in to her health issues.

ADVANCED PLANNING

As we were having lunch one Sunday, Mrs. Franklin was planning for her present and future needs. She informed us that she wanted the deacon from her church to give the tickets he gave her annually to someone else next year. She no longer cared to attend. She also mentioned that next year she may renovate the second bathroom in her home. Now that her arthritis was causing her increasing difficulty in getting up from her favorite living room chair, she was thinking of buying a new lift chair.

Mrs. Franklin had prepaid her funeral expenses and service expenses and kept a copy of her will, insurances, and financial documents in a small home safe. In these documents, she had also filed directives on what she wanted Robbie, her executor, to complete at the time of her death, from what clothing she was to wear to whom she wanted from the church to officiate the service, to the service itself, and what hymns were to be sung.

There was never any talk of her dying, nor dying anytime soon. Mrs. Franklin was a good example of an elderly and health-compromised person in retirement continuing to participate fully in life to the moment of her death.

THE DEATH OF MRS. FRANKLIN

Five months after her ninety-fifth birthday, Mrs. Franklin died. After falling one morning in her bathroom, she broke her hip, underwent hip replacement surgery, and survived the operation, even with her serious aortic stenosis condition.

While recuperating in the hospital immediately after hip surgery, Robbie and I visited Mrs. Franklin with her grandson and his wife, who both volunteered to live with Mrs. Franklin and care for her if she chose home recovery.

I was amazed at her immediate and clearly stated response to them as they informed her of their well-meaning intent. Here was a ninety-five-year-old woman, still with serious aortic stenosis, still in the process of becoming conscious after a long and serious operation. She turned her head, made eye contact with her grandson, and in her matter-of-fact way said audibly and clearly, "I will need only a few things done, but the things I need done I want done my way."

After spending a few days in the hospital, Mrs. Franklin decided not to return to her home but to move to a nearby rehabilitation center, where a friend from her church lived in an attached assisted living facility. Someone would be with her full-time in case she fell again.

"It is my decision to make, and that is where I want to go," she informed Robbie and me one day before her hospital discharge.

For the first few days, Mrs. Franklin improved during her stay at the rehabilitation center. She ordered and ate her meals, completed some daily walking and physical exercises in the gym, and received visitors. Then, she suddenly developed pneumonia and her oxygen levels began to drop. She stopped eating completely, entered a state of semi-consciousness and died two days later, approximately one month after falling at home and breaking her hip.

Even as she experienced poor health, physical decline, and the loss of loved ones, Mrs. Franklin adjusted to and integrated these unpleasant conditions as part of the aging experience itself. With this acceptance, she continued to live with inventiveness, involvement, and independence. She remained self-sufficient and self-functioning. In her remaining years, she remained living on her own terms, and with determination and purpose.

MY EIGHTH LESSON LEARNED: MASTER MAJOR LIFE TRANSITIONS

With Mrs. Franklin's passing, I realized I had learned, in just a few years, my eighth major lesson in my retirement. I had mastered, sometimes simulta- neously, many major life-transitions. These major life transitions required much resiliency, flexibility, careful thought, and personal determination. Mastering these life transitions, however, resulted in many new opportunities for me to experience a more purposeful and pleasurable life in retirement.

I resolved retirement dilemmas, met an unexpected family obligation, relocated to another part of the country, purchased a new home, began a new role in retirement as a part-time caregiver, and witnessed positive characteristics of aging while engaged myself in advanced aging. Perhaps most importantly, I became more aware of my own strong desire to age with an increased use of mindfulness.

AGING WITH INCREASED USE OF MINDFULNESS

Many people believe that aging with mindfulness represents a way of aging with greater use of awareness and reflection, thus providing us with more options and opportunities for further growth and development in our later years. However, my desire to make increased use of mindful awareness in my retirement did not make me superior to those who choose to age in other ways, such as on automatic pilot, like Mrs. Franklin. Rather, by aging with increased use of awareness, I was simply choosing to age with a different perspective, with a willingness to explore and examine myself from within.

Perhaps Mrs. Franklin chose to live her life less aware and mindful with some justification. Many people choose not to become more mindfully aware because they are not interested in, nor do they enjoy or find meaningful, the act of engaging in deeper self-exploration. Further, they are unwilling to devote the necessary time to the practices of self-reflection and examination that mindfulness requires. However, for those interested in becoming more mindfully aware, there are many personal and powerful benefits, especially as we age in retirement, and as I discovered in my ninth and next major lesson learned.

AGE WITH INCREASED USE OF MINDFULNESS

Reaching Higher Levels of Awareness: Experiencing Remarkable Moments of Oneness

Soon after my eightieth birthday, I was sitting in the Charlotte office of my new doctor, waiting for my annual physical. Many magazines and some books had been placed on a nearby table for reading while waiting. An article in one of the magazines I perused advocated becoming more mindfully aware as we aged.

QUESTIONING MY PRESENT AGING AWARENESS

Immediately, I questioned if I had been aging mindfully aware. I had reached my advanced age chronologically old, but still active and in good health, statistically outliving the average American male. However, I seemed to have habituated the aging process by adapting to aging with little thought. Was I, then, not aging mindfully aware? I recalled two recent incidences, while somewhat subtle, that may actually indicate more of a denial of the aging process rather than an awareness and acceptance of it.

THE PURCHASE OF AN AGE-RELATED SIGN

While browsing in a gift shop a few summers ago, I came across a sign with a fitting message on it: "Grow old later." I bought the sign and hung it in my kitchen, a daily reminder as to how I intended to live my remaining years.

Could my buying and hanging this sign in my home be more than a personal attempt to maintain a positive attitude toward aging? Could it also be a subtle and humorous way for me as well to deny my own aging process?

Or was it just a sign purchased to remind me daily to age with a positive attitude, as former President George H. W. Bush appeared to accomplish? When President Bush died, someone commemorating his life at his funeral stated, "He died young as late as possible."

Could our individual attempts to age positively actually be efforts, at times, to deny the aging process? I thought about another and more recent incident and questioned if it also could be another example of my attempt to deny my aging, of my reluctance to accept my physically aging self.

DRESSING SOMETIMES DIFFERENTLY

One late fall afternoon in Ogunquit, Robbie and I walked into the village for drinks at a local bar. We both were wearing shorts and shirts we had recently bought during a weekend trip to Montreal.

The shirts were different in that they had French symbols and wording embroidered on them. Definitely, they were different from shirts designed and typically worn here in the States, and to us most attractive and appropriate to wear by men of any age.

The bartender, a man with a jovial personality and good sense of humor, greeted us by saying, "You guys always dress like two thirteen-year-old girls." We both laughed. Many other people at the bar and within hearing range also laughed, joining in the humor and conversation, with some commenting positively about the attractiveness of our shirts, while others asked where we purchased them. Typically, when Robbie and I went for drinks and dinner, regardless of what kind of clothing we were wearing, we always felt included, embraced, accepted by neighbors, friends and acquaintances.

Abruptly, another older man across the bar, who must have been listening to the conversation, yelled loudly, with force and a tinge of anger, "They dress that way because they think they're still hot."

The laughing stopped. Caught off guard, I took a sip of my drink. Robbie looked down. The room momentarily became quiet. Then, other conversations resumed and the incident passed.

The stinging words kept vibrating in my thinking, because the incident made me question if there was any truth to this man's comment. Was I really wearing this shirt to appear younger and sexier, to still appear "hot," as I approached age eighty?

For years, I silently disapproved of older men dying their hair to look younger, wearing tight jeans without youthful bodies to fit in them, trying desperately to appear younger. Was I now as an older man doing the same by wearing a way too youthful and tight shirt? Was I compensating for my aging, for my loss of youth, by trying to recreate and present to others an image of a younger self?

Was I intentionally choosing not to see the ramifications of my aging because I had been strongly denying the loss of youth with the passage of time? Could accepting the inevitability of my aging also mean accepting the end of youth and hence my physical appeal and attractiveness? Could acceptance of the inevitability of my aging mean I might also be denying the inevitability of death? Was I at age eighty finally coming to terms with my aging self?

AGING WITH A POSITIVE OUTLOOK

After much reflection, I eventually concluded I was not denying my physically aging self by wearing a particular and unusual shirt. Rather, I had been accepting my natural aging with a different and positive perspective. Aging mindfully aware to me meant focusing more on *how* I was choosing to age and *why*, while at the same time accepting my aging. I had chosen to age with a positive outlook, a positive perspective.

I had purchased and worn this shirt that particular day because I desired as I aged to remain as attractive as possible in my appearance, and, in part, by the way I dressed. Even in my eighties, even if others may perceive me to be dressed age-inappropriate, I was dressed in a way that made me feel good about myself, confident and self-assured, in a different but still attractive manner.

I was choosing not to deny my aging, but to accept it while at the same time choosing to remain as physically active, healthy, and as attractive as possible. I suspect for the rest of my life I will always attempt to age with a positive outlook on life as I dress as attractively as possible, age-appropriate or not, "hot" or "not so hot" anymore.

AGING GRACEFULLY

The title of a book, also placed in the doctor's office on a nearby table, next caught my attention: *Healthy Aging: A Lifelong Guide to Your Physical and Spiritual Well-Being.* As I skimmed a few pages, I came to the author's description of aging, including a definition of aging gracefully. The author, the physician Andrew Weil, described the aging process and aging gracefully as follows:

> We can mask the outward signs of the process or try to keep up old routines in spite of it, but we cannot change the fact that we are all moving toward physical decline and death. The best we can do--and it is a lot--is to accept the inevitability and try to adapt to it, to be in the best health we can at any age. To my mind the denial of aging and the attempt to fight it are counterproductive, a failure to understand and accept an important aspect of our experience. That attitude is a major obstacle to aging gracefully. To age gracefully means to let nature take its course while doing everything in our power to delay the onset of age-related disease, or, in other words to live as long and as well as possible, then have a rapid decline at the end of life.[25]

I studied this definition of aging gracefully, and for some time. I agreed with Dr. Weil that as we age, we needed to adapt to the aging process. I recalled how Mrs. Franklin, Robbie's mother, had aged and died consistent with much of this definition. She had aged gracefully by adapting to her aging experience and then had a rapid decline at the end of her life.

While Mrs. Franklin and I both aged successfully in part by adjusting to the aging process, we also aged with different and often opposite perspectives on aging. As Mrs. Franklin chose to age primarily on autopilot, I had aged, to some degree, by making more use of reflection and self-awareness.

I questioned, however, one part of Dr. Weil's definition of aging gracefully: *No matter how much we try to remain healthy and fit, we are going to experience health issues in time, decline, and die.* I was not willing to view my remaining years as I aged as years of decline.

Of course, we are all going to age, change physically, and eventually die. As our society and culture have done for years, Dr. Weil's definition of aging gracefully focused, if only in part, on viewing our end years as a time when we are likely to experience primarily disease and decline. While I had chosen to age by not thinking much about it, I also chose to age with a positive perspective, a focus on aging Dr. Weil's definition of aging gracefully seems to omit.

Could a more positive focus on aging expand and reframe Dr. Weil's definition of aging gracefully? Could growing old be filled with many positive experiences for further self-growth and discovery? Could a definition of aging gracefully also include the realizing and use of the full spectrum of our abilities, interests, and emotions right up to the moment of death? Could we age gracefully by remaining positive in our attitude and productive in our actions as opposed to the view of aging as inevitable decline?

THE MANY PATHWAYS TO POSITIVE AGING

The possibilities of positive aging have been documented and recommended for years. Since the 1970s, many gerontologists have urged our society to move beyond a mindset of aging as concerned only with disease, physical deterioration, and death. This old and outmoded viewpoint on aging focused only on aging as a medical condition, they often reported.

While these same experts admitted aging was a time of life when many age-related problems did manifest, they also began to advocate for more positive approaches to aging, to move beyond a perspective on aging as only related to decline and disease to a new focus on the potential in the aging experience itself.

Gene D. Cohen, for one example, used the findings of impressive studies of the brain and mind during aging to show how healthy adults retain sound mental and emotional faculties and typically decline only gradually in their physical resources. The brain, he underscored, plays an important part in the way older adults remain healthy, for it is far more resilient, flexible, and capable than previously thought. Further, he noted our inner and authentic psychological selves continue to develop as we grow older and pass through different developmental stages of aging in the second half of life.[26]

Thus, many older adults later in life used an awareness of their individual authentic self and stages of developmental growth in retirement to reach their full potential, again, a basic and major premise within this book.

INDIVIDUATION AND AGING

As early as the 1930s, C. J. Jung coined the term, "individuation," to refer to the process of aging with the continuous use of a positive perspective. To Jung, individuation was the way to experience optimal personal development.

Jung called this process of positive aging "individuation" because it was an attempt to become more whole in the second half of life, to integrate as many parts of the personality as possible, to evolve into one's individual and authentic self. To Jung, individuation was a process of self-realization, the discovery and experiencing of new meaning in our individual and authentic lives.[27]

INDIVIDUATON AND AUTHENTICITY

Another purpose of individuation was to show how human traits and possibilities are combined in each individual in different and unique ways. Thus, individuation also implies being and becoming aware of one's own authentic self, as well as the experiences and transformations of self, both that would not have happened without engaging in the process of individuation.

A further purpose of individuation was to increase one's individual consciousness, or awareness. With greater consciousness, individuals engaged in ways of living that lessened the divide between conscious and unconscious, eventually resulting in the living of a more transcendent and spiritual life.

CONSCIOUS AGING

In the 1990s, other researchers interested in the study of aging continued to argue for a broader vision of aging and the aging process, one inclusive of a perspective on aging filled with opportunities for personal growth, transformation, and transcendence. Thus, the conscious aging movement began, bringing with it a perspective on aging that viewed aging as full of opportunities for finding further purpose, growth, and service as we age.

When we age consciously, we explore the many possibilities available to us. Our beliefs about what is possible for us and our intentions that spring from them hold great power in shaping who we become as we age. However, to age consciously requires the use of increased reflection, self-awareness, and time.[28] We can age gracefully, then, by becoming increasingly more mindfully aware of other positive and powerful choices and options available to us in retirement.

AGING WITH INCREASED USE OF MINDFULNESS

For the past thirty years, mindfulness has been the focus of much interest, study, and research. As a result, mindfulness has been described and defined in multiple and different ways, in general and specific terms and from psychological to spiritual perspectives.

MINDFULNESS AS AWARENESS

Broadly conceptualized, mindfulness has been defined as the state of being aware of one's thoughts, emotions, and experiences. Of late, many researchers from different fields of study have expanded this definition.

MINDFULNESS AS PAYING ATTENTION

Bishop and his colleagues have defined mindfulness in more detail and within two parts. First, these researchers view mindfulness as being self-regulating, a term used to describe how we pay attention with purpose. The second part of their definition refers to the willingness to remain open to, and curious and accepting of, those interests, issues, and events on which we pay attention with openness.

Bishop and associates further conclude mindfulness can be defined as a process of investigative awareness, one in which we observe the ever-changing flow of our individual experiences. The term, "investigative," refers to our intentional awareness to observe and gain a greater understanding of our thoughts and feelings.[29]

MINDFULNESS AND THE BRAIN

In the book *Aware: The Science and Practice of Presence*, Daniel J. Siegal defines mindfulness as what happens when certain mental faculties interact with one another in optimal ways. He identifies characteristics of mindfulness similar to those of Bishop and colleagues but expands upon them, particularly the third characteristic: Intention, the ability to maintain a positive attitude toward self and the world.[30]

In another and later book, *The Mindful Brain,* Daniel J. Siegel notes mindfulness involves, much more than just being aware. It involves being aware of the mind itself.

Mindfulness, to Siegal, is related to the brain's increased neural integration. This integration enables coordination and balance in both the brain's functional and structural connectivity, thus facilitating optimal functioning and well-being, such as improved self-regulation, problem-solving, and adaptive behavior.

Further, Siegel notes our mindfulness changes the way our individual brain functions. When we mindfully pay attention, we promote neural plasticity in the brain. As various dimensions of mindful awareness emerge within the activity of the brain, they stimulate the growth of neural connections, often in the social neural circuitry of the brain. This part of the brain has the potential to promote attunement, a sense of inner balance and harmony.

By reflecting on the mind in relation to mindfulness, Siegal believes change in our lives becomes possible because we think, feel, and behave differently. We explore further options and choices we may not have previously considered.[31]

MINDFULNESS AND AUTHENTICITY

In her book, *Mindful Aging*, Andrea Bryant reminds readers that the more mindful we become, the more we understand how our own choices and actions affect what we experience. To Bryant, mindfulness is an invitation to live more consciously aware each day so we can discover who we truly are and what we genuinely want out of life.

The problem, however, as Bryant warns, is that our perceptions may be in direct contradiction, at times, to the facts of what is possible. In other words, Bryant contends that in our efforts to age more mindfully aware and true to self, we may be actually sometimes limiting ourselves unnecessarily. Bryant states a way to stop such self-limiting behavior: fully acknowledge the reality of a situation. Once we grasp an understanding of our thoughts and feelings about a situation, then we are ready to change it.

Without question, Bryant's approach to mindful aging struck a powerful personal connection. In her definition of aging mindfully aware, she presents support for my strong desire and determination in my retirement to remain true to self: We become free enough to see who we truly are and what we genuinely desire out of life. Our self- awareness as to whom we truly are can help us fulfill our truest dreams and live as our authentic selves, because what we are doing is aligned with our true self, and with a sense of positivity.

Bryant defines positivity in aging mindfully as a focus on what we would love to accomplish simply for its own sake, and for pure joy. Positivity may not only make us feel good but empowers us and influences what we do and create. Positivity helps us create a life we love depending on our ability to reflect, to become aware of our own reality, and through increased use of mindful awareness. We use our mindfulness to entertain new possibilities as we become who we authentically or truly are.[32]

MINDFULNESS: SOME POTENTIAL PERSONAL BENEFITS

From these many definitions and descriptions of mindfulness, I deducted many personal benefits by increasing my use of mindfulness in retirement. I could improve overall aspects of my well-being, from physical, mental, to emotional dimensions. I could continue to learn and grow, to learn how to better focus, intend and respond. I could learn to pay attention with more purpose and openness. I could improve my problem-solving abilities and my adaptive behaviors. With the increased practice of mindfulness, I could gain greater understanding of my true or authentic self. Thus, my increased use of mindfulness could assist me each day to live true to self, and more fully in the present moment, as I continued to age with greater use of a positive perspective.

Most of all, by becoming more mindfully aware, I could cultivate the potential to discover and experience new and yet unknown spiritual dimensions, such as my desire to serve a greater good. Becoming more mindfully aware, then, was an opportunity to become more spiritually aware and transcendent, to potentially experience new and higher levels of self-awareness.

MINDFULNESS AND SPIRITUAL DEVELOPMENT

Throughout my retirement, I had made occasional use of prayer, meditation, journal writing, and nature as ways of increasing and practicing my spirituality. My spirituality, often minimal and overlooked in my past, slowly became a personal source of support, an inner source of well-being, and primarily through my increased use of my forementioned practices.

As I age in my retirement, I want to continue my earlier search for greater spiritual guidance and connections, but I also desired to expand them. I want to find and explore new ways of becoming more mindfully awake, more aware and present, and as a result, find different, deeper, and expanded spiritual practices and experiences. Specifically, I want to pursue the goal of cultivating a deeper inner life, a spiritually more transcendent life.

Since the beginning of my Reflection and Review stage of aging in retirement, I had been searching for deeper spiritual meaning and purpose. Frequently, I asked myself questions like the following: How can I become more aware? How do I allow spiritual energy to flow freely in my life? How, through spiritual reconnections and awakenings, can I grow and evolve? How can I better serve others by engaging in greater awareness and presence? How best can I find, and use effectively, my inner goodness? How can I best serve a greater good?

Eventually, I found answers to these questions as I experienced in my later retirement some memorable moments of connectedness and oneness, with some of these moments being truly remarkable, even profound.

AGING MINDFULLY AWARE: REMARKABLE MOMENTS OF ONENESS

I began my search for further spiritual development with the exploration of the word "goodness"—what it meant, and especially in relation to spirituality.

Goodness, I soon learned, is not a thing but an action. Therefore, the word is not easy to define. Just as Auden is credited with once saying, "Goodness is easier to recognize than define."

In Greek, the word for goodness, *agathosune,* means "an uprightness of heart and life." For many, goodness is associated with the qualities of being "upright of heart and life" through these actions: kindness, helpfulness, generosity, and honesty, with self and with others.

WITNESSING GOODNESS IN OTHERS

I continued my search for goodness by witnessing and recognizing it in other people. Immediately, I thought of Robbie, and how easy it was for me to recognize the goodness within him. For thirty-six years, I have observed Robbie, with his genuine desires to let the good within him naturally emerge—freely, generously, and unconditionally.

ROBBIE

While Robbie has exhibited many acts of goodness since I have known him, I remember vividly two recent examples which left a powerful impression. Usually, Robbie goes each day with me to the gym. Recently, he told he had something else to do one day, that he needed time to devote to something else.

Out of his strong desire to keep our environment green and clean, he spent that particular afternoon selflessly choosing to spend tireless hours outside, picking up litter on streets in our neighborhood and other nearby communities, and without any need for self-recognition or image-enhancement of any kind. As he sees necessary, he continues today to practice this self-chosen act of goodness.

I have also observed him employ his natural and instinctive goodness regularly to protect and care for feral cats and abandoned animals in our communities, both in Maine and Florida. On a regular basis, I have observed Robbie donate time, money, furniture, and clothing to numerous animal shelters and organizations while keeping these acts of goodness to himself. He continues today to make contributions of unconditional goodness to a number of animal shelters, and without the need for self-gain, recognition, or personal reward.

STEVEN

Similarly, Robbie and I have a friend who frequently displays many unconditional acts of goodness. We met our friend, Steven, an actor and artist from Maine, a few summers ago. To both of us, Steven epitomizes the word goodness.

Our friendship with Steven began one autumn evening after he had invited us to a fundraiser at his home for Camp Sunshine, an organization in Maine that supports needy children. We did not know Steven well at the time, so we did not know what to expect at the fundraiser.

Steven's home is situated on a large lot in the country, with a backyard of rolling hills. As we entered, we were greeted and invited for drinks and finger food served under tents. Other guests were in attendance and represented a range of residents from many of the neighboring seaside communities. Robbie and I introduced ourselves and mingled with other guests, and later previewed the items to be auctioned later as part of the fundraiser.

After the reception, Steven invited the guests to a musical presentation he had directed and arranged, as a gift back to them for their individual donations. Using a large tent in one section of his backyard, Steven had constructed a stage, secured a number of talented entertainers to perform, from singers and dancers to aerialists and comedians.

To this day, this setting, musical performance, and its design and intent, has remained for me an exceptional moment in time. That evening, I witnessed an example of a rare gift of goodness from Steven and a group of entertainers. All volunteered their time, talents, and unconditional goodness in two ways: first, to raise money for a noteworthy cause, Camp Sunshine, and second, to give back to guests a rare and unusual gift, a gift of collective goodness, the gift of an unconditionally shared creative performance.

EXPERIENCING GOODNESS

My participation in this event will always remain memorable because of my triggered feelings of authenticity, of being one with everything, with nature and the universe and the setting, with the event, the people, and the performances, as I witnessed and experienced the joy and exhilaration that comes from the unconditional acts of authentic goodness.

Not only had I witnessed goodness that evening, I felt the authenticity of that goodness, and, in turn, responded with authenticity. That particular evening became a time when the stars seemed to align with the moon and the universe, bringing me as a participant and witness along with them, an evening of magical moments frequently happening simultaneously, bombarding and interacting with one another, over and over, until everything that evening became connected, became one.

PRACTICING AND PERPETUATING GOODNESS

Later that same year, Robbie and I joined Steven and a few other members of our Maine community to support an entertainer who was new to the area but not yet established. These Sunday evenings likewise became memorable because they represented a subgroup of our community, led by Steven, working together for a similar and common cause, to support and help an entertainer and friend become established and independent in our community, another example of genuine and unconditional goodness and giving.

DISCUSSING GOODNESS

One day, I expressed to Robbie my desire to give back, to engage in acts of greater goodness, to serve a higher good, as I had observed him, our friend Steven, and others of our friends and acquaintances accomplish. I was having difficulty, I honestly shared, because my heart was not in making contributions of goodness in the same way he and Steven were choosing to use.

I informed him I could never be a volunteer of any kind or like anyone else. I explained to him my heart was not in that kind of giving back. For me, it would feel inauthentic, artificial and contrived, too much like belabored work.

Robbie responded, and with insights I had not previously considered. While I did not do any formal volunteer work, he informed me, I was constantly helping other people in my own unique, authentic ways. Instead of choosing to contribute in ways he and Steven had chosen for their individual selves, I enjoyed and gave back freely to others through telephone calls and conversations, writing email messages, genuinely caring, genuinely staying in touch, offering unconditional care, advice, and support.

He also reminded me I was constantly recommending and buying books for friends I thought would enjoy reading or find of bibliotherapeutic value. Then, Robbie said something that has ever since stayed with me.

He reminded me I was trying to mirror the goodness of other people rather than find my own goodness within. I could not do good by mirroring the good in other people, he informed me. That would be an artificial and false kind of goodness. "Remember our former neighbor," he asked.

A FORMER NEIGHBOR

Robbie and I often questioned the motivations of a former neighbor, a woman in Chapel Hill who owned a small, beautiful, and rare kind of dog. Once a week, our neighbor dressed in her best clothes and took her dog to visit ill patients at a local hospital. Upon her return home, she appeared to deliberately search for other neighbors, to eagerly share how much the patients enjoyed the visit from her and her special dog.

I often wondered, and shared with Robbie, if our former neighbor took her dog to visit patients to cheer them up, or did she go as well for another reason, for personal reward, to increase her own self-image and sense of self-worth, to fill a personal need for self-enhancement, a desire primarily to strengthen her own identity and self-image.

YOU DO NOT BECOME GOOD BY TRYING TO BE GOOD

"Your true goodness is who you are inside," Robbie emphasized, similar and consistent with remarks of Eckhart Tolle I later read:

> *You do not become good by trying to be good, but by finding the goodness that already is within you, and allowing that goodness to emerge. But it can only emerge if something fundamental changes in your state of consciousness.*[33]

For years, I had been entertaining a counterproductive path as I searched for ways to serve a greater good. I didn't do good by trying to be good, by mirroring the benevolent actions of others, and often without true commitment and genuine feelings. Goodness was not something I did for the sake of being virtuous. If I strived to do good for my own gains, it was not goodness I desired but personal reward.

I internalized Robbie's and Tolle's advice quickly. I had to find my own goodness within, and let that goodness surface genuinely, naturally, freely.

BECOMING ONE WITH GOODNESS

I had the wrong focus for serving a greater good. My goodness within was not end deeds or acts or accomplishments I sought to find and accomplish. My goodness within was not about pleasing other people. My goodness within was my authentic self, with multiple dimensions capable of doing good, of being good. My authentic self and my goodness within were one and the same.

My authentic self and my goodness within were reflected in my attitudes, beliefs, actions, and presence, my overall *beingness,* moments when I became filled with feelings of happiness, joy, satisfaction and fulfillment, moments filled with caring and compassion. In these moments, I made automatic and genuine use of my goodness within. In these moments of goodness, my feelings of authenticity flowed, with a desire to be and become of service to others.

In being true to self and letting my good within appear, I had to be and remain my authentic self in my remaining years, my inner source of goodness. I finally understood how I could be my authentic self, serve a greater good, and find deeper purpose and meaning—and all at the same time.

BECOMING MINDFUL OF MINDFULNESS

As I aged with increased use of mindfulness, I finally experienced the meaning behind terms I had read before but not fully understood, terms like "conscious of consciousness," or "aware of awareness." I finally grasped the meaning of these terms when I experienced firsthand what it means to become "mindful of mindfulness."

Much has been written about those moments in life when we learn how to detach from our thoughts so we can exist at deeper and more aware levels. In these moments, when we learn how to transcend the clutter in our minds, we become more fully aware by living more consciously. Once we experience these levels, we are experiencing higher and deeper levels of consciousness identified as conscious of consciousness itself, or aware of awareness, or mindful of mindfulness.

As we become more mindful of mindfulness, we become increasingly conscious of our present values and beliefs, ways to change and expand our worldviews, and opportunities to expand more clearly what gives us purpose and pleasure in life. By practicing becoming more mindful of mindfulness, we have the potential to transform our lives with deeper love and acceptance, of self and others, and thus bring enriched meaning to everyday life.

By increasing our awareness of our individual goodness within, we develop the potential to enrich our own lives and the lives of others. When we become mindful of mindfulness, we allow ourselves the potential of experiencing higher level of self-awareness, what Abraham Maslow first identified as self-actualization, for years the pinnacle in his hierarchy of human needs.

MASLOW'S HIERARCHY OF HUMAN NEEDS

In the early 1940s, the American psychologist, Abraham Maslow, developed his now famous hierarchy of needs, a theory of psychological health based on a person's ability to fulfill human needs with priority, with self-actualization being at the top.

Maslow argued that people first needed to build both esteem from other people as well as inner self-respect before self-actualization. When our deficiency needs have been met, we turn later in life to growth needs. The growth needs are the upper four levels of his hierarchy. Through knowledge and understanding of life circumstances, an individual is able to contribute to the betterment of others.

According to Maslow, our individual motivation to pursue growth needs increases as we age. The more our needs are satisfied, the more we want to pursue them. The more we come to understand, the more we become motivated to learn and grow.

SELF-ACTUALIZATION

Maslow defined self-actualization, the top level of his hierarchy, as the complete realization of one's potential as manifest in peak experiences involving the development of one's abilities and appreciation of life. More commonly, his definition of self-actualization became known as the full-realization of one's potential or one's true self.

SELF-TRANSCENDENCE

At first in his career, Maslow saw self-actualization as also involving self-transcendence and what he termed "peak experiences." Whereas self-actualization referred to the filling of one's potential, transcendence referred to attending to the needs of others. We can think of transcendence as having a concern for things beyond self, like altruism.

SELF-TRANSCENDENCE AS PEAK EXPERIENCES

In addition, self-transcendence refers to moments of spiritual awakening, self-liberation, and feelings of unity with others. Maslow further identifies these self-transcendent moments as peak experiences. To Maslow, peak experiences were moments of pure joy and elation that stand out from everyday events. The memory of such events is lasting, and people sometimes link them to a spiritual experience.

Maslow defined the concept of self-transcendence as associated with a spiritual or mystical peak experience, in part as the feeling of great wonder and awe, to the personal belief that something extremely important and valuable had happened, so that the person is transformed and strengthened in his daily life by the awareness and participation in such an unusual experience.[34]

A TERRIBLE MISTAKE

Toward the end of his life, Maslow realized he had made a terrible mistake in his hierarchy of human needs. Self-actualization and self-transcendence were not at the same level, he finally realized. Self-transcendence was the pinnacle of his pyramid of human needs, not self-actualization.

In spirituality, there is a word for Maslow's later realization of his highest level of human needs, one comparable with self-transcendence. Self-transcendence is sometimes called satori, a Japanese Buddhist term for awakening or greater understanding.

SATORI

Satori is an unusual experience that typically happens unexpectedly and suddenly, a moment of presence when we go beyond our thoughts to a higher level of consciousness.

Satori is a powerful, brief, and often ecstatic experience that occurs when we momentarily transcend the illusion of being a separate self, detached from others and the world around us. Momentarily, when we experience satori, we feel as if we are one with the world, a part of a universal consciousness, sometimes called a collective consciousness, or a unified awareness.

While not long-lasting in nature, satori is still a flash of insight, a moment of total presence profoundly liberating, capable for that limited time of creating feelings of inner bliss and expanded awareness. When satori happens, it seems to be beyond our will. Moments of satori are often associated with different facets of increased illumination, spiritual transcendence, and enlightenment.[35]

A TASTE OF SATORI

I have never before felt nor experienced a self-transcending spiritual moment as deeply or as profoundly as I did two summers ago in Maine. I attribute this event to a rare and unexpected moment in time when I became, for the first time in my life, conscious of consciousness itself, aware of awareness, or mindful of mindfulness.

Perhaps this self- transcending moment happened because of my efforts to meditate more deeply, or practice more deeply present moment awareness and mindfulness. Or perhaps not. I really do not know why this memorable and special moment happened, but I will never forget it.

In my brief moment of satori, I experienced new feelings and dimensions of self, elevated awareness, a new state of being, with a sense of peace and presence never previously attained, an ecstatic moment of bliss, peace, and self-satisfaction and, strangely, all occurring during a rather ordinary day in my life.

The following story is my attempt to put into words a description of my one moment of satori, a peak experience, and a kind of spiritual self-transcendence. I call my moment of satori "the perfect day."

THE PERFECT DAY

Robbie and I are fortunate to have among our friends two with the same name, David—one who lives in North Carolina and the other in Maine. Last summer, a day after Robbie and I returned to our Maine home, I experienced what I call "the perfect day."

Soon after we awoke, our Maine friend David, whom we had not seen for nearly six months, came by our condo for a reunion visit.

For over ten years on summer weekends, David and I have been participating in what we call our weekly "walks and talks," a time we simultaneously walk vigorously and talk freely and spontaneously, and on a wide array of unending topics.

Over these years of walking and talking, David and I have shared rich and deep conversations. During this particular activity, we both have learned much from one another and about one another, and over time we have become good friends.

David and I frequently have commented to each other how much we genuinely enjoy our weekly "walks and talks." No two of these experiences have ever been alike. Never has the conversation been meaningless or idle. Why, I have often wondered, did we both find much meaning and purpose from our weekly "walks and talks"?

After our walk on my perfect day, David and I stopped at an eatery in town and ordered two cups of Vietnamese coffee. While we continued to talk, we both greeted neighbors, friends, acquaintances, and visitors, many who asked about my winter and welcomed me back to Ogunquit for the summer season.

Later, during the afternoon of my perfect day, I took a short nap for approximately forty-five minutes, while David and Robbie visited and completed individual tasks in their daily itineraries. I mention my nap to illustrate the simple and unremarkable events unfolding during my perfect day.

That evening, the three of us went for dinner to a new restaurant in a nearby town. When we arrived, the restaurant was busy. As we waited to be seated, we began conversations with other people also waiting. Many were new acquaintances, and others were friends we knew from Ogunquit. We even met acquaintances we knew from Montreal, who were in Maine visiting the seacoast for the weekend.

After we were seated, we each ordered a different entrée, made comparisons, and all agreed our dinners were exceptional. Then, David drove us back to our condo before he left for his new home in nearby Portland.

Once Robbie and I were inside our condo, it happened, my brief taste of satori. *I kept repeating to Robbie, over and over, I had just experienced the perfect day. There was absolutely nothing more I could personally request from life on this perfect day, I kept saying to Robbie repeatedly. If I were to die in the night, or pass anytime soon, I would now have no regrets, for I had experienced a day of complete satisfaction and fulfillment, I continued.*

How could a rather ordinary day, I also thought, become for me a perfect day? I believe I now have the answer, or part of one.

STAYING PRESENT

During our walks and talks, David and I consciously stay present, in the moment. When we walk and talk, we let go of any prior thoughts or preoccupations. I stay as present as possible, enjoying the moment, walking and talking with David.

We listen with much attention and intensity and share information with genuineness, honesty, and integrity. I believe it is our ability to stay present with one another, to recognize and sense each other's presence, that makes our Saturday "walks and talks" both personally satisfying and meaningful.

During my perfect day, I was able to stay present in the moment and surrender fully to the events of the day as they unfolded, as unremarkable as they appeared to be. By being present, I was aware of the authentic essence in myself and in others I met during my perfect day. I experienced the relatedness of beauty, simple pleasures, fine company, and I responded to the people I met that day with genuine caring and kindness. On my perfect day, I experienced a form of authentic happiness.

STAYING AUTHENTIC

As David and I "walk and talk," we remain authentic with one another. During our walks and talks, we are each being our individual authentic self, our natural and spontaneous self.

On my perfect day, by being my authentic self, I experienced being my innermost and basic essence, my true self, and as a result, experienced heightened feelings of inner peace, joy, contentment, a sense of connectedness and oneness with the momentary unfolding events in my life, a sense of completeness, a need for nothing more.

During my perfect day, I had manifested a spiritual dimension of myself deeper and higher than my thoughts, a higher level of consciousness not ever previously attained. Consequently, I was functioning with heightened feelings within, coming from my authentic self, feelings of well-being, contentment, relaxation, and completeness. I needed nor wanted for anything more. I had experienced the perfect day.

Eventually, I realized it was not the events of the day, but what was happening inside me with my feelings that made this day the perfect day. My perfect day involved how I was choosing to respond to inside and outside events occurring in my life. On my perfect day, I was choosing to become one with self, one with other people around me, one with life.

STAYING ONE WITH SELF, ONE WITH LIFE

During my perfect day, I became immersed in and surrounded by a level of peace I had not experienced before. Within this level of peace, I momentarily changed the way I typically processed events in my life. For a brief time that same evening, I developed a sense of detachment from thought.

Although I am now in my eighties, I have rarely thought about death and even less about an afterlife. Regardless, toward the end of my perfect day, I had said to Robbie that if I were to die in the night, I had no fear nor regrets, for there was nothing more I could possibly request from life. During my perfect day, I accepted the inevitability of my death.

MY NINTH LESSON LEARNED: AGE WITH INCREASE USE OF MINDFULNESS

I had learned my ninth major lesson in retirement, the importance of aging with increased use of mindfulness. Throughout this lesson, l learned to age with a positive perspective, to not see aging only as a time of decline. I chose to age exploring new opportunities for continuous personal growth and self-transformation.

By choosing to age more mindfully aware, I sought further opportunities to fulfill my deepest dreams, realizing what I was living can be aligned with my true or authentic self with a sense of positivity. By living more mindfully aware in retirement, I developed more positive attitudes toward myself, other people, and the world around me. By continuously practicing mindfulness, I improved the overall quality of my life.

Most importantly, by becoming more mindfully aware in my retirement, I experienced new and previously unknown spiritual dimensions. I witness goodness. I discussed goodness and read about goodness. I experienced goodness. Eventually, I comprehended my authentic self and my goodness within were one and the same.

However, it was only after I became mindful of mindfulness itself that I reached my highest level of consciousness ever attained. On my perfect day, I had reached a level of profound integration and acceptance never before experienced, powerful feelings of making peace with the present moment. On my perfect day, I had become one with a Higher Power who continues to guide me toward goodness and grace, toward hope and love, toward authenticity and peace. On my perfect day, I had become one with self, one with life, one with eternity.

MAKE PEACE WITH THE PRESENT MOMENT

*Riding on a Limited Express: Living
One with Self, One with Life*

In the fall of 1960, during my first year of teaching, I remember introducing the poem, "Limited," by Carl Sandburg, to high school students. Now, some sixty years later, I still remember how quickly my students comprehended the poem's meaning.

At the literal level, the students stated the poet was riding on a train across a prairie. Moreover, they noted the train, called "a limited express," had fifteen all-steel coaches carrying a thousand people. At an interpretive level, students deducted that all passengers in the coaches will one day die, or pass to ashes, just as the coaches themselves will eventually turn to rust and be scrap.

Further, just like all the passengers on the train, my students inferred that they, too, one day will die. Thus, my students, then in their teens, were able to deduce that this poem served as an important reminder: Our time alive is limited, a point of which we should be more conscious at any stage of life.

RIDING ON A LIMITED EXPRESS

During those many years ago, my eventual death seemed so far away, in the far and distant future. Today, more than ever before, I am aware I am riding on my own limited express. Most of my years of life now are behind me.

Frequently, nevertheless, I find myself now asking how I can make use of my limited time remaining, and toward what possible best end? Recently, I have discovered my answer: by making peace with the present moment.

MAKING PEACE WITH THE PRESENT MOMENT

Throughout my life, particularly in retirement, I am aware I am most happy and peaceful when I am quiet, grateful, and content, one with the unfolding of life around me, engaged in things I genuinely enjoy.

I am at peace when I focus my attention on natural and spontaneous moments, when I am not resisting or judging, but authentically and unconditionally sharing and helping others. Essentially, I have learned to make peace with the present moment by being one with self, one with life, even in challenging and unfavorable circumstances.

MAKING PEACE WITH THE PRESENT MOMENT: COMING FACE-TO-FACE WITH DEATH

Throughout my life, I have not been a stranger to death. My father died in 1968, and my mother in 1971. Since then, my five siblings have passed, as have many of my former classmates. Many close friends have died, some naturally and others accidentally, as have many of my previous colleagues.

None of my experiences with death, however, has been as profound or traumatic as a recent experience of coming face-to-face with death during spring of 2020. This particular occurrence became not only a remarkable moment of synchronicity, but also an uncanny occurrence miraculous in nature.

THE EMERGENCY ABDOMINAL AORTIC ANEURYSM

One evening in early March, Robbie was complaining more than usual about a pain in his back. Over the course of the evening, he attempted to complete different exercises he typically performed in the past to ease his back pain. None seemed to be working. It was late in the evening, and I asked Robbie if we should go to the emergency room at our local hospital. He was more comfortable at that moment, he informed me, sitting upright on the sofa in our living room, as we waited for the pain to subside.

I left him sitting on the sofa and went to bed, thinking little more about Robbie's back pain, a reoccurring situation he had experienced for years. Robbie typically dealt with his back pain and its momentary treatment in his own ways until it subsided.

Two hours later, I awoke and returned to the living room to check on Robbie. He was frozen in position on the sofa, his eyes closed, his face white and his mouth open, looking much like his mother during her recent moment of death.

I yelled his name, shook his body, but there was no response. In shock, I immediately called 911 and requested emergency service. The dispatcher asked if Robbie was still breathing. I told her I did not think he was, that he must have died over the past two hours, from causes I did not know.

HESITATION TO COMPLETE INSTRUCTIONS

The operator instructed me to move Robbie's body to the floor, that he may be able to resume breathing in that position. I intuitively hesitated. I told her I was uncomfortable moving him, perhaps because Robbie had told me earlier, he had been more comfortable in a sitting position.

She insisted I move his body to the floor, but I still refused, informing her the emergency medics could do that once they arrived. Within seconds of my 911 call, a team of first responders was knocking on my door.

FAST TIMING AND THE SKILLED
EMERGENCY PARAMEDIC

A paramedic who looked like Santa Claus burst into our home, followed by his team of emergency technicians. "Just got the call as I was passing by your exit. Great timing," he said as he proceeded quickly to the sofa and shook

Robbie repeatedly and forcibly, until one of Robbie's eyes flickered slightly open. Robbie was still alive.

I heard the siren of another ambulance service approaching outside, as the paramedic next injected Robbie with fluids while requesting him to "hang in there" before he asked me what happened. I informed him of Robbie's earlier back pain.

The second team of responders was soon banging on the front door, followed by local police. All were asking questions. What happened to the patient? Who was I? What was our relationship? What were we doing at the time of the incident?

The first paramedic told the second team members he had things under control, that they could leave, that he and his team would soon transport Robbie to the emergency room at a local hospital.

He and his technicians next placed Robbie's body in an upright position in a stretcher and quickly but carefully placed him in an ambulance. In minutes, the red light was flashing again and a siren was roaring. Robbie was on his way to the hospital for further care and diagnosis. I followed the ambulance in our car.

THE FAST-PACED EMERGENCY ROOM NURSE

In the emergency room, a nurse named Stephanie asked me more questions, informed me what tests needed to be completed, and clarified why. All of Robbie's vital signs, she said, were "off the charts." His kidney levels were extremely high, and they would need to do an ultrasound of his abdomen.

Within a half hour, I learned that Robbie had suffered a rupture of his abdominal aortic artery, and he would need immediate emergency surgery. The good news was that the blood from his excessive internal bleeding had flowed into Robbie's back, most likely containing the flow of the blood to one area of his body, perhaps the reason why Robbie instinctively felt it best to sit in an upright position during the rupture, perhaps the reason why he was still alive.

With this latter information, I was pleased I had not moved Robbie earlier to the floor. If I had, the blood trapped in his back may have flowed to other parts of his body, causing more serious damage, even death.

The bad news was that an abdominal aortic aneurysm typically was a catastrophic event, and any number of issues could cause immediate death, as the surgeon on duty later informed me. With emergency surgery, the overall mortality rate was estimated as high as 80%. An emergency room doctor informed me that an open procedure was the standard procedure and would need to be completed as soon as possible.

THE HONEST SURGEON

Taking me aside, the surgeon assigned to perform the operation informed me that Robbie's prognosis was not good. Because Robbie's abdominal aorta had ruptured, he felt strongly that Robbie would not survive the operation. I informed the surgeon I thought Robbie had the determination to survive, and I hoped he and his team would work to that goal.

He smiled for the first time since he had arrived, and said, not in a condescending but compassionate manner, that he and his team would do their best. The first step, he continued, was to keep Robbie alive during the four-hour operation. He advised me to stay in the waiting area for periodic progress reports from him and his team.

As Robbie was being rolled into surgery, I noticed his mouth was now twisted down. He appeared to be having a stroke, in shock, or both. I followed him as he was rolled to the operating room. Robbie was sitting up, unconscious, his head turned to the right, his eyes glazed and starring off into the distance. Although I did not know if he could hear me, I told him I loved him, that I would be waiting nearby after the operation.

WAITING FOR THE PROGRESS REPORTS

As I waited for the surgeon's first call, I slowly absorbed the reality of this situation. As the surgeon privately told me earlier, Robbie, more likely than not, could die during the operation.

My immediate two regrets were that I did not foresee the seriousness of his earlier back pain, and if Robbie were to die, I did not have any time to say goodbye to him while he was conscious. After all these years of sharing our lives together, I suddenly regretted taking Robbie so often for granted, rarely telling him how much I loved and appreciated him, the personal and powerful contributions he made daily to enrich my life over the years, to fill my life with so much purpose and meaning.

MAKING PEACE WITH THE PRESENT MOMENT

Typically, in the past when traumatic events had occurred in our lives, I remained the one in control, questioning those people in charge about our options, informing them as to our preferences, and further questioning the procedures recommended in relation to our desired outcomes.

In contrast, this medical emergency had to be met immediately, by skilled and knowledgeable medical doctors, assistants, and nurses. Robbie was in good hands, I concluded. Moreover, whatever Robbie's medical team needed to do and how to keep him alive was beyond my knowledge and abilities. I could do nothing more than accept the fact I was not the one in control this time. There was nothing more I could do now but wait patiently and hope for the best outcome.

By accepting these facts, letting go of my tendency to control, I began making peace with the present moment. I knew there was nothing more I could do right now except to patiently wait nearby for the periodic progress reports. Suddenly, I felt less stressed and more relaxed, more at peace. I heard my inner voice say, "Let go, Let God," and I surrendered to the moment as I waited for the surgeon's first call.

I called our closest friend, David, in Charlotte, and he came immediately to the hospital to wait with me during Robbie's operation. He listened patiently to me as I reviewed the events leading up to the emergency operation.

WAITING FOR THE HOURLY CALLS

The calls from the surgeon came systematically, usually after about an hour. The operation had started, patient was doing well. The rupture is being treated with a graft. Patient is still doing well. The doctor is now closing Robbie's incision. The surgeon will be down to speak with me soon.

THE POST-SURGERY CONFERENCE

The surgeon was pleased to share that Robbie had survived the first stage, the surgery, and the insertion of a graft. Yet, he quickly informed me there were many risks to survival, especially over the next ten days. Robbie's heart, he informed me, had stopped twice during the operation. His heart, blood pressure, breathing rate, and oxygen levels all need to be monitored carefully over the next few days.

Also, Robbie's kidneys needed dialysis, and because Robbie had experienced a stroke on his left side, he would need an MRI of his brain to determine the seriousness of the stroke. The surgeon urged me not to become too optimistic. The risks were many, and the outcome could go either way.

Later that same evening in the intensive care unit, David and I were able to visit Robbie. I was shocked by his appearance. He looked huge and grotesque from the operation and addition of fluids, like a blown-up balloon of a person, nothing at all resembling his previous self.

Numerous tubes were attached to him. His arms and legs were bandaged and strapped down, to keep him from moving and doing damage to his recent surgical site. He was still heavily sedated and unconscious. The nurse said I could talk to him, that he might hear me.

I stayed only for a short time during these early visits, but I did not leave until I told Robbie how much I loved him, wanted him to recover, and would assist him in his recovery when he did.

HANGING ON TO HOPE

Whenever I visited Robbie over the next few days, the nurses and doctors were all helpful and informative, pointing out little signs of daily improvement. One nurse suggested I touch Robbie's left foot, to feel how warm it was, suggesting his circulation was improving. Another showed me how to read his vital signs on the different monitoring machines nearby. Robbie's breathing had improved, another nurse informed me, and his blood pressure was slowly improving and stabilizing.

However, on the third day, I happened to be visiting Robbie at the same time the surgeon came by for his daily evaluation. The outcome could still go either way, and quickly. Robbie's kidney scores, he pointed out, were still extremely high. Robbie would need another kidney dialysis, as well as another MRI of his brain, the surgeon informed me, to determine the degree of physical and mental damage Robbie may have experienced as a result of his accompanying stroke. Just in case Robbie did not survive, the doctor recommended I should inform Robbie's closest relatives, even make some preliminary funeral arrangements.

FUNERAL PREPARATIONS

The surgeon's objective statements were not what I wanted to hear. Nevertheless, if Robbie were not to survive, these were tasks I would have to do, and the time seemed right. David decided to stay with me at my home for a few days while Robbie recovered in the hospital.

Similar to me, David hoped Robbie would survive and recover. However, he encouraged me to consider the possibility that Robbie's quality of life may not be the same even with his survival. He kept reminding me Robbie would always want a quality life, not live just to stay alive.

That same afternoon, David accompanied me to a funeral home, to help me make funeral plans in case Robbie died. The director explained the options, costs, and procedures. David and I studied the urns and selected a green and brown marble one we felt was appropriate, one Robbie would select for himself. Strangely, after this meeting, I felt a sense of comfort, and I did not at first understand why.

COMFORTING THOUGHTS

As I sat alone in my home later that same evening, I finally understood the reason for my unusual comfort. For thirty-six years, Robbie and I had wasted little time living *other than* lives. We did just the opposite. We had lived true to self, lives filled with abundant moments of shared joy and bliss. We lived the best lives we possibly could. We did much, accomplished much, and enjoyed and shared much. For all these unusual and wonderful moments, I felt deeply blessed, grateful.

I would be distraught if Robbie were to pass, I knew without question. I would miss him immensely, but I would always remember and treasure all the memories we shared together as we lived our lives to the fullest. My reflection on these memories brought with it a deep sense of inner comfort, inner peace.

GRADUAL SIGNS OF IMPROVEMENT

With a second dialysis treatment, Robbie's kidney scores improved. His neurologist informed me that the MRI of Robbie's brain showed his stroke had the likelihood of improvement with physical therapy, and his cognitive functions and speech should not be impaired.

On the fifth day of Robbie's recovery, his sedation was lessened. Finally, Robbie could hear me and nod yes and no responses with a breathing tube still inserted. Knowing he could hear me and comprehend what I was saying, I told him how much I loved him over the years, how much I valued him, and how much he enriched my life. "Can you hear me?" I frequently asked him, and he would nod in the affirmative.

His breathing was monitored hourly, and later in the week, his breathing tube was removed. He was now breathing on his own, and his other vitals were being monitored often and carefully, minute by minute.

The nurses and doctors seemed as happy and excited as I was with Robbie's gradual recovery. Soon, Robbie was speaking words and short sentences aloud, with some breathing difficulty. On Robbie's sixth day in intensive care, his surgeon informed me that Robbie might be released to the next level of care, the surgical/medical unit, if he continued to improve.

During his second week of recovery, Robbie started to eat solid foods, respond orally to the nurses and doctors, take medications, and have his blood counts taken daily. Although he developed pneumonia, this serious but typical post-operative condition was treated quickly and successfully.

Toward the end of the second week, Robbie asked for assistance in using the bathroom. In the last few days of his hospital care, he was given some physical therapy in moving in and out of bed and walking with assistance using a walker. At the end of the second week, he was discharged to the care of a physical therapy rehabilitation center.

PHYSICAL THERAPY

For the next two weeks, Robbie was given occupational and physical therapy, learning again how to walk with a walker at first and later without one, independently. His day-by-day body vitals were taken and recorded, and his progress continued. His breathing and energy levels also improved, but there was much work yet to complete. The surgeon and doctors informed us that it could take four to six months for Robbie to recover in full, if not longer.

MEETING NEW RESPONSIBILITIES

Throughout our long relationship, Robbie had been the strong and focused home manager and caregiver. He did all the household work. He made and changed the beds, did the wash, stacked and emptied the dishes, fed and walked the dog, completed the weekly shopping and evening cooking.

He bought household supplies, changed the filters, watered the plants, took the car for servicing, and did most of the inside cleaning. He packed the car when we traveled, cared for the pets. Now with Robbie in need of much time to recover, I was the one who had to meet these necessary obligations, and my retirement lifestyle changed overnight.

With well-meaning intentions, I began doing many of these tasks, but with much difficulty. Basically, in the beginning, I was overwhelmed. I had not completed these tasks before, and to complete many of these tasks, although it may sound like a rationalization, I lacked the necessary skills.

Overnight, I became consumed with many home-management questions. Where did Robbie keep the dishwater detergent, and when should I do the dishes? Do I feed the dog first or have my morning cup of coffee? I only have an hour before I leave to see Robbie. What really has to be done now, before I leave?

I quickly realized the amount of time and energy required to complete all the household work Robbie had been expending on his own over our long relationship, his personal efforts to make our home lives as comfortable and enjoyable as possible.

HOMECOMING

Robbie came home a month after experiencing his aortic aneurysm. He could walk independently around the house, but he still lacked energy and breathed with great difficulty. For the first two weeks home, both a nurse and a physical therapist visited twice weekly to take his vitals, check on his progress, and give him exercise workouts and follow-up assignments.

Once Robbie returned home, I cooked his meals, gave him his pills according to his schedule, and literally hovered over him, to be sure he did not fall, become ill again, or die in the night, one of my early fears. Every time he coughed, I jumped. I woke him many times while he was sleeping in the night, to be sure he was still breathing.

MORE SIGNS OF RECOVERY

In time, as the weeks and months passed, Robbie improved. At first, he could get up on his own from bed, go alone to the bathroom, bathe himself while sitting in his shower chair, stay up for a few hours after breakfast, before returning to bed for at least a two-hour nap.

Robbie received home therapy for two weeks, three times a week, and began to take short walks outside, around the driveway, and to the mailbox and back.

Often, I drove him downtown, and we would walk the town block. Later, we found a paved path in a nearby neighborhood, and we walked this route each afternoon. In time, Robbie's breathing improved as did his energy levels.

Within a few weeks, Robbie stopped sleeping during the daytime and began completing some small household tasks, like making his bed, loading and unloading the dishwasher, watering plants, feeding the dog, and going with me to the vet and groomer. By the end of his first month at home, Robbie was completing many of the household tasks he did prior to his surgery, including doing the laundry and shopping with me at the grocery store.

Robbie had kept his appointments with his doctors, and he had walked independently in and out of their offices. One of his first appointments was a post-operation follow-up with his surgeon.

REASSURANCE FROM THE SURGEON

After we walked into the office and answered some preliminary questions, I thanked the surgeon for all his team had done to keep Robbie alive.

"No, no," he responded. It was nothing he did or anyone else, he further elaborated. He was most fortunate, he qualified, to have the help of another surgeon who just happened to be in the hospital the morning of Robbie's surgery. Robbie's recovery was well beyond anything he had done, he continued. It was only with God's grace that Robbie had improved and was doing so well, he concluded. "Robbie's recovery is a miracle, no doubt about it."

A SYNCHRONISTIC AND MIRACULOUS MOMENT OF ONENESS

Robbie's emergency surgery and recovery were another series of fortuitous and synchronistic events, this time more miraculous in nature than previous ones.

At the time of Robbie's aortic rupture, I knew instinctively not to move Robbie's body when instructed to do so by the 911 person. It may have caused the blood to flow upward and drown Robbie instead of remaining primarily in his lower back area. How miraculous a skilled emergency medic was driving right by my home exit at the same time when I called for assistance. How unusual to have a group of caring and competent emergency staff and personnel all working together on the same evening of Robbie's need for emergency surgery. How miraculous to have another surgeon onsite late that same night to assist the assigned surgeon in the insertion of the graft and the successful completion of the serious operation. How miraculous Robbie survived the operation and the rigorous recovery process.

Robbie now takes his medicines on his own. He has started separately related neck therapy for torticollis. In the afternoons, he frequently reads or gardens. Often, after I ask him how to complete a chore, he comes to where I am standing and shows or directs me, as when I recently changed the filters in the ceiling vents. Robbie has finished his tenth month of home care and daily displays signs of continuous recovery.

MAKING PEACE WITH THE PRESENT MOMENT: ENJOYING SIMPLE PLEASURES, SIMPLE MOMENTS OF ONENESS

The coronavirus pandemic overlapped with Robbie's emergency surgery and recovery. Both occurred in March of 2020, restricting what we both could do, in Robbie's recovery and our everyday living conditions.

During May of each year, Robbie and I typically traveled north to spend summers in Maine. We decided to spend this summer of 2020 at our North Carolina home, to make Robbie's full recovery our priority. With the additional necessity to socially distance and stay safe, we also decided not to travel north at all this season, to "hunker down" at our primary home, until the virus was under control or a vaccine had been developed and effectively distributed.

Without question, I missed the many person-to-person direct social contacts and activities I had enjoyed so frequently in my past retirement life, such as dining out, meeting friends for drinks, flying and traveling, being in large crowds with other people, like when we went to plays, museums, concerts, movie theaters, and sports events. Like most people waiting for a vaccine, I have lived day by day under new health guidelines.

However, I do not consider myself an individual who has become less than, less active, or less capable by adhering to the current pandemic health guidelines. Instead, I have found many new ways of finding purpose and meaning in our daily if somewhat restricted lives, particularly in ways to nest positively at home, with greater time for further self-exploration.

In small but meaningful ways, I have discovered personal strategies for nurturing positive self-growth and satisfaction while, at the same time, living homebound. Essentially, I have learned under these new living conditions how best to engage daily in simple pleasures.

For many, my simple pleasures may sound boring, routine, dull, and flat. For me, however, I find much joy and satisfaction in the daily completion of these daily tasks. I find ways each day to make these simple and ordinary experiences extraordinarily purposeful and pleasurable.

For this moment, if somewhat out of necessity, I still find much purpose and pleasure in daily living somewhat housebound. I still stay open to the daily possibility of experiencing an increasing array of new simple pleasures, pandemically influenced or not, daily events that happen sometimes naturally, unexpectedly, and spontaneously.

EARLY MORNING WALKS WITH TRIPP

After Robbie and I wake and enjoy our morning coffee, we go for a long morning walk around our neighborhood with our dog, Tripp. Tripp is a strong and determined dog. Often, it appears as if he is taking us for a walk.

For a long time during his recovery, Robbie did not feel strong enough to walk Tripp independently. At present, however, Robbie is now able to place a leash on Tripp and control him as we walk different routes in our neighborhood.

During our morning walks, we have met many of our neighbors, many of them dog walkers themselves. We all stay as safe as possible by wearing marks or staying at least six feet apart. Our unexpected morning connections and conversations with our neighbors remain a continual and enjoyable simple daily pleasure.

Later in the morning, after Robbie and I have finished breakfast, we sometimes go for another morning walk. We walk up and down a series of hills leading to the Catawba River, and we follow the river into another section of our neighborhood before circling back to return home, walking up two more challenging hills before reaching our destination.

Later in the evening, I sometimes walk by myself three additional routes, two within nearby communities, and one to a major intersection and back.

FOREST BATHING

Walking is my daily exercise of choice. I intend to walk daily in life as long as I am physically able. Recently, particularly on weekends, I have started to walk in deeply wooded areas, like local botanical gardens or along and around pathways surrounding nearby lakes. I call these walks my time for "forest bathing," a term coined by Japanese researchers who have studied how walking in forests and woods enhance health and happiness.

As I walk in the woods, I enjoy the many therapeutic effects of "forest bathing." Surrounded by trees, I take in nature with all my senses, and later feel more physically and emotionally restored. I boost my overall sense of well-being. I appreciate the silence that often comes with being alone walking in the woods, itself an invitation to reflect and meditate.

LONG COUNTRY DRIVES AND SHOPPING

At least twice a week, Robbie and I drive to our four favorite grocery stores, wearing our masks and staying socially distant from others. The car drive to each store has become an opportunity for us to get out of the house and enjoy a leisurely drive in and throughout neighboring and country towns. Many times, we take a different route just to experience new and more pastural and peaceful scenery and settings.

While shopping, I go in one direction, and Robbie in another. During Robbie's early recovery, I worried Robbie might fall, accidentally get hurt, faint from exhaustion, or experience a relapse while on his own. I no longer do. Robbie is now well enough to shop independently, without my assistance.

Moreover, Robbie likes his independence as he shops, purchases items he specifically wants, like magazines and books, household items and supplies, to inside and outside plants and gardening tools.

We go to a variety of grocery stores for different and select items. One store we favor carries weekly fresh seafood from the North Carolina coast.

Another store we frequent carries a wider variety of fresh vegetables and imported nuts, and another our favorite homemade breads.

Although one store is a fifteen-mile drive, we enjoy the drive and find our visits well-worth our efforts. This particular store is one of those shopping venues with an inventory of just about anything any shopper may ever need, an unusual all-in-one kind of store.

Years ago, when I was much younger, I remember observing some retirees who lived next door to one of my relatives. When I visited this relative, I noticed her retired neighbors often left their home and returned with bags of groceries. I remember thinking what boring, routine lives they must live, spending so much time, it appeared, simply shopping. Today, I feel just the opposite. For many, retired or not, the simple pleasure of shopping can be an enjoyable, creative, and fulfilling adventure.

PREPARING SUNDAY BRUNCHES

We both enjoy cooking and dining out, but in this age of the coronavirus and restaurant restrictions, Robbie has started a new tradition for us—Sunday brunch at home. Last Sunday, he prepared a feast: scrambled eggs, sliced cheese, fresh tomatoes, turkey bacon, hash browns, pancakes with homemade syrup, and fresh fruit. He seems to enjoy our Sunday brunch at home ritual, and I view the event as another strong indicator of his continuing recovery.

PLAYING MUSIC

Since I first met Robbie in 1984, he has possessed a love for music of all kinds but particularly current popular culture music. He has an extensive CD collection and library. Often, he plays different selections at different times of the day, many I have heard before, many that I have not, soothing sounds in these uncertain times.

This past Sunday, for example, before and after our brunch, he played a number of CDs we had purchased during our travels in Montreal, from

Thomas Orton's *Portraits* to Vangelis's *1492*, followed by *Enigma, Era*, and Emma Shapplin's *Carmine Meo*.

Robbie knows I particularly enjoy listening to Gregorian chants. During one of our recent Sunday brunches, he played "Saint Benedict," the Gregorian chant of Fontgombault, followed by "Chant" by the Benedictine Monks of Santo Domingo De Silos.

Before dinner recently, Robbie played CDs with a Latin theme, including *Portuondo*, by Omara to Kim Kuzma's *Acustico* as we enjoyed a glass of a new Spanish wine we found while recently shopping.

Because Robbie is more knowledgeable than I about each CD played, from the selection to the artist and theme of the song, I ask him numerous questions and he answers and I learn, as I listen to both him and the soothing music.

GARDENING

Over the past three years of residing in our new home, Robbie has installed and maintained a large garden along the entrance and back of our home. He has bought and planted a variety of trees, shrubs, and plants; created gravel pathways and sitting areas among them; installed bird feeders; and purchases when we shop an array of garden items, from gloves and birdseed to mulch and more plants.

ONLINE SHOPPING

We both enjoy shopping and ordering any number of items online, but in this age of recommended social distancing, washing hands, and wearing masks, shopping online has become safe, convenient, fun, and efficient. We also do not need to drive long distances. Many prices are typically lower than in stores. Further, online shopping often offers a wider selection of products than many physical stores. Most of all, we both enjoy the online shopping experience.

Recently after watching the televised documentary "As I See It," we shopped online for two books published by Pete Souza, the official While House photographer during the Obama administration: *Obama: An Intimate Portrait*, and *Shade: A Tale of Two Presidents*.

DOCTOR APPOINTMENTS

At first, I thought the follow-up appointments with Robbie's doctors would be obligatory, time-consuming, burdensome, inconvenient, even unsafe in the age of the coronavirus. Surprisingly, none of these meetings has been anything but pleasant and informative.

I have learned much from these visits, and primarily by asking each doctor and specialist necessary questions, gaining in the process new knowledge. Equally important, I know Robbie is receiving exceptional medical care from his team of doctors and health care personnel.

From Robbie's cardiologist, I recently learned the importance of an annual test, an ultrasound of his unblocked carotid artery and another of the left side of his abdomen, to measure the size of another but less serious aneurysm in his iliac artery. From his neurologist, I learned that Robbie's neck neuropathy is not caused by his previous 100% blocked carotid artery. Instead, Robbie has torticollis, a painfully twisted and tilted neck condition involving the muscles of the neck. Robbie's neurologist has further recommended Robbie have botulinum toxin injections every three months to help relieve the muscle pain.

Robbie's physical therapists have recommended Robbie receive neck massages regularly after the injection treatment. From Robbie's new physical therapist, I have learned about the many benefits of neck therapy for neck pain.

Robbie's primary care doctor has completed a number of necessary follow-up procedures, including blood work since Robbie's discharge from his hospital care. She has explained to us how Robbie's red blood count and blood pressure have improved since his aneurysm, and informed us that Robbie's kidney function has remained stable.

COMPLETING HOME PROJECTS

Once Robbie returned home, we discovered a need to rearrange the furniture, to make his movement around the home both safe and convenient. Because Robbie lived primarily downstairs, I moved our larger television from my den upstairs to the living room downstairs. Then, I moved Robbie's lift chair from the corner of the room toward the center, so he could watch the screen more easily, without unnecessarily twisting his head.

Three months into Robbie' recovery, I suggested to him we should rearrange the whole downstairs sometime, to give our living space more flow and ease. I did not like sitting somewhat in back of Robbie while we watched the evening news together. Nor was it comfortable to sit on the sofa on the side of the wall facing Robbie and, at the same time, watch television.

Neither of us physically was able to move anymore by ourselves our large pieces of furniture. We mutually decided we would need to hire the people we used regularly for completing these kinds of household tasks.

One following Saturday morning, Robbie shared with me a blueprint he had drawn. In the plan, he had placed our living room furniture in a new and more open floor arrangement, with the heavy pieces of our furniture all on the other side of the room. Immediately, I liked the new furniture placement design and wondered why we had not placed the furniture in this arrangement earlier.

I shared with Robbie my intent to call our handyman, to come help us move the heavy pieces of furniture as soon as he could. I spent much of the rest of the day upstairs doing desk work, until I decided to go downstairs and make a late afternoon cup of coffee. As I did, I was momentarily shocked.

Robbie had rearranged by himself most of the living room furniture, in accordance to his recent blueprint. He had found an old carpet in the garage, and used it to pull the furniture from one side of the room to the other, and all on his own, and without doing any damage to his abdominal incision that was still in the healing stages.

Robbie continues to find new and creative ways of decorating our home. He has purchased numerous plants for our indoor solarium. He has bought hand-carved local statuary for the patio, and a moss bird cage to place near the bird feeder in our outdoor garden. Each time we go shopping, he buys a different plant to place somewhere inside our home, in front of the dining room window, in the bathrooms, or near the window in his bedroom overlooking our patio.

MAKING GREATER USE OF MY AGING BRAIN

As I age at home, I make conscious efforts to remain flexible and adaptable, to be and become more resilient and capable. Even as I age, I know my brain has the capacity to grow new brain cells. As Cohen states:

> *New dendrites, new synapses and even new neurons continue to be cre-ated—especially when the older adult is actively engaged in activities that are physically and mentally stimulating.*[36]

In particular, I make greater use of my aging brain by remaining a lifelong learner. As I continue to read, listen, view, and respond to events in life, I continue to use and develop my inquiring mind. I enjoy remaining curious. I enjoy stretching my thinking as I gain new ideas and information.

STAYING CONNECTED

Before the pandemic, Robbie and I participated in local politics, commu-nity meetings, local events, and causes. We attended many local functions, museums, libraries, and lectures. Through our participation in and support of these community activities, we remained socially connected. We not only pursued new interests, but we expanded our social connection and formed many new friendships.

Through our past and active social participation, we have developed a small but strong group of meaningful friends, many of them much younger than we are, a core of close friends on whom we can continuously rely for friendship and support. We learn from one another, support one another, and enjoy the company of each other.

Our core group of friends enrich our lives on many levels. Robbie and I both have few family connections. Therefore, in many ways, our friends have become our family, and we are all right with this situation, for our friends help keep us healthy, happy, and connected.

Some of our friends are now scattered across the country, but most live in Florida, North Carolina, and Maine. While our core group is small, we value the quality of our friendships over the quantity of friends. In this age of the coronavirus and social distancing, we stay in touch with our friends through telephone calls, text messages, Facebook, and email messages.

Socially, as I age homebound, I no longer search to become the center of things. I no longer need the external validation from others to justify my self-worth. Nevertheless, I still need a core group of people in my life to value, love, and support, and especially to share special events in my life as they occur.

ENGAGING IN DEEP CONVERSATIONS

While social distancing, Robbie and I have started the practice of engaging in more conversations with one another, deeper and more serious conversations. We turn off the television and music, shut down our computers, silence our cell phones, and just participate together in longer, deeper, and sometimes more intimate conversations, some influenced of late by Robbie's near-death experience.

We both feel blessed to be both alive, still together, with more time to share, more time to care for one another. We both want to take advantage of the present moment by experiencing more quality time together, more moments of joy and bliss.

In our past conversations, we have talked intensely about politics, different books we have read and are reading, and our individual daily activities and projects. Slowly, however, we now have moved into deeper conversations about issues we privately have been keeping to ourselves. We both seem now more content to share with one another what matters most to each of us at this stage of our lives.

The beginning of our more serious conversations started recently when we revised and updated our wills with our lawyer. Before we did, we had a serious discussion with our lawyer about how best to meet our future legacy desires, and with necessary and protective procedures.

We further discussed the necessary and additional document preparation we desired, such as financial power of attorney, health care power of attorney, and the necessary paperwork to complete our individual requests for natural deaths. Later, alone in our home, we continued to engage in more intimate conversation, sharing with each other some of our hidden feelings.

I began by sharing with Robbie my fears of taking appropriate and adequate care of him during his recovery, my inner feelings of vulnerability if I did not do an adequate job, how I worried when he first came home, that he might die unexpectedly in the night.

After my confession, Robbie asked me specifically for more detail about what happened the night of his aneurysm, how I found him, what happened in the emergency room and during the operation, for details I was reluctant to share with him earlier in his recovery, afraid I might unintentionally upset him, lower his morale, cause an unnecessary setback.

Robbie later shared with me his dreams of a full recovery, to do things on his own without relying on other people, to be able to drive again. I told him that also was my goal, to get him healthy and independent, so we can resume our lives as in past years, with greater independence and freedom.

PRACTICING GRATEFULNESS

As we stay more homebound than ever before, I have developed a new approach to journal writing. I have started the practice of keeping a gratitude journal, my preferred way of expressing my thankful appreciation for daily blessings, both inside myself and outside, blessings sometimes larger than myself.

In my gratitude journal, I keep a short summary of my daily blessings, a record of those grateful events that occurred each day. In my gratitude journal, I have divided each page within three columns, and I record my daily blessing comments wherever they seem to fit best. I have labeled my three columns as follows: (1) Daily Moments of Happiness, (2) Simple Pleasures Experienced, and (3) People for Whom I Feel Grateful and Why.

Today, for example, in my first column, Daily Moments of Happiness, I wrote, "unexpected gift." In the second column, Simple Pleasures Received, I wrote "basket of heirloom tomatoes." In the third column, People for Whom I feel Grateful and Why, I recorded, "neighbor, for helping me recall a treasured memory of my childhood days."

This particular moment of gratitude occurred this morning after a neighbor brought Robbie and me an unexpected gift, a basket of heirloom purple Cherokee tomatoes, grown by herself in her summer garden. After my neighbor left, I toasted a piece of twenty-grain bread, spread it with light mayonnaise, sliced two pieces of tomato and placed them on top, drizzled the tomatoes with olive oil and sprinkled them with salt and pepper.

As I enjoyed eating my tomato sandwich, many powerful and past moments of gratitude poured forth, and surprisingly, from many years ago, from my early childhood days. I was grateful as a child for my secure life on a farm, where my father grew our vegetables in his garden. I was grateful for an abundance of delicious and sweet-tasting fresh tomatoes, often fetched directly from our garden before eating. I was grateful for the opportunity to have shared love and communion with my mother, father, and siblings as we ate our tomato sandwiches, usually at lunchtime. I was grateful for this special memory, a snapshot of my childhood life growing up on a farm, some seventy years ago.

In my recalling and recording of my moments of gratitude, I give thanks for all the favors I daily receive. I am especially appreciative of the many contributions of others to my well-being, and I am thankful for all the simple pleasures as they occur daily in my life. As I record and compile my moments of gratitude in my journal, I have noticed I often become more hopeful, optimistic, happy, and content, a few of my many personal benefits of practicing and expressing gratefulness.

Consequently, this coronavirus has not caused us to grow old or approach our lives in needless and negative ways. Rather than view our now socially restrictive lifestyles as inconvenient and interrupted, we both have individually found, instead, a myriad of ways to let our simple pleasures unfold. Through our opportunities to engage in these daily simple pleasures, I have learned my tenth major lesson in retirement, make peace in the present moment.

MAKE PEACE WITH THE PRESENT MOMENT: BEING ONE WITH SELF, ONE WITH LIFE

With the luxury of more time to reflect in this age of the coronavirus, to think about and determine what now seems of most significance, I feel I am most at peace in the present moment when I am living more fully one with self, one with life. My full acceptance of my authenticity, however, did not happen until after our society increased its acceptance of many more recent advancements in the gay rights movement.

The Gay Rights Movement has made many significant advancements since I first retired, in 2001, with the following among the most important. In 2009, President Obama signed the Matthew Shepherd and James Byrd Jr.

Hate Crimes Prevention Act, expanding federal law to include protection to individuals, regardless of sexual orientation, from violent crimes.

In 2016, the US military lifted its ban on transgender people serving openly. Just recently, on June 15, 2020, the Supreme Court ruled that the Civil Rights Act of 1964, which prohibited sex discrimination, also applied to discrimination based on sexual orientation and gender identity. Until this decision, workplace discrimination against lesbian, gay, bisexual, transgender, and questioning (LGBTQ) individuals was legal.

Perhaps the most powerful gay rights advancement occurred in 2015, when the Supreme Court ruled against Section 3 of the Defense of Marriage Act (DOMA), which allowed the government to deny federal benefits to married same-sex couples. Later in the same year, the Supreme Court ruled that states cannot ban same-sex marriages, thus making gay marriage legal throughout our country.

SOCIETAL SUPPORT FOR MARRIAGE EQUALITY

At least six in ten Americans have supported gay marriage in almost every Gallop Poll reading since the 2015 Supreme Court decision to legalize it, making gay marriage legal in all fifty states, just eleven years after Massachusetts became the first state to legalize gay marriage.

On October 21, 2020, the Pope called for civil union laws for same-sex couples, a major departure from past Vatican doctrine. On the same day, the Eleventh American Values Survey conducted by the Pew Research Center, noted the highest approval of same-sex marriage, 70%.

Approval across the political divide, with religiously unaffiliated Americans as the most supportive, 90% endorsed same-sex marriage. Today, more mainstream Americans have a greater acceptance of same-sex couples than ever before in history. Many heterosexuals today also view same-sex members of our society as more like them than different.

I never thought I would live long enough to see the day the Supreme Court recognized that the Constitution guarantees marriage equality, offering same-sex couples the dignity of marriage. As President Obama said in his speech on June 26, 2015, "All Americans are entitled to the equal protection of the law. All people should be treated equally, regardless of who they are or who they love."

Now a few years later, I believe the passages of all these acts has now made it easier for me to stay out and open in mainstream America. The acceptance of gay marriage should give us all hope that many of the issues in society with which we grapple, and often painfully, can bring with them real societal change. As President Obama further reminded us in his speech on June 26, 2015, a shift in hearts and minds is possible. "We are one people, stronger together than alone."

OUR MARRIAGE

On September 6, 2013, after living for twenty-nine years as life partners, Robbie and I legally married in our beautiful summer town of Ogunquit, Maine. Our closest friends often have asked why we decided to marry, reminding us that we have lived together as life partners for twenty-nine years. I typically respond with these reasons: Marriage equality, full self-acceptance, and love, of self and others.

MARRIAGE EQUALITY

Our legal marriage brought with it the acknowledgment of responsibilities we had been meeting for years, along with the benefits of our mutually shared love and companionship. Now that we are legally married, we are viewed as more alike than different from other married couples, gay or straight.

We love each other unconditionally. Similar to heterosexual couples, we have our pets, projects, interests, obligations, and challenges. We want the best life possible. We practice discipline and take responsibility. We want to leave the world a better place. We want a stable and genuine relationship in which we continue to share and care, to work together, to learn, create, contribute, and grow.

Most importantly, only after Robbie and I married did I fully accept myself as a gay and married man equal to other married individuals, gay or straight, no longer with a further need to censor or justify my true identity. With these feelings of equality, I finally felt freer and prouder. I was now living in a country in which I could continue to plan my own destiny, develop a stronger belief in myself, remain who I genuinely was.

FULL SELF-ACCEPTANCE

When I retired in 2001, I came out to friends, family, and society, but only partially, not fully. Over many of my past twenty years in retirement, I have remained only as honest and open about my gay identity as I thought necessary, depending on my evaluation of the situation in which I found myself.

In other words, I was only cautiously and partially out. I placed my own judgments and evaluations of circumstances into action first, before determining to be "out" or "not out" in self-selected situations. In short, I had admitted my gay identity to myself and a few other people, but I had not fully claimed my gay identity, without efforts to first self-censure.

Since our marriage, however, I have become fully out, fully accepting of myself as a gay and married man. While I came out at the time of my retirement, I often shared my gay self with others as the situation required. Sometimes, I was out, sometimes I was not, depending on the situation. Once married, however, I became fully out, regardless of the circumstances.

Being fully out did not mean I had no boundaries, or flaunted being gay. Being fully out meant I was finally comfortable enough to acknowledge and claim my gay identity as situations required, and without hesitation or reluctance.

To illustrate, Robbie and I have made many trips by car from our Maine home to Montreal. Coming and going in and out of each country at the border, we typically are asked by the attendant about our relationship. Before our marriage, I would always say "friends." Since our marriage, I now say "married," and without any discomfort or reluctance, without any guilt or shame.

This self-acceptance was important. I realized if other individuals in our society could not understand nor accept my gay identity, it was their problem, not mine. As a gay man, out and now married, I was not willing any longer to accept unnecessary rejection.

Since our marriage, I now follow my passions and desires in retirement with greater ease and authenticity. I have learned how to allow new and more intimate and honest relationships to develop, to allow true acceptance and love in my life, of self and others.

I now claim fully my most basic self, my gay identity, by living fully out as a gay and married man. I find the act of meshing who I genuinely am with all that I do a natural, easy, and self-rewarding experience.

HE'S MY HUSBAND

After Robbie and I were married, a good friend and her husband introduced Robbie and me to another heterosexual couple, stating in her everyday voice, "This is Bill and his husband, Robbie."

I remember this incident vividly, because it was the first time anyone introduced Robbie as my husband. Although we were legally married, I had not thought of ourselves as husband and husband in our same-sex marriage. That kind of terminology was reserved for straight people, I first thought. As a result, I felt embarrassed and somewhat artificial, as if I were trying to impose heterosexual norms on my gay marriage.

Then, a few days later, I realized my straight friend's intent. Like straight couples, the Constitution now guarantees gay married couples marriage equality. If, as a gay and married man, I am equal to heterosexuals in marriage, then surely the love Robbie and I have committed to each other also must be equal. Just as President Obama stated in his second inaugural address, "If we are truly created equal, then surely the love we commit to one another must be equal as well."

Gradually, over the past seven years of our marriage, I have called Robbie my husband with increased acceptance and comfort, often to be more honest and open but also direct, practical, and efficient.

For example, when Robbie experienced his recent aneurysm, I called 911, and immediately our home became filled with men and women from two rescue squads and police departments. While one medic was resuscitating Robbie, another asked me a series of questions, the first being the nature of our relationship. I informed the person that Robbie and I were married, that he was my husband.

As I made this statement, I noticed a policeman standing in the back of the living room, near the entrance door. He turned his head upward, rolled his eyes, coughed lightly, shifted his weight from one foot to another before folding his arms firmly in front of his chest.

He was obviously uncomfortable with my gay identity and my declaration of it, but most of the other people present did not appear to be. The person asking questions quickly continued. Had we been doing any drugs? Had Robbie taken any new medications?

Similarly, when Robbie was recovering from his recent aneurysm, we were asked repeatedly by various health care personnel to identify our relationship. My standard reply has become "He's my husband." Within the past few months, I have used this form of identification so frequently, I no longer feel awkward or embarrassed by this admission. Instead, I now feel more natural and sincere, more authentic.

I have allowed my relationships with others to be based on self-honesty and respect through my identification as a gay and married man. I feel more confident, proud. I recognize the transformative power in my full self-acceptance. I am now allowing for more intimate and open relationships with others, who more readily accept that love is love.

Regardless of all our differences, we are as a nation all one people, stronger together than we ever could be alone. Through its increased acceptance of gay marriage, our country has come to realize that love is love. Through my acceptance of myself fully as a gay, out, and married man, I have increased my self-love, as well as my love of others.

LOVE OF SELF, LOVE OF OTHERS

In *Man's Search for Meaning,* Victor Frankl records his personal story of finding a reason to live after being captured and placed in a Nazi concentration camp during World War II. An Austrian psychiatrist, Dr. Frankel has written about the importance of having a purpose in life regardless of the circumstances.

Frankl underscores this important point: Everything can be taken from a person but one thing: the ability to choose one's attitude in any given set of circumstances. Thus, Dr. Frankl reminds us that mankind is driven by a strong desire to find meaning and purpose in life.

A further premise Dr. Frankl underscores is that meaning in everyday life reveals itself in the capacity to love:

Love is the ultimate and the highest goal to which man can aspire... The salvation of man is through love and in love. I understand how a man who has nothing left in this world still may know bliss, be it only for a moment, in the contemplation of his beloved.[37]

Love was what Robbie's and my long relationship has been all about, love of self, each other, and those loving individuals in our lives. For thirty-six years, we have shared, and continue to share, a life of bliss. For the past twenty years in my retirement, Robbie has been my retirement companion and guide. His affirming love has become indispensable to my happiness.

MY TENTH LESSON LEARNED IN RETIREMENT: MAKE PEACE WITH THE PRESENT MOMENT

Nearly twenty years after I retired, I learned my tenth major lesson in retirement, the significance of finding peace in the present moment regardless of the circumstances, whether they be life-threatening moments, or moments when we are temporarily inconvenienced, or powerful self-actualizing moments when we decide to become fully our individual authentic selves.

I have finally mastered the tenth lesson in my retirement. I now feel the powerful emotions of societal acceptance that comes with marriage equality. I am now fully out and support the advancements of the gay rights movement. I am legally married, with deeper feelings of love and acceptance, of self and others. Daily, I am living one with self, one with life.

A GOLDEN MOMENT OF ONENESS

On September 6, 2020, Robbie and I celebrated our thirty-sixth anniversary as life partners and our seventh year of marriage. The date was significant, for it was also Robbie's sixth month of recovery from his recent emergency aneurysm.

We ordered a dinner to be delivered from one of our local and favorite restaurants. Our friend, David, had sent us earlier two bottles of Schramsburg Blanc De Blanc, our favorite champagne, to celebrate these occasions. I remember well this special moment of oneness, as if it were happening now, in the present moment.

As we move about our spacious home in anticipation of the evening, we accidentally keep bumping into each other. Robbie jokingly reminds me how we often move in two different directions, and thus occasionally collide. Robbie now moves his head more often to the left, because of his neck muscle spasms, and I slant my body to the right, from years of walking and pronating my feet and body in this direction.

In recent years, we have become aware of the passage of time and the preciousness of each moment remaining in our individual lives. As we go about the completion of our daily tasks and activities, we have developed the habit of toasting one another with the expression "for this moment," a simple but conscious effort to remain at peace and anchored in the present.

"For this moment," Robbie said, as he lifts his glass and makes a toast.

Suddenly, I remember a wonderful quote I read that morning about being present and at peace. I leave Robbie momentarily and go to my office upstairs to locate the source. On my return, I read to him the following paragraph from Eckhart Tolle's *A New Earth: Awakening to Your Life's Purpose*:

How to be at peace now? By making peace with the present moment. The present moment is the field on which the game of life happens. It cannot be anywhere else. Once you have made peace with the present moment, see what happens, what you can do and choose to do, or rather, what life does through you. There are three words that convey the secret of the art of living, the secret of all success and happiness: One with life. Being one with life is being one with the Now. You then realize you do not live your life, but life lives you. Life is the dancer, and you are the dance.[38]

Robbie listens carefully. "One with life, one with the present moment," he repeats, as he cautiously lifts himself out of his lift chair and walks carefully to his nearby computer table.

Robbie had been playing computer music in the background most of the day, from his extensive collection. Mika begins singing "We Are Golden," and Robbie turns up the volume.

We are not who you think we are,
We are golden, we are golden.
We are not who you think we are
We are golden, we are golden.

Robbie and I start singing along, at first softly and slowly:

We are golden, we are golden.

Then Robbie slowly begins to dance, moving his body carefully and awkwardly, two steps to the left, two steps to the right.

I jump up from the sofa to support him, and as I do, I likewise begin to dance, moving my body in my own strange way, enjoying the moment, enjoying being blissful.

Robbie raises his hands in the air and continues to dance more confidently, and as he navigates a turn, he loudly sang: *We are not who you think we are. We are golden, we are golden.*

I likewise continue to dance and sing: *We are golden, we are golden.*

"For this moment, we are the dance," Robbie said, and then adds, "Life really doesn't get much better than this."

I smile and nod in agreement.

CONCLUSION:
CONTENTMENT AND INTEGRATION
Completing the Circle of Retirement

For over two decades, I have lived a quality life in retirement, a life with numerous options and choices, an ever-changing and transformative life. While the practice of staying true to self did require much effort at times, I typically viewed this challenge not so much as work but as an opportunity to live a more conscious and meaningful life.

In my Freedom and Adventure stage of retirement, I began a whole new life, one with a strong focus on living and remaining true to self. Free from past constraints, I developed a new and powerful attitude, "the world is mine to explore."

Inspired and reenergized, I stayed true to self as I discovered daily new ways of living. I engaged in a new lifestyle within new communities. I met and made new friends. I reached a level of financial freedom I had not previously attained. I found purpose and pleasure in everyday life, primarily by pursuing those interests and activities of most enjoyment and meaning.

Ten years later, when I began my Reflection and Review stage of aging, I assumed a much different focus in retirement, one filled with deep and reflective moments of increased inner contemplation. I began to evolve, to grow and develop into a more transcendent self, as I searched for new ways of finding deeper purpose and meaning, to serve a greater good. I shifted my values as I engaged in new behaviors, many spiritual in nature.

As I reviewed my life in retirement, I resolved and met new obligations. At the same time, I explored new opportunities. By becoming more mindfully aware and present, I experienced remarkable feelings of oneness, with self and with life, new and higher levels of consciousness. With the use of these new levels of awareness, I discovered new and powerful ways of making peace with the present moment.

Essentially, in both my second and third developmental stages of aging, I met the two basic premises set forth at the beginning of this book. Because of my efforts to remain aligned with my authentic self in retirement, I have experienced many intense and elevated feelings of joy, happiness, and fulfillment, memorable moments of connectedness and oneness. I have lived a life in retirement unspoiled by worry or regret.

Moreover, my awareness of my developmental stages of aging has assisted me in the finding of new and different opportunities to continuously learn and grow, to transcend and transform myself, to find deeper purpose and meaning in my remaining years. Twenty years after retiring, I continue to live some of the best years, if not my best years.

A HEART STILL SINGING, A SOUL STILL SOARING

Often, especially when I least expect them, memories of the major lessons I have learned in retirement suddenly popped into my consciousness, still singing, still soaring. These pleasant intrusions serve as a reminder my retirement journey is not over. I still may have a few years ahead, a fair shot for a longer life, with time to complete unfinished projects and begin new ones. I still may have some remaining time to enjoy new and powerful moments of connectedness and oneness.

A NEW STAGE OF DEVELOPMENTAL AGING

Now, nearly eighty-three, I am entering my fourth stage of developmental aging in my second half of life. I identify this stage, most likely my last, by how it appears to be unfolding and how it presently feels. It is a stage I identify as Contentment and Integration.

CONTENTMENT

My feelings of contentment have never been as pronounced as at present. I am experiencing strong feelings of self- acceptance, satisfaction, and peacefulness while basically living somewhat confined at home, somewhat housebound as the coronavirus pandemic continues to rage in the outside world.

I am content, nevertheless, with my present and somewhat restricted life, knowing eventually the world will return to a life of more normalcy. However, for now, for this moment, I am enjoying being relegated to home, with more time and opportunities for Robbie and me to engage further in our daily and simple pleasures.

Robbie tends to his garden outside, his inside solarium, and his many other home-based projects, like his recent landscape renovation of holly shrubs in the front of our home and the planting of two crepe myrtle trees on the side entrance.

I find great pleasure in witnessing and sharing with him his passions as we now spend more time nesting and anchoring. However, while we both are anchoring more, we are not necessarily simplifying our lives more.

Recently, I shared with Robbie my growing desire to simplify my life, how just discussing the idea of getting down one day to one home, with less possessions, less stuff, appeals to me. He smiled and quickly replied, "Well, you better find someone else to move in with you."

While we agree to disagree, we both concur that for now it is important for us to keep our Maine condo, and for as long as we can comfortably travel back and forth. My roots to New England are extremely strong and, most likely, I would have serious regrets if we ever sold our home in "Paradise North."

Further, Robbie reminds me how extremely hot the weather can become in North Carolina during the summer months, and how life at our Maine condo during this time of year is a welcomed reprieve. For now, for this moment, we feel content, peaceful and happy as we continue to anchor and age in one place.

INTEGRATION

My new and satisfying sense of contentment, however, does not mean that I am willing to spend my remaining years becoming a stereotype of a person "over the hill." As I age, I have no desire nor intentions to withdraw from life, to isolate myself from others. Rather, in my remaining years, I want to continue to grow and learn. I want to integrate and sustain, even enlarge, my involvement with those interests, activities, and people of most meaning to me. I want to continue to matter in life.

INTEGRATION AND MATTERING

By mattering, I am not referring to achieving more tasks just for the sake of accomplishment itself. Nor am I referring to the acquisition of more and seemingly impressive possessions. I want to matter by making great use of my inner-push as I age, that force and fuel inside that motivates my desires and actions. I want to matter by participating as fully as I may desire at any given moment, in my life and the life around me. I want to matter by staying current, active, and involved, and in my own self-chosen ways.

INTEGRATING OLD EXPERIENCES

For as long as possible, I want to continue to enjoy and engage in enjoyable and meaningful activities. I treasure my continued shared life of bliss with Robbie. I exercise daily, take care of my health, and remain independent. I find productive ways to learn. I read widely and stay well-informed and engaged in current events. I expand my thoughts and improve my thinking skills and abilities. I stay connected to those people of most meaning to me. I find deeply meaningful my recent cultivation of a more spiritual life. I continue, and plan to continue, living my life with vitality and purpose.

INTEGRATING NEW EXPERIENCES

I understand there are no guarantees for any of us at any stage of life. Adverse situations can happen and at any time, from unexpected accidents, profound loss, to debilitating illnesses. Nevertheless, I intend to integrate, with a positive outlook and much determination, all my new experiences as explorations themselves in retirement. Whatever they may be, these new experiences have the potential to guide me to an older self capable of living with integrity and authenticity, with new purpose and deeper meaning, with contentment and integration, with wholeness and completion, what Erikson and Erikson call generativity.[39]

THE CIRCLE OF LIFE

In many ways, the completion of the circle of my retirement is analogous to the possibilities often implied within the completion of the circle of life, often described as uroboros.

UROBOROS

Since ancient times, uroboros has been depicted as a snake or serpent forming a perfect circle by eating its tail, a symbol of our lives from beginning to end. The uroboros also is a symbol of birth and continued growth, of wholeness and infinity.

Further, the uroboros has been said to symbolize one who is authentic, and thus constitutes the secret of prima materia: The formless root of matter within each of us from which all things emerge, the authentic self, that powerful source within us that helps us transform ourselves and thus become more conscious, more awakened and integrated.[40]

PRIMA MATERIA

Thus, prima materia can be interpreted as our authentic and natural self, our true self. Rather than define our worlds by the use of form alone, by outside things we can objectify and see, the symbolic use of uroboros becomes more of a reflection of what we cannot see but what we often feel inside, our individual and formless authentic self.

COMPLETING MY CIRCLE OF RETIREMENT

Like uroboros and the circle of life, I anticipate new opportunities for further growth and transformations. Hopefully, I also will complete the circle of my retirement in a fashion similar to the circle of life as described by Thomas Moore:

> My end is my beginning. The secret to life lies in the image the alchemists and Hermeticists frequently used: The snake formed in a beautiful circle; its mouth open to receive its tail. The beginning is always present, as is every moment between then and now, both as a memory and as a present element in the construction of self.[41]

In my remaining years, I will construct and integrate many different and inner dimensions, from the emotional and psychological to the physical, mental, and spiritual. Within this construction and integration, I will honor and make central the present element, the core of my being, my authentic self—my own prima materia--my formless root of all matter within.

I will continue to live one with self, one with life, with my heart frequently singing and my soul forever soaring. In and throughout my retirement, as with other major transitions I have experienced and mastered over time in life, I have found no better way to be and journey.

REFERENCES

1   Cohen, Gene D. *The Mature Mind: The Positive Power of the Aging Brain*. New York: Basic Books, 2005, xvii-xix.

2   Moore, Thomas. *Care of the Soul: A Guide for Cultivating Depth and Sacredness in Everyday Life*. New York: Harper Collins, 1992, 53-177.

3   McGraw, Phillip C. *Self-Matters: Creating Yourself from the Inside Out*. New York: Simon and Schuster, 2001, 30.

4   Stewart, Chuck. *Documents of the LGBT Movement: Eyewitness to History*. Santa Barbara, California: ABC CLIO, 2018, 96-129.

5   Moore, Thomas. *Care of the Soul*, 127.

6   Peck, M. Scott. *The Road Less Travelled: A New Psychology of Love, Traditional Values and Spiritual Growth*. New York: Simon and Schuster, 1976, 16-159.

7   Ibid, 159.

8   Schlossberg, Nancy. *Retire Smart, Retire Happy: Finding Your True Path in Life*. Washington DC: American Psychological Association, 2005, 99-100.

9   Schlossberg, Nancy. *Revitalizing Retirement: Reshaping Your Identity, Relationships, and Purpose*. Washington DC: American Psychological Association, 2009, 149.

10 Cameron, Julia. *The Artist's Way: A Spiritual Path to Higher Creating*. Jeremy Tarcher/Putnam, 1992, 20-21.

11 O'Mara, Shane. *In Praise of Walking: A New Scientific Exploration*. New York: Norton Press, 2020, 6-28.

12 Schlossberg, Nancy. *Retire Smart, Retire Happy*, 103.

13 Tolle, Eckhart. *A New Earth: Awakening to Your Life's Purpose*. New York: Penguin Group, 2005, 81.

14 Tornstam, L. "Gerotranscendence: The Contemplative Dimension of Aging." *Journal of* Aging Studies. 11. 2, (1997): 143-154.

15 Hopcke, Robert A. *There Are No Accidents: Synchronicity and the Stories of Our Lives*. New York: Riverhead Books, 1997, 172.

16 Jung, C. G. "Synchronicity: An Acausal Connecting Principle." *The Collected Works of C. G. Jung*. Princeton: Princeton University Press, (1960), 441.

17 Hopcke, Robert H. *There Are No Accidents*, 6.

18 Ibid, 3.

19 Mackey, Chris. *Synchronicity: Empower Your Life with the Gift of Coincidence*. London: Watkins Press, 2015, 2.

20 Ibid, 7-202.

21 Hopcke, Robert H. *There are No Accidents*, 46-47.

22 Ibid, 183.

23 Csikszentmihalyi, Mihaly. *Flow: The Psychology of Optimal Experience*. Cambridge, UK: Cambridge University Press, 1998.

24 Nelson-Isaacs, Sky. *Living in Flow: The Science of Synchronicity and How Your Choices Shape Your World*. Berkeley, California: North American Press, 2019, 7-47.

25 Weil, Andrew. *Healthy Aging: A Lifelong Guide to Your Physical and Spiritual Well-Being*. New York: New York: Alfred A. Knopf, 2005, 5.

26 Cohen, Gene D. *The Mature Mind*, 23.

27 McNeeley, D. A. *Becoming: An Introduction to Jung's Concept of Individuation*. Carmel California: Fisher King Press, 2010, 38-43.

28 Schmidt, M. A. "Individuation: Finding Oneself in Analysis-Taking Risk and Making Sacrifices." *The Journal of Analytical Psychology*, Vol 50, 5, (2005): 96-616.

29 Bishop, S. R. et al. "Mindfulness: A Proposed Operational Definition." *Clinical Psychology*: 11, 2, (2004): 232-234.

30 Siegal, Daniel J. *Aware: The Science and Practice of Presence*. New York: Penguin Random House LLC, 2018, 96-97.

31 Siegal, Daniel J. *The Mindful Brain: Reflection and Attunement in the Cultivation of Well-Being*. New York: W. W. Norton & Company, 2007, 5.

32 Brant, Andrea. *Mindful Aging: Embrace Your Life After 50 to Find Fulfillment, Purpose, and Joy*. Eau Clair, WI: PESI Publication & Media, 2017, 8-15.

33 Tolle, Eckhart. *A New Earth*, 13.

34 Maslow, Abraham H. "A Theory of Human Motivation." *Psychological Review*. 50, 94, (1943): 370-396.

35 Mackey, Chris. *Synchronicity*, 175-187.

36 Cohen, Gene D. *The Mature Mind*, 84.

37 Frankl, Victor. *Man's Search for Meaning*. Boston: Beacon Press, 116.

38 Tolle, Eckhart. *A New Earth*, 115.

39 Erikson, Eric H. and Joan Erikson. *Life Cycle Completed*. New York: W. W. Norton, 1997.

40 Liddell, Henry G. and Robert Scott. *A Greek-English Lexicon*. Oxford, England: Oxford University Press, 1940.

41 Moore, Thomas. *Ageless Soul: The Lifelong Journey toward Meaning and Joy*. New York: St. Martin's Press, 2017, 282.